TIMEWORKS PUBLISHER COMPANION – DTP on your PC

Ray Morrissey

SIGMA PRESS
Wilmslow, United Kingdom

Copyright © R. N. Morrissey, 1989.

All Rights Reserved. No part of this publication may be reproduced, stored in a retrieval system, or transmitted in any form or by any means, electronic, mechanical, photocopying, recording or otherwise, without prior written permission.

First published in 1989 by

Sigma Press 1 South Oak Lane, Wilmslow, Cheshire SK9 6AR, England.

British Library Cataloguing in Publication Data

A CIP catalogue record for this book is available from the British Library.

ISBN: 1-85058-149-5

Laser typesetting and design by

Sigma Hi-Tech Services Ltd, using Timeworks Publisher on an NTS NEAT 286 PC, attached to an Apple LaserWriter.

Cover design by

Professional Graphics, Warrington, UK

Distributed by

John Wiley & Sons Ltd., Baffins Lane, Chichester, West Sussex, England.

Acknowledgement of copyright names

Within this book, various trade names and names protected by copyright are mentioned for descriptive purposes. Due acknowledgement is hereby made of all such protection.

Preface

This book arose out of my enthusiasm for a piece of software which, at such a low cost, enabled me to do all sorts of manipulations with documents which I had previously farmed out to professional design houses at considerable expense.

Running my own small company meant I had a frequent need for short run literature and information sheets which often did not justify the high costs involved, and second best had to suffice. Using Timeworks Publisher I became able to produce my own literature at a much more reasonable cost.

As mentioned in the book, however, I do restrict my activities to the more straightforward projects, and leave the complicated work to the professionals. This is only because I am not a good graphics designer, and not due to any shortcomings of the program.

Chapter 1 of the book is largely for the bookshop browsers who have not committed to purchasing a DTP system, but who want a quick review of what it all means. The rest of the book is quite specific to Timeworks Publisher, which still seems to represent the best value in this type of software available today.

In writing the book I have used all the versions of the program from the initial release up to the current version 1F.12. If you have an earlier version, though the modifications are minor, it still remains worthwhile upgrading to the latest version. This is not expensive and you should contact the software publishers to obtain this. As the manuscript was being completed I had a preview of the new version to be launched in the not too distant future. Substantially this has few superficial differences from current versions, and all the contents of this book will, in general, apply. It will, however, offer a number of improved features, particularly with respect to text and graphics file handling, and I am looking forward to getting my hands on it.

For the technical amongst you, I have run Timeworks Publisher chiefly on the Amstrad 1640 ECD with Hard Disk, and all the screen dumps were produced with the GRAFPLUS software, producing *.PCX files, which has given excellent results. Clip art files used in the production of my final example newsletter are from the SNIP ART series from Electric Studio. The text of the book has been produced on

Microsoft Word 4 and 5, and the final preparation for printing, including most of the illustrations, has been carried out with Timeworks Publisher itself, which is an excellent demonstration of its power.

I would like to acknowledge the enthusiasm and support given by Graham Beech in the process of the preparation of this book. GST Software, of St Ives, the publishers of the program, and their Softline technical support line have been very helpful in ensuring that I made no blunders in any of the technical aspects of the program, and reviewed the first manuscript to assist in this. Millbank Computers Limited kindly supplied me with a copy of the GoScript PostScript emulator, for which my comments in the text do not do full justice, as my application was very limited.

To all of you who purchase the program and the book, I hope you have as much enjoyment from its use as I do.

Ray Morrissey

Contents

1. DTP or Word Processor?	1
Word Processing Basics	1
Desktop Publishing Systems	4
Buying a DTP Package?	5
DTP Terminology	6
Typography Terminology	7
Typographic Measurements	9
Text Measurement	10
Page Definitions	11
GEM (Mouse) Definitions	13
Hardware Requirments	14
The Printer	14
The Computer	16
2. Getting Started	19
3. Page Manipulations	41
Frame Manipulations	45
4. Text Manipulation	57
Text Copying	64
Text Files	68
Headers and Footers	75
5. Paragraph and Style	79
Using and Modifying Paragraph Styles	90
Creating a Style Sheet	93
Importing Style Sheets	98
Tabular Paragraph Styles	100
Bullet Paragraph Style	104
Header and Footer Paragraph Styles	105
Modifying the Default Document Style	105
6. Graphics Functions	107
Timeworks Publisher Internal Graphics Function	107
Importing Graphics Files	118
Dot Image Files	122

7. Document Layout and Design — 129
Applications — 130
Basic Design Principles — 130
Practical Projects — 137
    Form Design — 137
    Creating the Master Page — 139
    Headline Section — 141
    First Text Entry Frame — 143
    Main Body Frames — 145
    Community Newsletter — 151
    The Master Page — 153
    Travel Club Newsletter — 171

8. A Little Bit More About ... — 175
Printers and Printing — 175
    Selecting the Printer — 175
    Paper Alignment — 177
    Changing Your Printer — 179
    Fonts — 180
Text and Paragraph Formatting and Effects — 183
Item Lists — 189
Hyphenation and Word and Letter Spacing — 189

9. The GEM System — 201
The Mouse — 201
    Mouse Definitions — 203
Installing GEM and Timeworks Publisher — 204
    Select Display — 205
    Select Mouse — 206
    Select Printer — 206
    Select Communications Port — 206
Graphics Environment Manager (GEM) — 207
Files and Directories — 208
Loading and Using GEM — 211
    Creating New Folders — 219
    Copying and DeletingFiles — 221
    Other File Functions — 225

1

DTP or Word Processor?

In this first chapter we are going to look at the general background issues involved in starting to use desktop publishing (DTP). We will be reviewing, quite briefly, the development of the word processor and desktop publishing software and systems, and how recent improvements are clouding the difference between these two groups. It is possible to see that a significant distinction still exists, but that this may become less obvious as software develops. The second section of the chapter will examine the jargon associated with publishing and typography, to the extent required to make good use of the DTP facilities. Finally, as this book relates specifically to the Timeworks Publisher software, we will determine the particular hardware requirements for a functioning desktop publishing system.

Word Processing Basics

Traditionally word processors have been regarded as electronic typing machines, with the screen providing a substitute for paper as the medium for entering and editing the text. When all the processes are complete the text is finally committed to paper for despatch to its intended destination. The traditional output device for the word processor has been a daisywheel printer. This enables the production of text that is indistinguishable from that produced by the conventional electronic typewriter. A high quality appearance is guaranteed by the printing mechanism. The introduction of such wonders as spelling checkers has eliminated one of the other problems of manually produced text. With the on-screen editing features of all word processors it is now possible to produce error free, professional standard documents in any office or home.

However, one of the main limitations of the earlier word processors was due to the features of the daisywheel printer. Despite offering high quality printed output, these printers are generally limited to using a single simple text style, with little opportunity to improve the appearance of the printed material. In practice, the only enhancements available were the production of bold text, by causing the wheel to strike twice in the same position, or by adding an underline character to normal text. At this stage printers, and word processors, which allowed additional features such as text justification (i.e. even right and left margins) or text centering were considered quite advanced.

There was, nevertheless, a clear distinction between typewritten text and that produced by professional typesetting systems. The most obvious distinction was in the uses of different sizes of text, and different text forms within the same document. While office printing technology was limited by the characteristics of the daisywheel printer, word processor requirements remained relatively simple.

This situation changed significantly with the introduction of other low cost office based printing options. The first of these was the dot matrix printer, which, instead of using the pre-formatted characters of the daisywheel, made use of an array of pins which were 'hammered' onto the page in patterns corresponding to the required characters. However, the early devices using only nine pins were not capable of the high quality output required for professional work. They did offer the opportunity for very much faster, and quieter, output. As a consequence they have found, and retain, an important place in the production of work for internal office use and data processing, where appearance is not critical.

Word processors soon developed to use the capabilities of these new printers, but the daisywheel remained the primary printer for professional use.

Inevitably, the dot matrix technology improved to provide systems which, using a 24 pin printing head assembly, coupled with 'Letter Quality' software control were able to offer a significant improvement in text quality. Even now, however, they are not a full substitute for the daisy wheel in stringent professional applications.

The main characteristic of the dot matrix printer, however, was the ability to manipulate the printer mechanism to provide additional printing features. Traditionally, the printing head assembly is driven to form the patterns required for character printing, replicating the daisywheel as closely as possible. However, it was only a relatively short step towards providing control of the printing head so that any formation of character could be produced. As software can now effectively drive each individual pin in the head assembly, any combination of the total number of pins can be driven onto the paper. This, coupled with fine control of paper feed in the printer, means that graphics can be built up using these pins to produce combinations of small dots on the page. These graphics capabilities can be used to build up pictures, or to change the format or size of the printed characters. This brings us one step closer to the features of the typesetting systems. On a modern 24 pin printer graphics can be generated with a density of 180 dots per inch, which can provide quite high quality output. Higher densities of 360 dots per inch are available, but as yet little software is capable of exploiting this feature.

Word processing software has continued to develop to make use of these additional printer facilities, and newer packages such as Microsoft Word 4, WordPerfect 5.0, etc. offer the opportunity for substantial enhancement of text produced with these printers. These systems make allowance, for example, for larger text sizes, and for different character forms such as italic print, etc., within the same document.

There is little doubt, however, that the development of the small sized, that is "Desk Top", laser printer has been the factor which has advanced the technology of office printing by the greatest degree. For the first time we are no longer dependent upon 'impact' systems for the production of text.

Laser printers use a technology similar to that used in small photocopiers, and induce an electrical charge pattern on the paper. This pattern attracts and fixes the powdered "toner" to the paper to form the printed text, etc. In the true laser printer a charge pattern is produced by manipulating the output from a small solid state laser diode, by means of rotating mirrors, to form the pattern on a sensitive drum. This pattern is then transferred to the paper, which attracts the toner to form the printed page. With this mechanism effective print resolutions of 300 dots per inch are standard. However, although this appears to be no higher than the most recent dot matrix printers, the quality is generally very much better. Although still inferior to the professionally typeset systems, which can offer an effective resolution of better than 1200 dots per inch, there are few normal professional applications where laser printers cannot be used successfully. As with the dot matrix printers, it becomes relatively simple to produce graphics output from these printers, and hence to provide greatly enhanced appearance.

Recent developments in laser printer technology have eliminated the need for rotating mirrors, and new LED (light emitting diodes) and liquid crystal shutter devices are now available. Potentially, with the elimination of some moving parts, these should be more reliable.

There is an inevitable penalty to this progress, however, and that is in the cost of these new printers. Adequate dot matrix, and even daisywheel, printers can now be obtained for around £200, whereas the cheapest practical laser alternative will cost in the region of £1200. In addition, laser printers, like photocopiers, need to be recharged periodically and the replacement toner cartridges are quite expensive. This adds to the on-going running costs of these systems.

Although it is almost inevitable that the laser printer will become the choice for many professional applications, it should not be assumed that all other types of printer should be considered redundant. High quality 24 pin dot matrix printers are more than adequate for many text applications. They can be substantially faster than laser printers, and can cope more easily with different paper sizes. They remain the most suitable for many professional applications. In the area of personal computing these printers are still the best option available for both text and graphics applications.

The most important development, for our purposes, is the high quality graphics ability of laser printers, which separates them quite clearly from all other mechanisms available.

Word processors, then, have tended to follow printer technology in providing increasingly complex text facilities. The latest versions, compatible with the laser printer, provide many of the functions formerly the exclusive province of typeset systems. Multi-column pages, different text styles and sizes, as well as some additional graphics facilities are now available from the top word processor packages.

Desktop Publishing Systems

What, then, is desktop publishing, and do we need it? It would appear that there is no clear definition of this term available. It has been coined quite loosely by many software houses to describe various text enhancement programs, without regard to any universally accepted meaning.

It seems likely that we can best describe the function, as being that provided by the first such system. There is little question that the birth of DTP occurred with the introduction of a system using the Aldus Pagemaker software running on the Apple Macintosh computer, and driving a laser printer. The term 'Desk Top' could be taken quite literally, as the hardware for the system fitted comfortably on a standard office desk.

The particular feature which made the Macintosh stand out from other computers at the time was the graphics orientation of its screen display, as opposed to the strict text applications of the more traditional systems. By creating text in a graphics environment there is a much greater freedom to control the appearance and size of this text, in the manner achieved by the professional typesetters. This, coupled with the graphics capability of the laser printer, meant that it was possible to create a page on screen, and reproduce this precisely on the printed page. The graphics functions of the system meant that pictures could, for the first time, be included both on the screen, and transmitted onto the page.

DTP systems became available on the PC only when the graphics ability of these systems began to approach that of the Apple Macintosh. The transfer of Pagemaker to the PC, and the creation of the Ventura PC system were dependent on the improved graphics abilities of these computer systems. The introduction of increasingly high resolution PC graphics screens (e.g. Hercules, EGA/VGA, etc.) has made this transfer practicable. Of equal significance, though, was the development of graphics interfaces, such as the Digital Research GEM , and the Microsoft Windows systems.

The term 'What You See is What You Get' (WYSIWYG) was coined to describe word processors which gave a close representation, on screen, of the final printed page. There are still only a few word processors which can achieve this in practice. DTP packages, however, come much closer to this reality. The only practical limitations lie in the relative resolution of the screen display, and the final printed page.

Consider that with a EGA/VGA screen we get a Horizontal resolution of 640 dots, representing about 6.5 inches of paper width. That is approximately 100 dots per inch. This is substantially lower than even a dot matrix printer, but compares even less favourably with the laser capability of 300 dots per inch. Within this limitation, however, DTP packages come nearest to achieving a true WYSIWYG environment

This, then, is probably one of the major features which discriminates between the DTP and word processor systems. DTP is predominantly a graphics orientated system. It has, or at least should have, the ability to use pictures, and to provide a high degree of control in placing, scaling and editing these.

Above all, publishing is a visual art. The skill in publishing is not only to create good text (that is my job!), but also to create an attractive visual impact (that is the publisher's job!). To achieve this end, the DTP program must give freedom to manipulate text and graphics on screen to create good 'Design', and to transmit this faithfully to the printed page.

Another important feature of DTP programs is the need to operate in conjunction with other software systems. Where a large amount of text is envisaged, then this is best produced using a word processor. Graphics, too, have to be created outside of the DTP program, and "imported", for use in the final document. Graphics can originate from art packages, or from scanned images, and can be stored in a number of formats. A good DTP package will be able to accept text and graphics from a number of sources.

In summary, then, we have noted that a word processor is used chiefly for the manipulation of text. By using more sophisticated output printers, in particular the laser system, a number of text enhancements are made available.

Desktop publishing, on the other hand, although requiring the manipulation of text, is predominantly a graphics orientated process. Its aim is to allow on-screen manipulation of the appearance and layout of text, and to integrate this with graphics images, to create an attractive visual impact.

Despite the continuing development of the graphics capabilities of word processing systems, the true DTP software still retains a substantial advantage in overall page design manipulations.

Buying a DTP package?

Should we, then, be attempting to choose between the two systems? The simple answer is "no!". The two systems are in many ways complementary, rather than competitive. If you are serious about publishing even the simplest document, then a word processor is an essential tool in any event. It is, and will remain, one of the more valuable functions of the computer, whatever other applications may arise. Selecting which type of word processor to purchase is quite another problem altogether, with an extremely wide range of prices and features available.

A DTP package becomes essential if you agree with the basic premise that visual impact is as much a part of communication as is content. Only with such a package can you achieve the control required.

When deciding whether or not to purchase a DTP program there are some other factors to consider. One very important point to make, early on, is that no DTP package will make you into a good graphics designer. Unless you have a good basic design ability, or specific training in this area, step carefully when deciding to follow this path. The advent of low cost DTP software has been the trigger for some quite appalling documents, where there was clearly no design ability on the part of those preparing them. Some examples of these still assault the eye in many journals that appear regularly on the newsagents' shelves.

Also consider carefully what it is that you are trying to achieve. In the professional environment, where you may wish only to include graphics in the form of spreadsheet graphs, etc., some of the more powerful word processors may be the best vehicle. Driving laser printers, these are quite capable of producing high quality, attractive documentation. The page design options may be more limited, but in some cases this may be a good thing.

The choice of DTP packages is not as overwhelming as that of word processors. Here the choice must be made on the basis of need, but more particularly of cost. There are the group of systems, such as Aldus PageMaker and Ventura, which provide excellent features, but which are expensive to buy, and require expensive computer systems to operate. For these, as a corporate image is inevitably involved, laser printers are mandatory.

On the other hand there are a group of programs, of which Timeworks Publisher is the principal example, designed to operate on basic PC systems, with the capability to drive both dot matrix and laser printers. These software systems are available at very low cost, yet provide excellent features. Where laser printers are supported they are capable of full professional quality output, largely indistinguishable from the more expensive programs.

The principal benefit of these systems is that they enable you to assess the requirement for a DTP system, without the risk of a large investment. In many cases, indeed, these will prove to offer all the necessary facilities, in software terms. Hardware, particularly the printer, can then be upgraded as and when appropriate.

In the author's business Timeworks Publisher continues to provide all the facilities that are needed from desktop publishing. That is, chiefly, to produce information brochures, price lists and training materials, and the occasional newsletter.

DTP Terminology

Inevitably, when discovering a new application, we come up against the barrier of 'Jargon'. This is true in the world of publishing, just as it is in many other cases. To add to the confusion, some of the terminology which has become more widely used is used incorrectly and/or inconsistently. The definitions which follow have been researched as thoroughly as possible, to ensure that they represent the widely accepted view. More importantly, however, they will be adopted for this book and used consistently throughout.

To this end, I am also going to define some GEM orientated terms to reduce the need for clarification later in the book. To those already familiar with GEM, this will be largely redundant, except to ensure that we are speaking the same language. For those for whom Timeworks Publisher has been the first introduction to such Graphics systems, it is recommended, although not obligatory, to read the chapter on GEM first.

Typography Terminology

Typeface: This is the basic pattern that defines the shape of the characters as they appear on the printed page. Most typefaces are known by a unique name, e.g. Times, Helvetica, etc., and many are protected by some form of copyright or proprietary ownership. Timeworks Publisher comes supplied with two typefaces, Swiss and Dutch, which are generic variations of some standard typefaces. The construction of typefaces varies enormously, and there is a whole terminology involved in this area alone. As far as our requirements are concerned, it is a case of 'What You See Is What You Got!'

Style: (Also referred to as "Typestyle"). This is a description of variations made on the basic typeface. One variation is made by changing the *weight* of the text, i.e. making it bold (heavy) or light, by varying degrees. The second most common variation is to slope the typeface to produce an *italic* version. Of course, the effects can be mixed. For example, with the typefaces supplied with Timeworks Publisher the following options are possible:

    Normal
    Bold
    Italic
    Bold Italic
    Light
    Light Italic

Size: This is the third of the parameters which describe the text we are using. Rather obviously, this relates directly to the actual size of the typeface as viewed. The unit of measure of size is the *point*. We will be returning to a fuller discussion of type measurement a little later, as this is important when looking at the physical layout of a page.

Font: This is one of the terms which appears to have suffered the greatest misuse. A font refers *only* to a single size of a single typeface, but may include the possible

Dutch Font

NORMAL
BOLD
ITALIC
LIGHT
BOLD ITALIC
LIGHT ITALIC

Swiss Font

NORMAL
BOLD
ITALIC
LIGHT
BOLD ITALIC
LIGHT ITALIC

Figure 1.1 Typestyle variations

variations or styles (this is one area where the literature was unable to produce an agreed final definition, as some would exclude the variations). For example, 12 Point Swiss and 10 Point Swiss are different *fonts*. A font contains all the printable characters available.(i.e upper & lower case letters, numbers, and special characters)

From this, then, we can see that to properly define a font we would have to specify the typeface, the style, the size and the character set. Fortunately, in most DTP applications we work with a relatively limited range of fonts in any single publication. Within the operation of Timeworks Publisher, even with the recently introduced extended range of fonts, there is little problem in coping with the options available. We will discuss this further in the chapters on the use of text, and on the principles of design.

Typographic Measurements

It was hoped to avoid a serious discussion on this topic, as it can become quite involved. However, as certain aspects of the terminology are used within the program, and as they will have an impact on the appearance of the finished product, some discussion is inevitable.

Point: The basic unit of measure in Typography is the *point*. For obscure historical reasons this is effectively equal to 1/72". Stated conversely, there are 72 points to the inch. The other principle unit of measure is the Pica (pronounced "Piker"), which is equal to 12 points, or 1/6 of an inch (that is, there are 6 picas to the inch). As we will see later, within Timeworks Publisher, we can choose the unit of measure with which to work, using either Inches (Subdivided into 1/10" or 1/8"), Centimetres, or Picas and Points.

Using this latter unit of measure has some benefits, but it can lead to some confusion in understanding how the units are expressed. The number 1,10 in this system means 1 Pica AND 10 points (the (,) has been used deliberately here to try to differentiate from the decimal point). Remembering that there are 12 points to each Pica, it is important to remember that the number after the (,) must not exceed 11. For example, 1,12 would be 1 Pica AND 12 points, and would be taken by the program as 2 Pica. Similarly, the number 1,60, which appears acceptable in decimals, is very misleading in Pica/Point measure, as it actually means 1 pica and 60 points, which is taken as 6 pica.

It is interesting to note that the standard line spacing on every printer is 6 lines to the inch, which corresponds exactly to a line spacing of 1 pica, or 12 points.

It is important to understand these measurements, as, although we can control the general page dimensions in either inches or centimetres, *text* measurements and line spacing are always given in picas and points. Reconciling the different units of measure can be quite confusing, most especially so when trying to work with metric units, for which there is no straightforward conversion between measurements.

EM: The final unit of measure that we are going to be faced with is the 'em' (there is also an 'en', but I pray that this can be avoided). The 'EM' is slightly difficult to cope with in that its actual size depends on the size of the font that we are using. An 'em' is defined as the width of the lower case 'm' in the particular font under consideration. An alternative definition, which may not necessarily conflict with this, is that an em represents a square of the point size in question (i.e. an em in 12 point text will be 12 points wide).

In true typography, as opposed to printing with typewriters, each character has it own width. (Note that with a typewriter all characters are assigned the same space). Each character, then, occupies a different amount of space along the line. Generally, in computerised applications, such as with Timeworks Publisher, we do not have to worry about this as it is all handled automatically. However, there are cases, particularly when using larger sized text, when the normal printing controls give an unattractive appearance. In order to achieve a pleasant look it is sometimes necessary to move individual characters closer together, or further apart. This procedure is termed *kerning*, and we will discuss this a little later. In addition the spacing between individual words will be adjusted to assist in achieving a uniform appearance along the line. However, the relevance, at this time is that within Timeworks Publisher we specify the amount of space between individual words in 'ems'. In practice, this unit is not much help, and we will have to rely on visual judgement. Also, in many cases the screen resolution, even with VGA, is just not adequate to show the effects of small kerning and spacing adjustments, and these need to be printed for final assessment.

Text Measurement.

We have defined the Point as the basic unit of measure in typography; we will now see how it is actually applied in practice. Referring to the illustration (Fig 1.2), we see that size is defined as the height of the text, measured between the highest and lowest points of the typeface. In strict typographical terms this also makes allowance for a small (though un-defined) amount of white space above the text. The example shows 36 point text, with the indicated lines defining the upper and lower points. The diagram has been constructed so that the lines are exactly 36 Points apart, and do show a small amount of white space at the top.

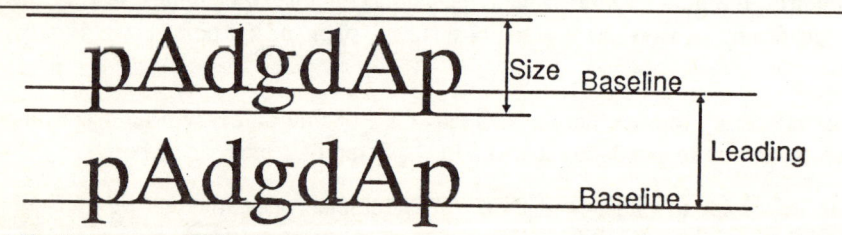

Figure 1.2 Text Measurement Definitions

The *baseline* is also illustrated, as this is used as the reference point for text on the page. In the example shown, the text descenders (i.e. those bits below the baseline) have a height of 9 points, and the capitals and ascenders (i.e. those bits above the base line) have a dimension of 27 points. This ratio, however, may vary from typeface to typeface.

The distance between two successive baselines is termed the *leading* (pronounced 'ledding'), and this can be adjusted to get the best visual impact. In the example shown the Leading is set at 43 points.

The presentation of text on a page is usually referred to as a factor of both point size and leading. In our example, then, the text is 36 point with 43 point leading, usually given the notation 36/43 or 36 on 43.

We will see, in some of the practical examples later, the effects of changing these dimensions.

The point size of text, then, is a measure of the text height. Obviously, the width of text is related to its height, but only loosely. Different fonts, even of the same point size, will have different widths. The fonts, Swiss and Dutch, supplied with Timeworks Publisher have significant differences in width. Also, adding variations to the text, such as Bold and Italic, have an effect on the text width. There is no fixed relationship between height and width, even with different sizes of the same typeface. The established typefaces are designed more on the basis of attractive appearance than to any strict formula.

This becomes important when trying to achieve any sort of text alignment when using different fonts, etc,. and requires serious attention when designing page layouts. As this is something we have to learn to cope with, and cannot change fundamentally, we will look at this later in the practical sessions.

Page Definitions

Timeworks Publisher is equipped to work with four different page sizes:

Letter	8.5 x 11.0 inches
Legal	8.5 x 14.0 inches
Note	5.5 x 8.5 inches
A4	210 x 297 mm

Of these, only the A4 size is in regular use for documents within the UK. The 'LETTER' page is the standard listing paper used by default in most computer printers. It is now, however, becoming easier to get true A4 size continuous paper, and there is less need to use the US format. Most modern software can now be set to use standard A4, which gives a total of 70 lines of text. Beware, however, that many systems still come with a default setting of 66 lines of text, again corresponding to the US size of paper.

The page can be used either in *Portrait* mode, which is the normal configuration, with the longest side vertical; or it may be used in *Landscape* mode, that is, with the longest side horizontal. This selection is made as you start your session.

The default selection for Timeworks Publisher is A4 Portrait.

Margins are also important in setting out the page. These are basically the blank borders around the text area, top and bottom, and left and right. As we will see, it is possible to print in the margins, if we require it, to achieve special effects. Where a document is to be bound, it is usual to leave a deeper margin on the appropriate side of the page. This additional margin is termed the *gutter* margin. Note that on left hand pages the gutter margin is on the right, and on right hand pages it is on the left. Fortunately, if you are using multiple pages, Timeworks Publisher can keep a track of left hand and right hand pages for you.

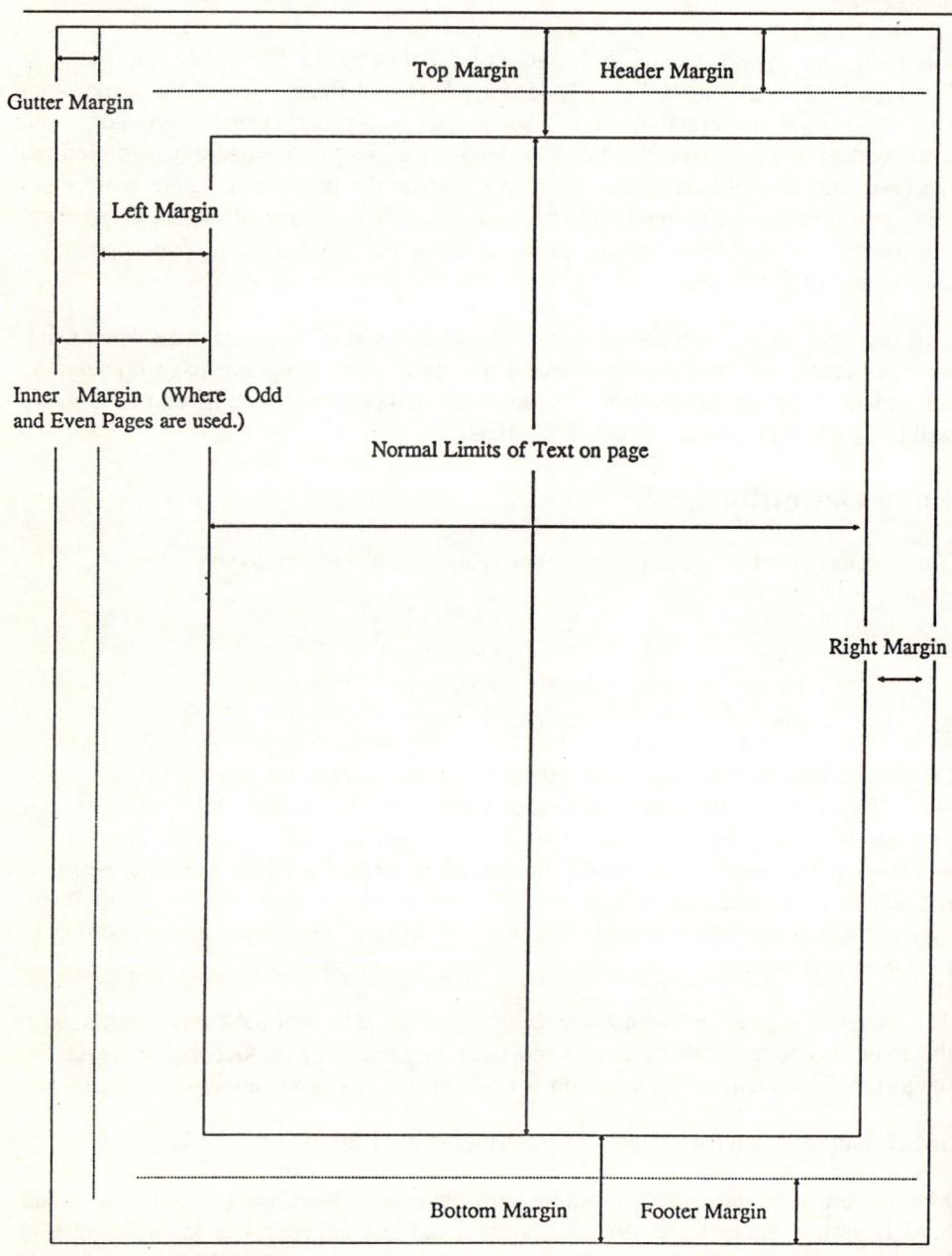

Fig 1.3 Page Layout Definitions

A definition which seems superfluous, but which will avoid confusion later, is the *paragraph*. In Timeworks Publisher, and in most word processors, a paragraph is defined as a section of text which begins on a new line on a page, and is ended by the use of the [RETURN] key on the keyboard. Using the [RETURN] key issues an internal computer code which is recognised by most software in the same way.

The final terms for definition here are *footers* and *headers*. Looking at different software applications, there is some misuse of this terminology, and our definitions are those used within the Timeworks Publisher package.

A FOOTER is a fixed section of text which appears along the bottom of each page in the document, below the normal text bottom margin. It can include some variable information, such as page or chapter numbers, but the basic layout remains consistent.

A HEADER has the same function, but applied to the top of the page, above the normal text top margin.

It is possible to omit headers and footers from individual pages, for example at the beginning of a document, or at the start of a chapter, etc.

When headers and footers are used within a document it is important to take care that the relevant settings for header and footer positions, and the text upper and lower margins, are compatible, and do not overlap in any way.

GEM (Mouse) Definitions.

As mentioned earlier, these definitions are introduced here so that we are all using the same terms when working within the Timeworks Publisher graphics environment. They will be understood even if you have not used GEM previously. It is advisable for those not familiar with this system to read the chapter on GEM soon, to make some sense of some of the filing options which will be presented by Timeworks Publisher.

Point: Use the mouse to move the screen pointer to the chosen menu/option, etc.

Click: Press the left button on the mouse.

Double Click: Press the left button on the mouse twice in quick succession. Sometimes the timing is critical, so if at first you don't succeed.. ....!

Drag: Hold down the left button while moving the mouse pointer to a new location.

Select: Point to the option/menu and click.

Accept: When presented with a menu with an [OK] box, point to this and click.

Cancel: When presented with a menu with a [CANCEL] box, point to this and click.

Hardware Requirements

Before we can get down to the more enjoyable business of loading up our software, and seeing just what we can do with it, we will first look at the hardware aspects of our system. Then, without duplicating the lessons in the Timeworks Publisher manual, we will look at the basic structure of the program. In later chapters we will look at each of the program facilities in detail.

As we considered earlier in the book, the main purpose of a DTP package is to make it possible for us to produce documents that can be both meaningful *and* attractive. The part of the hardware system which has the greatest impact on the finished product is the printer. Consequently, we will look at this first.

The Printer

Timeworks Publisher, through the GEM interface, is capable of driving a wide range of printer types, broken down into the following general categories:

9 Pin Dot Matrix	Resolution 120 X 144 dpi
24 Pin Dot Matrix	Resolution 180 x 180 dpi
LaserJet+ Compatible	Resolution 150 x 150 dpi
Laserjet II Compatible	Resolution 300 x 300 dpi
PostScript Compatible	Resolution 300 x 300 dpi

In general, the standard of output is related to the resolution of the printer. The last two laser printer groups can be expected to give the same level of quality, but the PostScript compatible will have the greater range of fonts available. (PostScript is a language specifically designed for control of page printing).

Which printer to choose is more a matter of budget than anything else. If you just wish to produce a club newsletter, or something similar, then a 9 pin dot matrix is quite adequate. It is worth noting that, as the printer is driven in graphics mode, the quality of text from Timeworks Publisher is frequently of a higher quality than any "Letter Quality" pretensions that your printer may have. The author first used this program driving such a printer, and felt it quite acceptable for use within his business for limited applications. With 9 pin printers available for less than £200, this is a practical option. Anyone already using a computer will have a printer of some type available. With the exception of daisywheels, most are capable of producing satisfactory output at this level.

The move up to a 24 pin printer does achieve noticeable improvement. Although a little more expensive, starting at a price of around £300, they are probably a worthwhile upgrade for most applications. Their text quality for other uses is so much better in any event.

The only justification for going to a laser printer is either that you have one already available, or if you are envisaging a major business application. Even the cheapest laser type printer is around £1200, and in many cases you will need to purchase additional printer memory and/or font cartridges to get the full benefit. This adds a significant amount to the investment. Postscript compatible printers are significantly more expensive than standard lasers, and are a serious investment for any business. Using a laser printer, however, you will achieve full professional results.

Another important feature in the selection of the printer is that this has a significant impact on the range of fonts that are available. With both the 9 pin dot matrix and the HP LaserJet models, the print range is limited to a maximum size of 36 points. Using the 24 pin dot matrix printers, or either of the Postscript compatible laser printers, allows a greater range of fonts, with the latter giving by far the greater selection. However, even this is not an absolute benefit as the Postscript printers do not allow the use of the graphic 'Bullet' symbols available with the less expensive printers. One further limitation with the 9 pin printer is that it cannot print in landscape mode, thus further reducing the options available.

This sample of text and graphics has been printed on a 9-pin dot matrix printer, with a resolution of 120 X 144 dots per inch.

This sample of text and graphics has been printed on a 24-pin dot matrix printer, with a resolution of 180 X 180 dots per inch.

This sample of text and graphics has been printed on a Laser printer, with a resolution of 300 X 300 dots per inch.

Figure 1.4 Comparative Printer Output Quality

The Computer

Timeworks Publisher works extremely well on a wide range of computers. It was first available on the Atari 520 system, before being re-written for the IBM compatible PCs. It is also now available as the software part of the Acorn Archimedes DTP system. The author has used Timeworks Publisher on a range of display adaptors, from basic CGA (mono) to VGA (full colour) and the system is workable on all of them. Obviously, as the screen resolution becomes higher, then it is easier to relate screen appearance to printed output.

Timeworks Publisher has a mode (Double Size Page View) which allows operation at twice the normal screen resolution. This overcomes many of the problems of lower resolution displays, enabling most documents to be displayed on screen with good relation to the printed output. Colour is a nice addition, but is by no means important as it is not used to give any special information.

The result of this is that, in most practical situations, the monitor is the least critical of the elements of the computer, although there is little doubt that the greater the screen resolution the easier it is to preview the final results. This means, as with the printer, that almost any existing system will give you access to the most important features of the program with few restrictions.

Timeworks Publisher, to quote the manual, "makes intelligent use of all memory up to the 640K DOS limit". It will work on the basic 512K machines, but there are significant benefits in expanding up to 640K, chiefly in respect of speeding up the processes by reducing disk accesses. If you have extended memory above this level then this can be configured as a RAMDISK, with significant benefits.

The author's initial experience was with Timeworks Publisher installed on a Twin Disk Amstrad PC1512 (although it had previously had expanded memory to 640K added), and it worked extremely well. There is some disk swapping required in order to read data files, and to use the printer drivers. Outside of this, all procedures are handled internally, with program overlays being drawn from the overlays disk permanently in Drive B:.

The one exception to this comfortable state of affairs is when trying to print documents with a significant graphics content. To produce print files of the resolution required Timeworks Publisher has to create temporary files on disk during the printing process. With the original 360K disks there simply was not enough room to achieve this, and the printing could not proceed. This problem is also true of the Atari Floppy system, even with 720K disks, and inevitably also of the Archimedes system. (The same restriction will apply to all such applications)

In practice, this was a significant incentive to add a hard disk to the basic system. Suddenly life became very much easier, and the limit on graphics printing was eliminated immediately. There is little doubt that a hard disk is by far the most useful enhancement to a basic system. This makes DTP very much easier, but also reflects a major benefit with most other software. Here also, although not essential, a hard disk is strongly recommended.

In addition, if you are going to work with long documents, and are in danger of running into memory limitations, then a hard disk becomes quite important. The program has the ability, explained in more detail a little later, to use the hard disk for file 'slaving', to enable work on much longer documents (Extended memory, above the 640K limit, can also be used in this way)

One further point, relating to machine memory, is that for Timeworks Publisher to operate on a floppy-based system, there is insufficient space to allow for a RAM disk larger than the 34K required by GEM. If your start up procedures require the creation of a larger RAM disk, then the installation will abort (although with a proper explanation). If this is the case, as happened with the author's initial installation, it will be necessary to create a separate Startup disk, which excludes the automatic creation of this RAM disk. With the Amstrad machines this may also mean adjusting the NVR values for the RAM disk. GEM will create the necessary RAM disk for its own operations, as a part of its normal start up procedures.

In all of the above there is some element of choice. Primarily, you have to balance your requirements against your budget. Remember, however, that you can get excellent results from even the most basic system. So, use and enjoy the system, and then think about necessary enhancements. You will be in a much better position to assess your actual requirements after some experimentation.

However, there is one element of the system which is definitely not optional. You must have a *mouse*. Those of us introduced to the PC world by courtesy of Alan Sugar, and those using either the Atari or the Archimedes, will all be familiar with the workings of this happy little rodent. It is only on applications so strongly tailored to the use of a mouse that its real benefits become apparent. When changing from a long background working only with DOS, this is at first a little confusing. However, it takes only a little experience to become quite happy with this way of working. Having used the mouse for a period with Timeworks Publisher, it then becomes much easier to get to grips with GEM, and to determine some of the benefits of that system.

Those of you who have not used a mouse need not fear. There are a number of such beasts available, many of which will plug directly into your RS232 port. Prices are relatively low, between £50 and £120, and they are extremely simple to install. Generally, all that is required is to load in the mouse driver program (usually called MOUSE.COM), as part of your startup AUTOEXEC.BAT function, or by direct call before starting the Timeworks Publisher program. The instructions supplied with the mouse are usually quite clear. In most cases, the mouse can remain connected without any problems, and may even be effective in other applications. (Microsoft Word 4, for example, makes good use of the mouse in some of its editing functions).

In summary, then, Timeworks Publisher is an effective program on even the most basic machine, requiring either 2 x 360K disk drives, or a single 720K drive as the minimum configuration. Adequate output can be achieved from basic 9 pin printers, and any monitor can be used. Increased memory, to 640K, and the addition of a hard disk are the most beneficial enhancements to consider in the short term.

For professional work a laser output of some form is almost mandatory. With this, Timeworks Publisher is capable of producing documents which compare with even the most expensive alternative systems.

2

Getting Started

The installation of the Timeworks Publisher program is, happily, a quite straightforward process, only briefly discussed here. Those of you who are quite happy with the normal processes of software installation should carry on here. If you need a little bit more encouragement to proceed, then turn to the appropriate pages in the final chapter, where this is explained more fully.

The process is driven by the INSTALL program on the DTP master disk, and is a simple process of following on-screen instructions as they are presented to you. For a floppy based system you will need to have five formatted floppy disks ready before starting the process and, as mentioned in the previous chapter, to ensure that there is no large RAM disk created.

The installation process firstly installs the required parts of the GEM system onto the appropriate disk(s), and then adds the Timeworks Publisher program and files. During the process you will be asked to define the following:

    Type of mouse;
    Type of screen display; and
    Type of printer.

In each case you are offered a short list of choices, and it is necessary to pick that which most closely corresponds to your own system. Unusually, Amstrad users are specifically catered for in this process, with the choice of the Amstrad mouse in the list of options available.(As the Amstrad mouse simulates the cursor movement keys it is frequently possible to make use of this in software which does not specifically use a mouse)

Once the installation is complete, it is necessary to run the FONTWID program, following the instructions given, in order to enable Timeworks Publisher to work with the screen and printer fonts available.

Any subsequent changes in the system can be adapted by running the INSTALL program again to specify any changes. Note, here, that the GEM system provided also has a file called GEMSETUP, which is normally used to load GEM into the computer. This would *not* work with the disks supplied with earlier versions of Timeworks Publisher as there was a conflict in the disk-naming conventions. With current versions of the program this has been eliminated.

If you have a hard disk system, on which an earlier version of GEM is already installed, then there is a small conflict in the organisation of the GEM files and directories, and it may be necessary to remove the earlier version. Timeworks Publisher will only operate with the GEM version provided (Version 3). This, however, does have some improved features, chiefly in relation to its output functions, which make it worthwhile in any event.

Now that we have sorted out the hardware system, and satisfactorily installed the software, we can get down to the real business of this book, using Timeworks Publisher . If you are new to GEM it will help first to read the chapter on GEM. Although you will be able to progress without it, there may be some actions required which will be explained there, but which I will take for granted in this section.

Before starting the program you must be sure that the mouse driver is loaded. If this is not done by the AUTOEXEC.BAT file, then do it now. (Again, this procedure is covered in more detail in the chapter on the GEM system, as this is more appropriate to newcomers, and of no real importance to those already familiar with GEM)

To start Timeworks Publisher with floppy disks, insert your Startup disk in drive A:, and type PUBLISH. When prompted, insert the specified disks, and follow the on-screen instructions. At the end of the opening sequence you should have your Overlays disk in drive B:, and your Fonts disk in drive A: (Or the combined 720K disk in Atari/single floppy systems).

If you wish to run the program from within GEM, on a floppy system, then you must first use the GEM disks created during the install process (See Chapter 9), to start up the GEM Desktop, and then proceed as normal.

From a hard disk, either type PUBLISH, from the root directory, or open the PUBLISH.APP file in the PUBLISH sub-directory, created when the program was installed. (In older version of the program the PUBLISH.APP file was placed in the GEMAPPS sub-directory, arising from the difference in the organisation of the GEM files)) In all cases, after the opening title screen you will be presented with the first working screen, as illustrated in Figure 2.1.

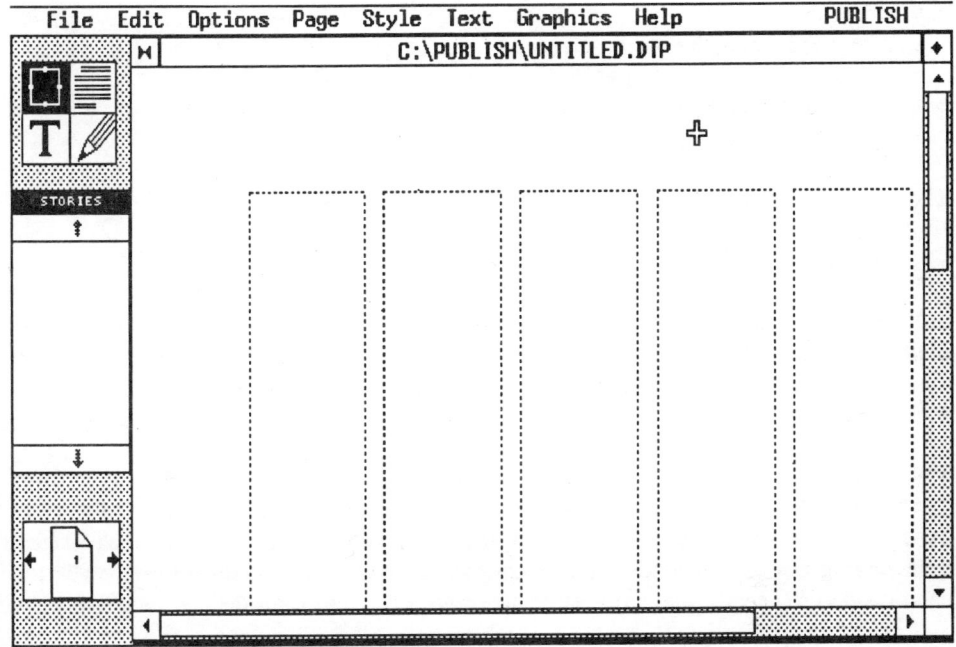

Figure 2.1 Timeworks Publisher Opening Screen

When the loading process is finished, the screen cursor will appear as an outline cross-hair.

The top bar of the screen shows the 8 menu options available for controlling all aspects of the program. Pointing at these will automatically bring down the menu lists, and you should move the cursor along this bar to demonstrate the action. Those options which are available at any particular point in the program will be displayed as dark characters. Those which are not available currently are shown in light text. Note that when the cursor moves out of the page area it changes shape to an arrow.

Alongside some options there is a key code, which can be used as an alternative form of instruction. Pressing the [ALT] key, and the character shown, will have the same effect as selecting the option using the mouse. However, this will not work while the menus are open on screen, so the keyboard controls will need to be memorised. Some of the selections are simple on/off toggles, whilst others will bring up further choices, as we will see in detail later.(Note that one option labelled 'Soft hyphen', shows the (^) character, and this requires the use of the [CTRL] key, rather than the [ALT] key to activate it)

Along the left hand side of the screen is the Toolkit display area. From this area you will select the modes of operation, and some additional features.

The upper block, showing a rectangle of four Icons, is used to select the current mode of operation. The reverse highlight is used to show the current selection. Four options

are available :
> Frame mode (The initial selection)
> Text mode (T symbol)
> Paragraph mode
> Graphics Mode. (Pencil Symbol)

The mode is changed simply by selecting the appropriate box with the mouse controls.

Below this is a further block, termed the *browser*, and currently headed *stories*. The heading and contents of this will vary, depending on the mode of operation. *Stories* is the Timeworks Publisher term for Text Files, and will, normally, show a list of all text files currently in use in the document. Again, we will look at the contents of this as we progress through the work.

The third block shows a representation of the current page selection. At the moment this shows a normal right hand page, as symbolised by the small fold in the top right hand corner. If we are working on a multi-page document this will show two pages, representing both the left hand, and right hand pages of the document.(We will first have needed to specify that we wish to work with left and right handed pages, but we will get to that later).

The rest of the screen is occupied by the conventional GEM working area. In the top left hand corner is the *close* box (Butterfly). If we wish to abandon the current document, and start another, then we can click on the close box and follow the selections offered. Alongside this is displayed the current document title and path information, as set by the program defaults at this stage.

The *full* box (Diamond) in the top right hand corner enables you to expand the screen display by removing the Toolkit display to give us a larger working area. This can be restored by a second click on the box.

Along the bottom and right hand side, the *scroll bars* enable us to move the viewed section of the page around, by dragging the solid bars, or by clicking the appropriate arrow heads.

The page shown in the display area represents an 'actual' size view of the Timeworks Publisher default page. The light outlines represent *column guides*, which provide a basis for controlling the page layout. These guides do not appear on any printed output, but are included as an important convenience feature.

We will get a better idea of the actual page layout if we choose a different view.

Point to {PAGE} to drop the page menu, then click on the [Full page] option. The display will change to show a reduced scale replica of the default page. See Figures 2.2. and 2.3

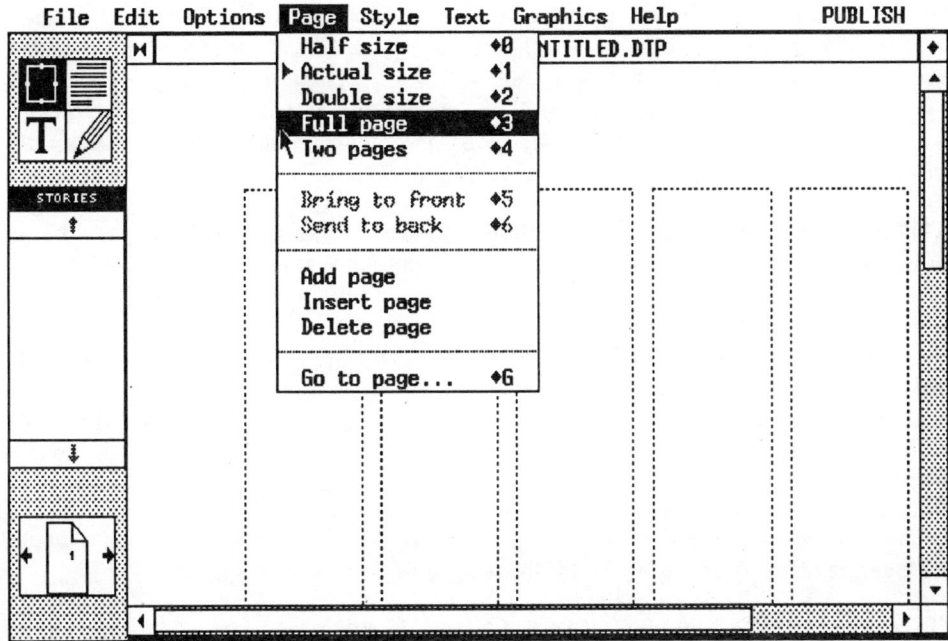

Figure 2.2 Page Menu

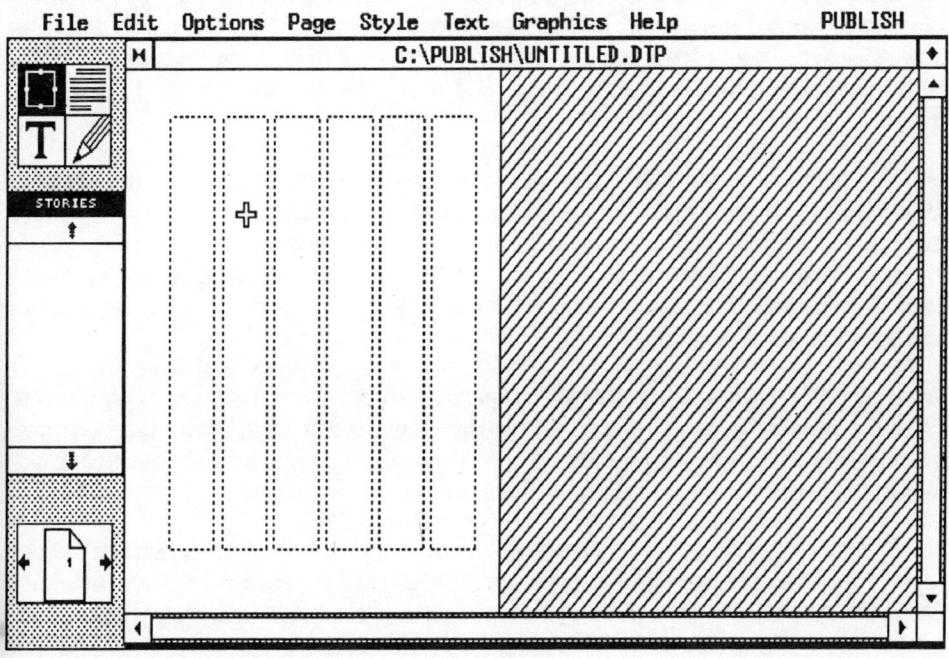

Figure 2.3 Full Page View

Figure 2.3 shows a standard A4 page, with six uniform, and equally spaced, column guides. The guides indicate an overall text area which has 1 inch margins top and bottom, a 1 inch left hand margin, and a 0.5 inch right hand margin. For many applications this is quite a sensible base layout but, as we will see later, this is entirely under our control. The presence of the column guides does not necessarily inhibit us from working outside of that area.

This full page view is very useful for looking at the overall layout of our page, but is not adequate for detailed work, and you would normally revert back to a larger scale view for most of the time.

If you are using a high resolution monitor (e.g. Atari or Archimedes monitors, or IBM EGA/VGA/Hercules monitors) then the 'Actual size' view is adequate for most purposes, and we will work chiefly in that. If using a lower resolution monitor, such as television view on the Atari, or the IBM CGA display, then you should switch between Actual size, or Double size, as appropriate.

In order to have a brief view of the capability of Timeworks Publisher we can take a look at one of the files supplied with the program.

Go to the {FILE} menu, and select the [Open...] option, and you will be presented with the standard GEM Item Selector menu. (The function of this is fully explained in the GEM chapter) Use the pointer to select the DTP folder from the listing. Now select the TIMEWORKS.DTP file, and accept it. Wait for a short time while the file is loaded. Various things will be seen happening in the browser, but ignore these for now. You will finally be presented with an actual size view of the first of two pages of the demonstration document, shown in Figures 2.4 (a) and (b) on the next two pages.

Use the page menu, and the scroll bars, to view different sections of the page, at different magnifications, just to see the impact of the various options. This page has a large graphics file, which appears to be an image of the same page. In the large scale views this can take some time to appear, so a little patience is required. When you have played with this feature enough to demonstrate the various functions we will take a look at the second page.

In the {PAGE} menu select the [Go to page...] form, which brings up a sub-menu. Enter the number 2, where requested, and accept. After a short while the new page will be displayed, showing further features of the Timeworks Publisher package. Again it is worth moving around this, using the various view options.

There is an alternative, and much more direct, way of moving between adjacent pages. Move the pointer into the page icon in the Toolkit, and note the arrows along either side. These allow us to turn the pages in the document, and if we click on the left hand arrow (i.e.Turn to previous page) we will see page 1 appear. As this is the first page (obviously) any further clicks on this arrow will be ignored. We can now switch back to view the following page by clicking on the right arrow. If you click a

Desktop Publisher PC

Another first from GST

GST SOFTWARE of Cambridge announce the first professional Desktop Publishing package available for under £200. The program, developed for US software publisher Timeworks, is published in the UK by Electric Distribution.

Breakthrough

Timeworks Desktop Publisher is a real breakthrough in price-performance, with a feature list that rivals that of *Ventura* or *Pagemaker*, but at a price that brings professional DTP power within everyone's reach.

Features

- Frame-based page layout
- Five page view modes
- Style sheets
- Multiple fonts
- Multiple text styles
- European character set
- Direct text input and editing
- Text import from WP programs
- Automatic justification
- Automatic hyphenation
- Text block cut, paste and restyle
- Vector and raster graphics import
- Picture scaling and cropping
- Automatic picture runaround
- Raster image paint mode
- Vector graphics draw mode
- Wide range of printers supported

Electric Distribution, 8-10, Green Street, Willingham, Cambridge, CB4 5JA. Willingham (0954) 61258.

What the press say...

Program of the month is *Timeworks Desktop Publisher*. Those incredible wizards at GST ... have put together the finest DTP package possible. Straight from the box I put together a ten-page document of text and pictures without a problem or a single setback. The ease of use with *Publisher* is incredible. It allows for your mistakes and yet gives scope to your creativity.

Dale Hughes, ST World, April 1988

Timeworks DTP represents remarkable value. Other budget packages such as *GEM Desktop Publisher*, *Finesse* and *Fleet Street Editor* bear little comparison. Excellent value for money and highly recommended.

Bruce Smith, PC, April 1988

Figure 2.4 (a) First page of TIMEWORKS.DTP document

FONTS, SIZES & STYLES

This is 36pt Swiss roman
This is 28pt Dutch bold italic
This is 20pt Swiss bold superscript

This is 14pt Dutch italic

This is 10pt Swiss

This is 7pt Dutch

This is a 220pt Space Shuttle!

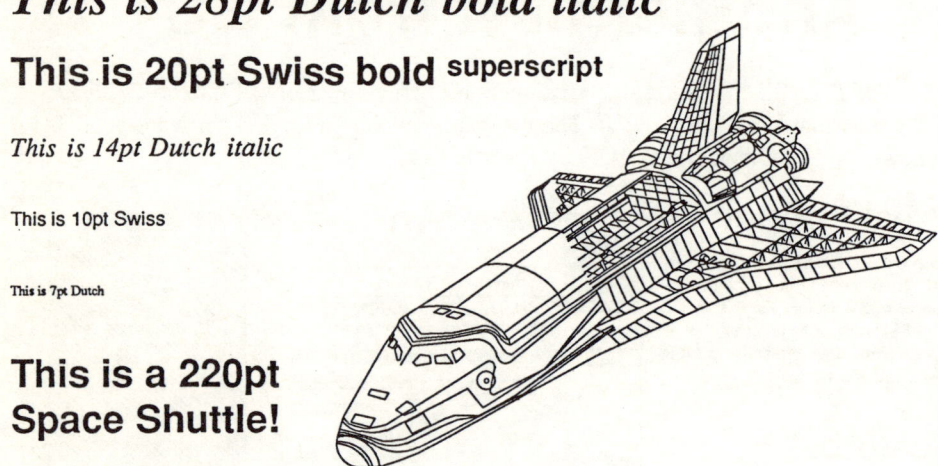

This is a picture from GEM Draw Plus, with scanned logos and text

Figure 2.4 (b) Second page of TIMEWORKS.DTP document.

second time on this arrow, and as this is the current last page of the document, you will be asked if you wish to add a new page. At this time we do not, so, if you have brought up this option box click on [NO].

Within the {PAGE} menu there is an option to select a two page view. However, this is restricted to showing a left hand and a right hand page, in the proper relative position on the screen. The first page of any document, numbered page 1, is always a right hand page. Thus, when we call up a two page view of this document we will get page 1 (a right hand page), with a blank area to the left.

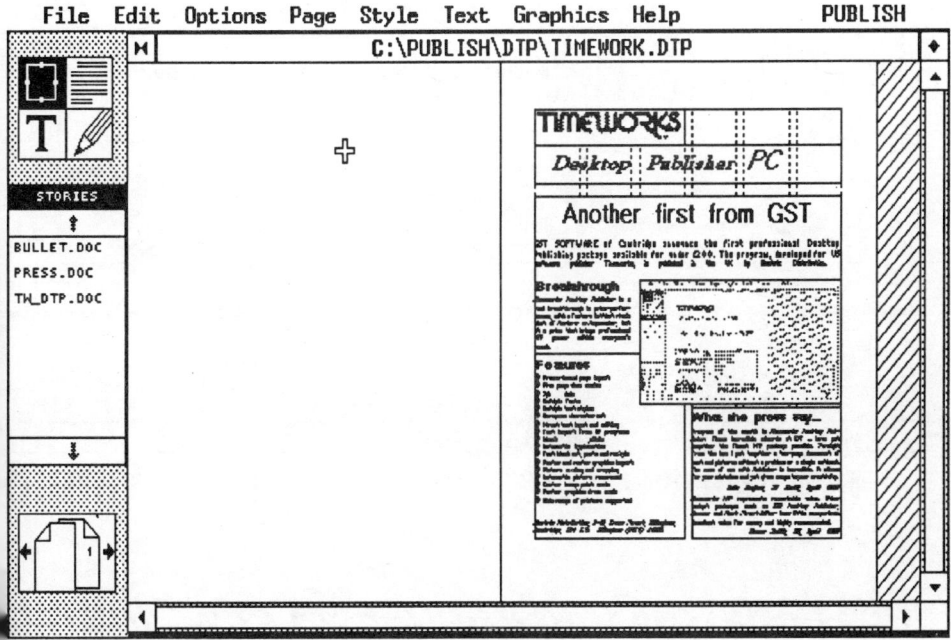

Figure 2.5 Two Page View Showing Page 1 (Right Hand)

Following from this, page 2 must always be a left hand page, and consequently if we view this page using the 'Two pages' view, this will appear on the left hand side of the screen, with a blank (unused) page to the right.

The result of this arrangement is that it is not possible to view pages 1 and 2 of a document together. To remain consistent, the left hand part of the screen will only display a left hand page, which is always even numbered (2,4 etc.). The right hand part will therefore only display a right hand page which is always odd numbered (1,3 etc.)

Whichever view you are using, you will notice on the display that a number of areas are surrounded by solid lines. These lines, unless specifically selected, do not print, and are only there to show the "Frames" which are used in constructing the page. To

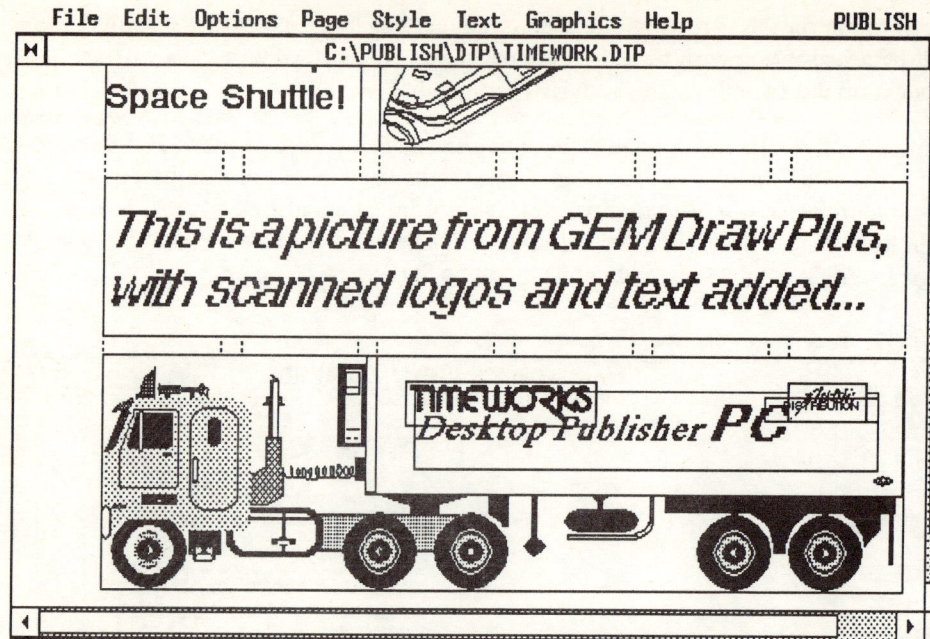

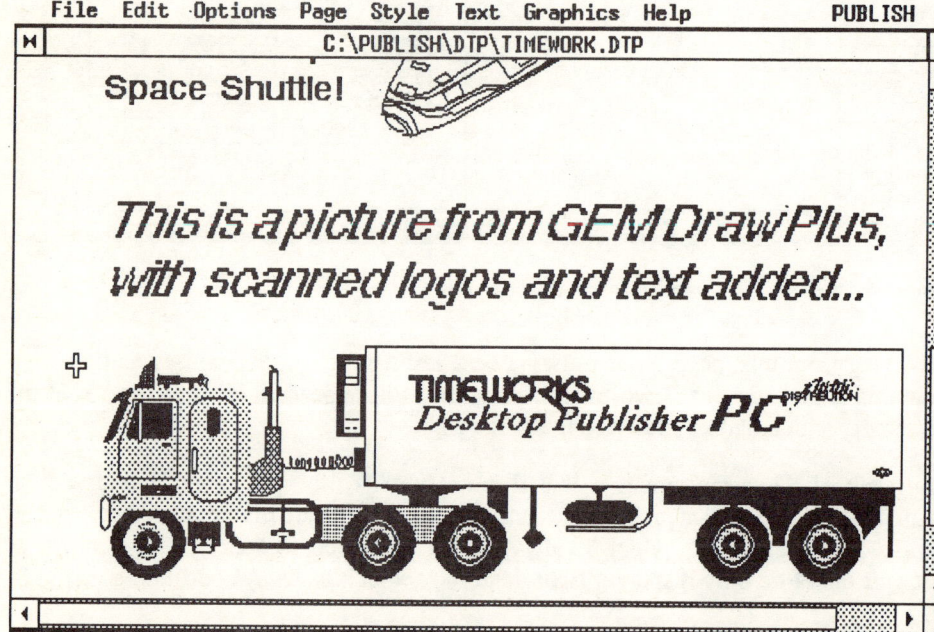

Figure 2.6 Document Page Frames ON (top picture) and OFF (bottom picture).

eliminate these, and get a clearer view of the document, go to the {OPTIONS} menu, and click on the [Show frames and columns] option, which will now hide these elements of the display. This is one of the toggle functions on the menus, and can be reversed by following the same procedure. We now see the page as it would be printed. Only frames where we have chosen to retain an outline will display as such.

It would be possible to print this page if required, to compare the screen and final output presentation. If you are the adventurous type, and you have a printer connected and correctly installed, then explore the print functions yourself. Others may prefer to refer to the notes on printing, later in the book, before proceeding with this.

You are obviously free to play around with these pages as much as you like. You should now have learned a little bit about moving around the display, using different views, and obtained an impression of a few of the possibilities that will open as you learn to use this package.

We will now go on to look at some of the procedures required to start producing our own documents. To finish your current session you may select the NEW or QUIT options from the File menu.

The QUIT option takes you out of the Timeworks Publisher program completely, first asking you if you want to save any changes to the document. At this stage it is unlikely that you would, so select the [ABANDON] option, as this will leave the original file undisturbed.

The NEW option from the menu will likewise ask if you wish to save or abandon the current file. Abandon it, and the program will start with a new file.

At this point you will be asked: Do you want to load a stylesheet?.

As we have not discussed this topic yet we will select [NO]. You will then be offered the Page Format menu, which allows you to decide what paper to use, and some other options that will be covered later. For the moment, accept the default settings. We will now be presented with a clear page, using the initial defaults discussed earlier.

Either by continuing from the preceding session, or by starting a new session, we should be faced with our normal opening screen. Use the [Full page] option in the {PAGE} menu or press [ALT] 3, to display a full page view. If you are continuing on from the above, you may also need to restore the [Show frames & columns] option from the {OPTIONS} menu.

Before we can do anything in Timeworks Publisher we have to define a *frame* Everything we wish to place on a Timeworks Publisher page has to be contained within such a frame.

To define a frame, we must first be in *frame mode*, so ensure that the appropriate icon is highlighted in the Toolkit. The screen pointer will be a 'Cross-Hair' cursor. Move this to the top left hand corner of the leftmost column guide and *drag* it down to the bottom right corner of the second column guide. (That is, move the mouse while holding down the left button). When the button is released a solid line will surround the frame. You will also notice that, provided you moved the pointer close to the column guides, the frame will have aligned itself with these guides. This is a [Snap to guides] feature, controlled from the {OPTIONS} menu, which is useful for ensuring alignments. Where small position adjustments are required this can be toggled on or off as necessary.

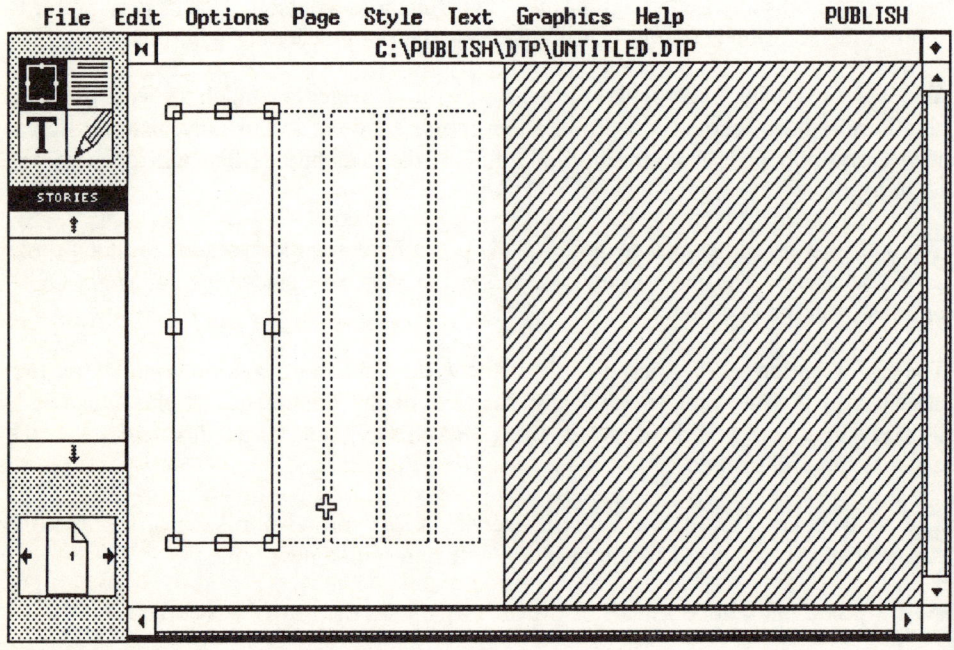

Figure 2.7 Basic Timeworks Publisher Frame (Activated)

Also notice, on the frame surround, the presence of small boxes, or *handles* , at each corner, and at the centre of each side of the frame. These handles appear on the currently selected frame, to identify it, and to enable us to further manipulate the frame. If we place our cursor in one of these boxes, and hold down the left hand mouse button, the cursor should change to a pointing finger. With this displayed, the handles can be moved to change the size of the frame.

If you are a little off target with this action, two alternatives may occur:

If you are just *outside* the correct position, that is, outside the frame, when the button is pressed then the handles may disappear, showing that the frame selection has been cancelled. To restore this you must move the pointer back into the frame, and click once to select it again; or

If you are *inside* the frame when the button is pressed, the cursor will change to a *flat hand*, which indicates that you are about to move the whole frame, which may not be desired.

In either case, you should release the button, and position the cursor more accurately to achieve the correct function.

Try this out a little, but finish off with the original frame shape, covering the first two columns. Click the mouse with the cursor outside the frame and the handles will disappear, enabling us to work on a new frame.

Now create a second frame to cover the next two columns of the guides, in the same fashion.

We are also going to create a third frame, but we will approach this in a different way, as we merely wish to have a third column the same as the first two. Ensure that the second frame is still active, i.e. the handles are showing. If it is not, move the cursor inside the frame and click once. Now move to the {EDIT} menu and select the [Copy] option. Although nothing seems to have happened, internally, Timeworks Publisher will have registered this command and copied the frame to a *clipboard* (i.e. a temporary storage area in memory)

The program allows one item to be copied to a clipboard in each mode, except Paragraph mode, i.e. we have three clipboards in total. If we attempt to copy a second item onto the clipboard the original will be lost. However, as long as we do not do any further copying, this frame will be held for us.

To use this we again go to the {EDIT} menu, and this time select the [Paste] option. Be a little careful here, because if you select either of the other options in error you will lose the original copy, and will have to start the copy process again. On the screen you will see a selected frame appear, just offset from the original. Move the cursor into the selected frame, and press and hold the mouse button. The cross-hair cursor will change to a flat hand, so that by DRAGGING the frame we can move the copy to any position on the page. Move this to cover the last two column guides and let go. The frame will remain active until we select another. Note, also, that the copy is still stored in the clipboard. Should we require to use it we just select the paste option again, and proceed as before.

The technique we used above to move the copy frame into position is the same used to move any complete frame around the page, and the general sequence of actions is:

1) Click in the frame to make it active, and release the button.

2) Click and hold the button so that the flat hand appears.

3) Drag the frame to the required position on the page, and release the button.

The steps (1) and (2) above MUST be quite distinctive; that is, the mouse button must be pressed AND released in step (1), before being pressed again in step (2).

Failure to do this will often result in a stray frame being created on the page. This will have to be removed using the [Cut] option in the {EDIT} menu.

Note, however, that the [Cut] option also makes use of the Clipboard. That is, if you have a frame stored in the clipboard following either a *CUT* or *COPY* procedure, and you then require to cut another frame, the original is overwritten, and therefore lost.

The use of the terminology *CUT, COPY* and *PASTE* may give rise to some confusion, particularly as it is not always applied consistently in different applications. We will pause here, to try and explain this a little further.

The term *CUT* can be used to mean 'remove entirely' (i.e. delete), or 'remove and place a copy somewhere else'. Within Timeworks Publisher this latter meaning is used, and hence the use of the clipboard to provide temporary storage for the element. (In some software the term MOVE is used to describe this second option).

The term *COPY* is used to mean "leave the original in place, but make an additional copy elsewhere in the document", and again there is a need to use the clipboard.

The *PASTE* function is used, simply, to place a copy of the contents of the clipboard at another place in the document (not necessarily on the same page, or even in the same document)

This use of these functions is consistent throughout the operation of Timeworks Publisher, and a single clipboard is available in each of the operating modes.

Once the three frames have been placed on the page, it would be a good idea to have a little practice at repeating the procedures, and get used to the functions described. Then we can move on to look at some further features of the program.

We can enter text into a document either by directly typing onto the page, or we can create a text file using a word processor, and *import* this into our document.

For the moment move the cursor outside all the frames, and click, so that none are currently active.

We will make use of a text file provided with the program to see this function in operation. Point to the {FILE} menu, and select the [Import text] option. You will be presented with the appropriate Timeworks Publisher response screen, as illustrated in Figure 2.8.

This Figure shows the range of word processors supported by Timeworks Publisher. However, there is much more to discuss about this, in a later section. For present purposes we see that the 1st WORD PLUS option is highlighted, and we will accept this, as the file available is stored in this format. We are then presented with the GEM Item Selector screen, and we should select the *stories* folder, and from this the only file available, EXAMPLE.DOC.

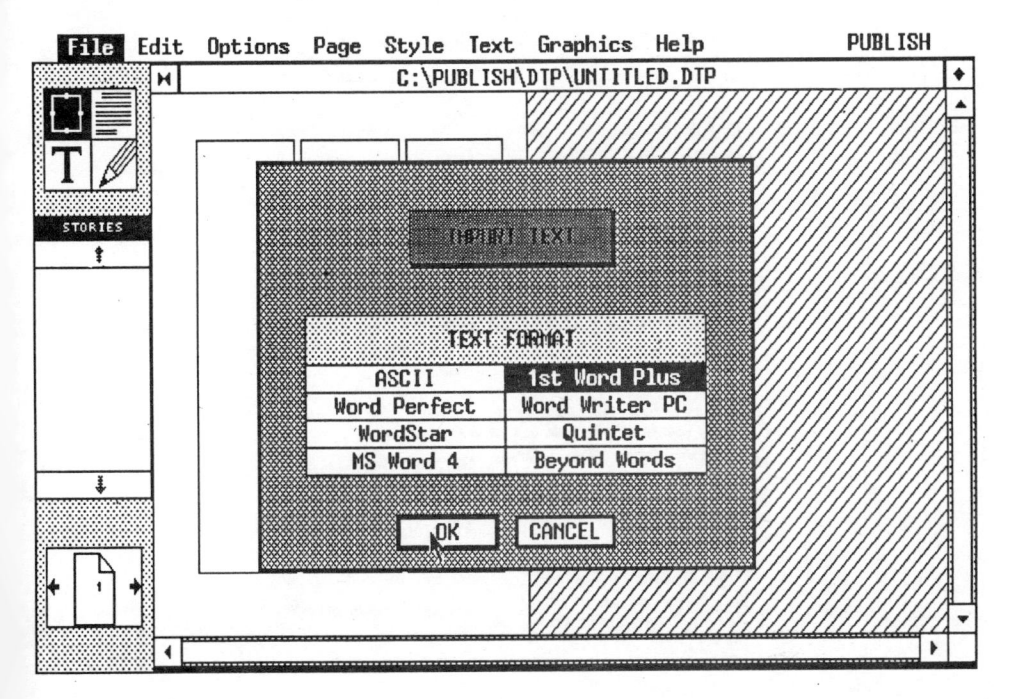

Figure 2.8 Import Text Control Screen

This is loaded into the computer, and if we look in the BROWSER, we will see this file name listed under the heading 'STORIES'. This means that the document is now available to the program.

Note that if any frame is active when we import a text file, this file will immediately flow into the frame, without any further action. Always make sure, before using the import facilities, that only a suitable frame, or none, is active.

Now make the leftmost frame active, and then click on the filename in the Browser. This file will then flow in to fill the active frame. If we now select the second frame, and click on the file name once again, the remainder of the text file will flow into the second frame.

In full page view it is probable that the text is illegible, so change the page view to Actual Size ([ALT] 1) or Double Size ([ALT] 2) depending on your monitor. We will now see the text file in the two columns.

If we use the options available to us to move around the page we will see that some of the text enhancements have been imported into the DTP file. For example, we can see Bold characters, Underlined characters and Italic characters, just as they would appear in the original document. (Sadly, this ability is not universal, even with the word processors listed in the selection page, but we will look at this later)

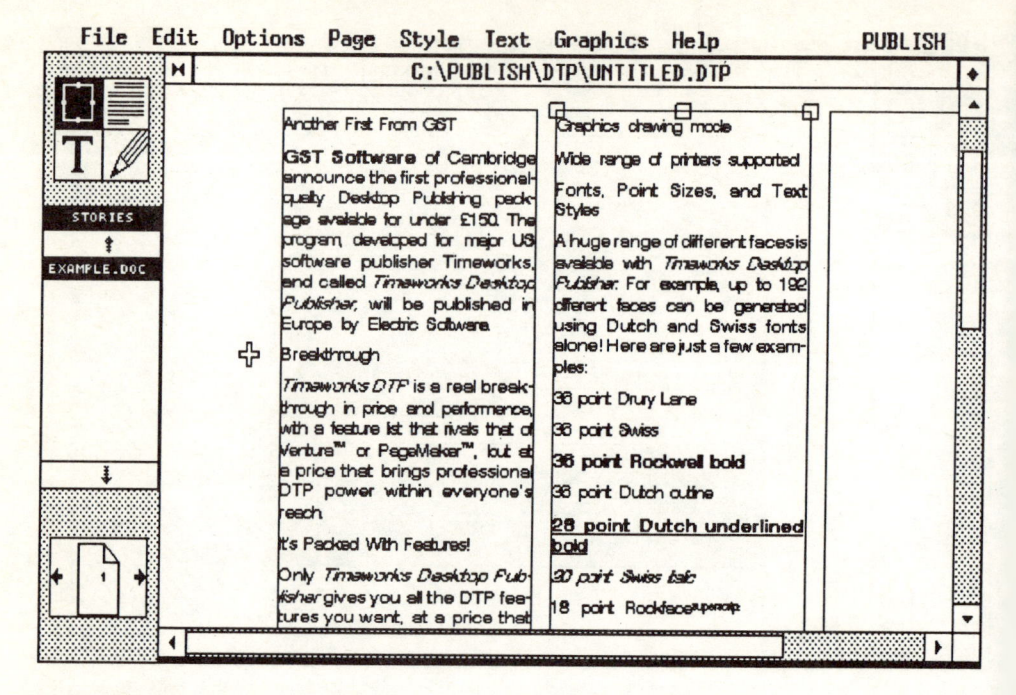

Figure 2.9 Imported Text

Once we have the text in our page we can use some of the features of the program to change its appearance. For now we will use some of the text options, and for that we will need to select the Text box from our Toolkit selection. Move the pointer to the box containing the letter 'T' (for TEXT), and click. This option becomes highlighted, and we note that the Browser has now changed to show the available text enhancements, and is headed 'TEXT STYLE'.

The text cursor appears as an 'I' bar. To change any of the text features we must first highlight that text. Move the text cursor to the beginning of the first line of text in the first frame; 'Another First from GST'.

To highlight this text we have to drag the cursor across to the end of the line. Do this by holding the button down while moving the mouse, and we should see the line appear in inverse. (i.e. white text on black background).

It is sometimes a little difficult to line up the text cursor exactly. The 'I' bar is used as a position guide, but when the mouse button is pressed this places a second, thin line, cursor on the page, in the correct text position. It is occasionally possible for this to be one character position different from that expected. To ensure the correct position move the 'I' bar and check the location of the true text cursor before proceeding.

If the text cursor position is not correct place the 'I' bar closer to the required position and click again, and the true text cursor should follow.

Having highlighted the required text block, now move the cursor into the browser, and click on the Bold option, and we will see the text change. Note that the text remains highlighted, so immediately select the Underline option from the browser, and note a further change in the text. Now click the mouse with the cursor outside the line of text, and the display is restored showing the new text format for this line. We can change any of the text in this way.

As each individual change is made to the text the whole page is re-drawn to accommodate the changes, and to make allowance for any changed spacing that may arise as a consequence of the particular action.

Note that changes in the text within the Timeworks Publisher page are not reflected in the original file. When we save our DTP document the changes are stored within that, and the original file remains untouched. Pick out some more of the text, particularly some of the isolated lines, and add some enhancements of your own choosing.

Using the Browser we can affect the *style* of the text, but we may wish to do more than this. We can, for example, change both the size and typeface that we use, within the limits of the fonts supplied by Timeworks Publisher.

Select the first line of text again, but now move the pointer to the {STYLE} menu, and we will see there the options shown in the Browser, with two others. The outlined option in light text is not available with the PC versions of the program. The other important selection is the FONT/SIZE selection which we will choose now.

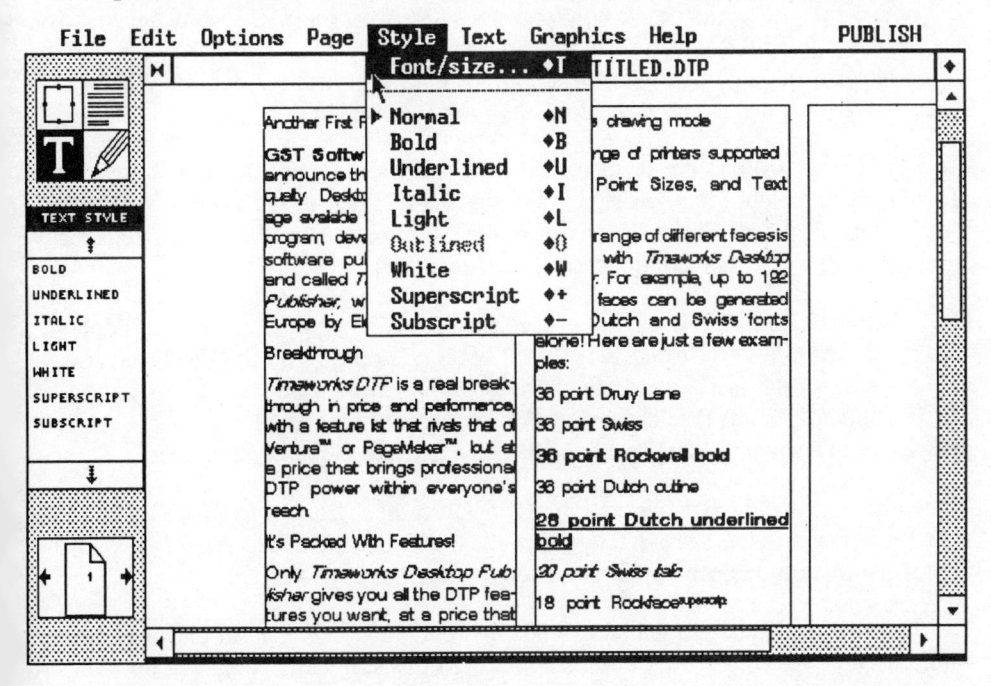

Figure 2.10 (a) Changing the font – Style Menu

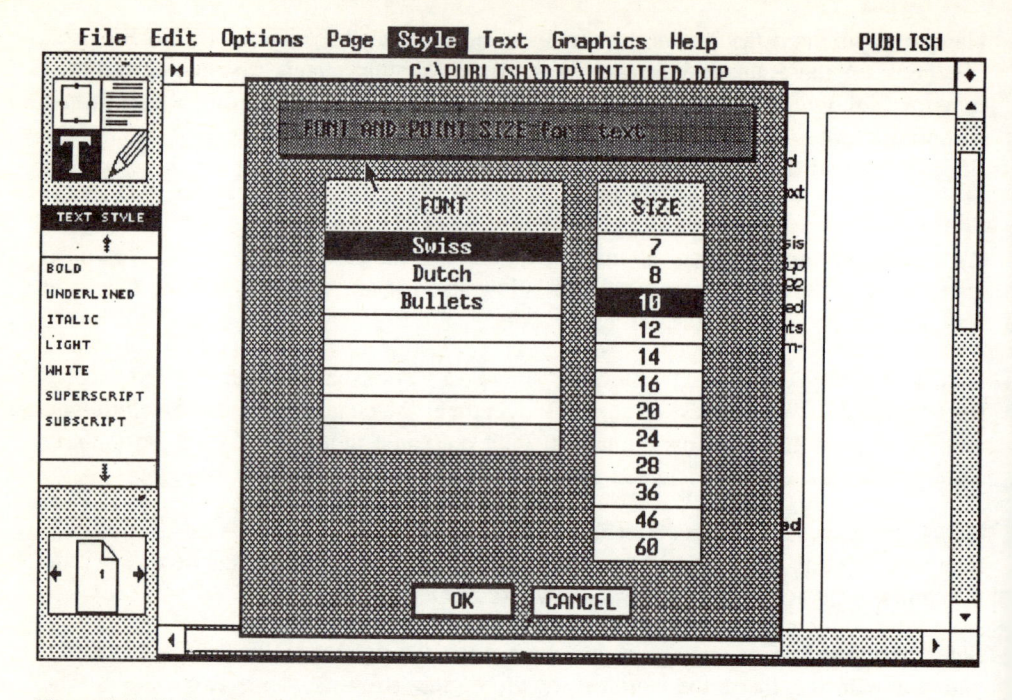

Figure 2.10 (b) Changing the font - Font/Size menu

The actual options available do now depend on the version of the software that you have and, in particular, the type of printer selected. The illustration shows a version of the menu using an EGA monitor and a dot matrix printer for output. Whatever is displayed, the actions required to adjust the print size are similar.

For now, let us just choose an increased point size, say 16 or 20, by pointing to the appropriate selection. Click on [OK], and we are returned to the normal screen with the changes displayed. (With Postscript printers you may enter the point size directly from the keyboard in one point increments, if required)

Note that the Bold and Underlined specification still applies, as we would hope. Again, now have a go at using the various text style options on the displayed text to obtain a feel for the facility. Do not at this time, however, select the *bullets* option, as this is a little different. (Well, do so if you really want to, as no harm can be done; it just produces a slightly unexpected result which I would rather explain later)

Remember that within Timeworks Publisher you can experiment as much as you like with these basic functions. At this stage you will not risk losing anything, and the very worst that can happen is that you need to clear the page and start again.

The Timeworks Publisher manual extends this particular exercise, in one way, and it would do little harm to follow their examples. At this stage this book will do things a little differently; we will add a few more manipulations to our repertory, and then go on to a very detailed look at the various modes of operation

Change the page view to [Full page], and CUT all the different frames from the page. (Go on, you know how to do it!). Although the frames, and their contents, are removed from the page entirely, the basic document remains intact in the program, and is listed in the browser, and can be used within a completely changed layout.

For this exercise we will create one single frame to cover the first three column guides on the page. We then want two equal sized frames to occupy the upper and lower halves of the remaining part of the page. These frames are easily created in the same way as we did for the first exercise.

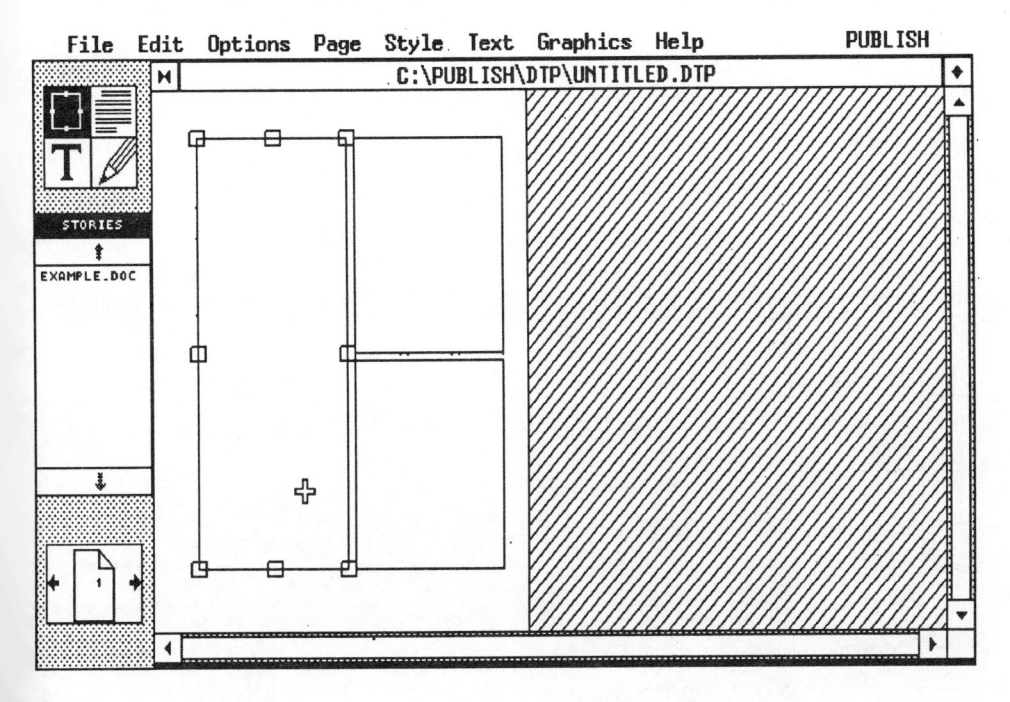

Figre 2.11 Modified Frame Layout

Now select the first full column frame, and click on the EXAMPLES.DOC file in the browser, and see the text flow into the frame. Click on the upper of the frames on the right hand side of the page, and the remainder of the text file will flow in.

Use the {STYLE} menu to change the characteristics of the first line of text, as before. Now move to the line, which says 'Breakthrough'. Select the 'PARAGRAPH' mode icon in the tool box, and note the cursor change to show the paragraph symbol. If we now click on the word 'Breakthrough', the whole word will become highlighted. Note, also, that the browser now lists 4 items, headed paragraph styles, and the one called 'BODY TEXT' is currently highlighted.

Paragraph styles contain complex text style and layout instructions which can be brought into effect by a single action. With the text still highlighted, move the cursor to 'SUBHEAD' in the browser, and click once. Notice that the text immediately changes to a new appearance, which incorporates both size and style features.

Move down to the line 'Its Packed with features', and repeat this procedure. Now move to the first of the list of features 'Frame based page layout', and highlight this. Use the cursor to select the BULLET style, and note the changes. Select each of the points in turn and assign the bullet style, to improve the clarity of the listing.

This gives a little taste of the power of Timeworks Publisher to control page and text layout, and we will be looking at this feature in very much greater detail later.

Note that as we make all the individual line and text changes, the whole document is adjusted automatically to make room for the new sizes and layout of the text.

As the final exercise in this session we will add a picture to the page using the final, empty frame.

Change to Frame mode and ensure that none of the frames are selected by clicking the mouse outside all frames. Move to the {FILE} menu and select the [Import picture] option, and you will get the appropriate Timeworks Publisher response screen.

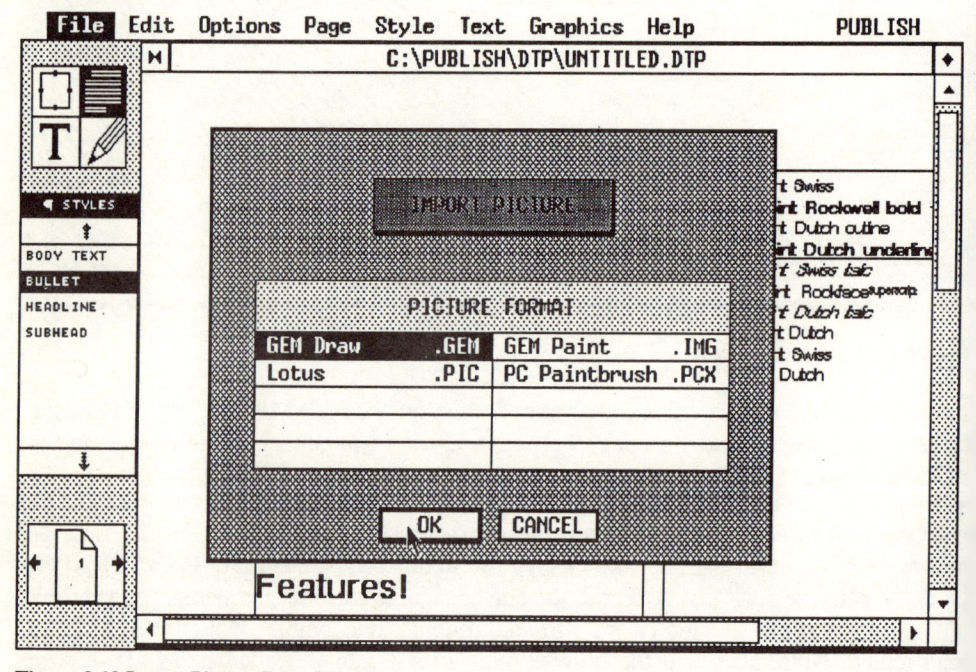

Figure 2.12 Import Picture Control Screen

As with the text screen, we are shown the picture formats that can be accepted by Timeworks Publisher, and although this does not look impressive we must remember that the PC Paintbrush format (PCX) is one of the most widely used standards.

However, the picture we will use is stored in the default selection created by GEM Draw, although there are others supplied on the disk which use the GEM Paint (.IMG) format (There are important differences between these formats which we will return to later) Accept the offered selection, and we are once again presented with the GEM Item Selector display.

There is only one file available to us at this point, PC.GEM, which is in the Pictures folder, and we will select this. We now notice that the Browser has changed, with the title LINE ART, appearing at the top with the PC.GEM file listed below. If the browser doe not show 'LINE ART', in the title bar, then click on this bar and the browser title will rotate between the three options available, namely, line art, images and stories. If we now select our last frame, and click on the PC.GEM file in the browser, the picture will appear in the frame. As this is a *Line Art* drawing it will arrange itself to fill the available frame, and we have no editing control over this. In order to get the drawing to appear in acceptable proportions, we can change the frame size to achieve the desired overall appearance. Using the handles, manipulate the frame size until it looks satisfactory.

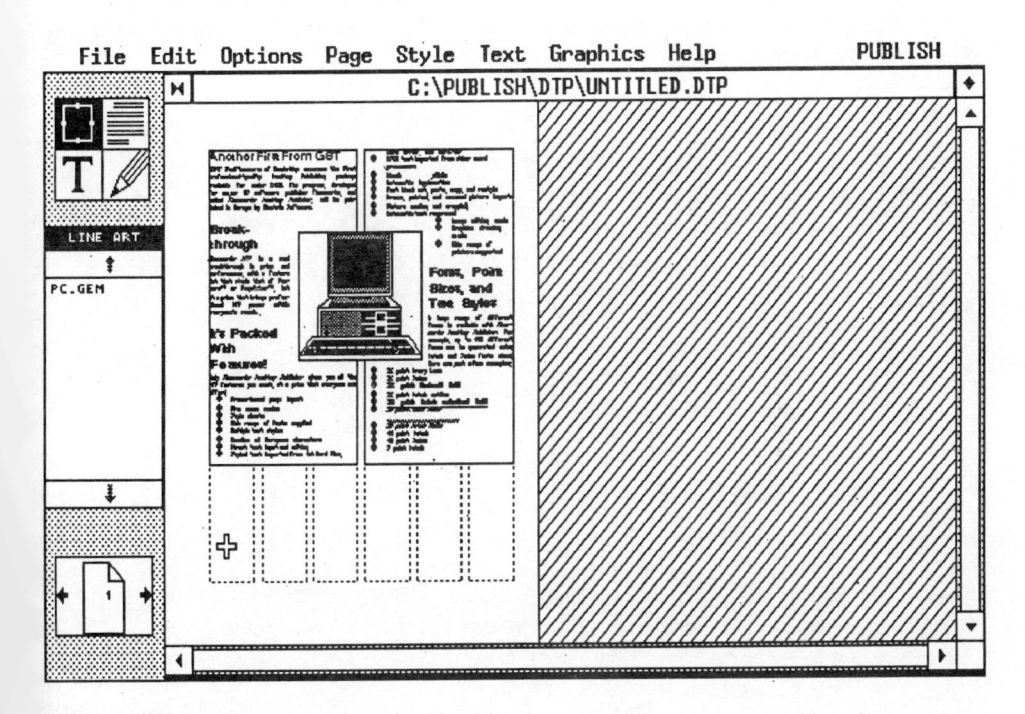

Figure 2.14 The Finished Document

Now that we have the picture on the page we can choose to position it wherever we wish, even over some of our text. Move the picture frame so that it sits in the middle of our left hand column, just below the paragraph headed 'Breakthrough'. You will notice immediately that all the text has flowed out from under the picture frame, and where necessary moved into the second frame. By changing to a larger scale view we can move the picture frame to the most suitable point in the text, and further change the size to suit the position if necessary.

Return to full page view, and now move the picture frame so that it bridges the two columns of text. Notice that once again the text is rearranged to fill up the available space. We can continue moving and manipulating the various frames on the page to achieve the desired layout and, of course, we can add additional frames, and type in headlines, etc., to further enhance the appearance of the page. Once again, you should refer to the original manual if you wish to pursue this now.

The above, very briefly, is intended to give a general view of some of the features of Timeworks Publisher , to enable you to perform some of the basic manipulations, and to generate some ideas of the type of results that can be achieved. You are in a position now to experiment with some of these techniques, and to start to achieve some practical results.

In the chapters that follow we will look in detail at the various modes of operation available, and identify some of the techniques that will be required in more advanced work. We will also try to point out any traps in using the software, and to show any shortcomings that may appear.

3

Page Manipulations

To work on any examples in this section we will need to start with a clean sheet on the screen. We can either abandon or save an existing file, or we can start the program again. Whichever way you get there, once there is a clear screen, select the NEW option from the file menu.

When we first select the NEW option, we are asked if we wish to load a style sheet. We cannot address the matter of style until we have looked at some of the other functions, so we will simply reply [NO] to this. (In practice, however, Timeworks Publisher will actually use its own internal default styles, which correspond to the original DEFAULT.STY sheet specification)

We are then presented with the page format options screen. The first item, paper size, is self explanatory, and we are just required to highlight the paper we expect to print upon. There is no facility for changing any of these fixed options. If you have an unusual paper size requirement, then choose an option which is larger, but use the column controls to ensure that all your printing is confined within the real size of your paper. You may also be faced with some difficulties when it comes to printing and page alignment, but these can be overcome, fairly easily.

Likewise, the orientation option offers no problems, so just select the appropriate type. During printing the printer will simply print out the page on its side, for the landscape option, so this does not require a wide column printer, or any other difficult adjustments.(It is not possible to use landscape (i.e. wide) mode using a 9 pin dot matrix printer)

The concept of master pages requires a little more explanation. In most applications for producing documents, a fairly narrow range of page layouts will be adopted, in order to maintain a consistency of appearance. In this sense master pages are used to

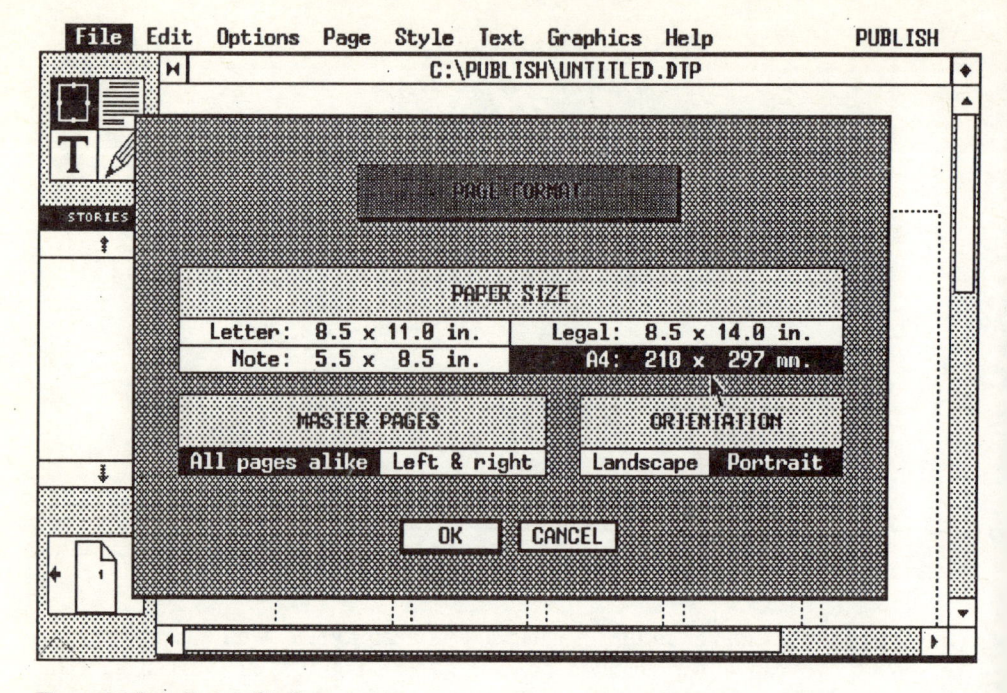

Figure 3.1 Page Format Display

provide a basic reference page for such documents, and will incorporate custom column guides and other features. If the document is only going to be printed on one side, that is, there will be a binding margin only on the left side of any page, then we need only define a single master page, and select the [All Pages Alike] option on the page format menu.

If, on the other hand, we are producing a long document, or book, which will have printing on both sides of each sheet, then we will require to create left and right pages, in particular to take care of the *gutter* Margins, and any other variations that we may require.

To see the impact of this, select the following options from the page format menu:

Paper Size	A4
Master Pages	Left and Right
Orientation	Portrait

When these are selected Timeworks Publisher will load its default style and display page 1 of your document, (as yet blank). Note that the column guides shown indicate a wider margin on the left, to allow for binding. This shows that page 1 is a 'right' page and this is confirmed by the page icon in the Toolkit column.(Look in any book and you will see that page 1 is always a right hand page)

Point to the {PAGE} menu, and select the [Go to page..] option.

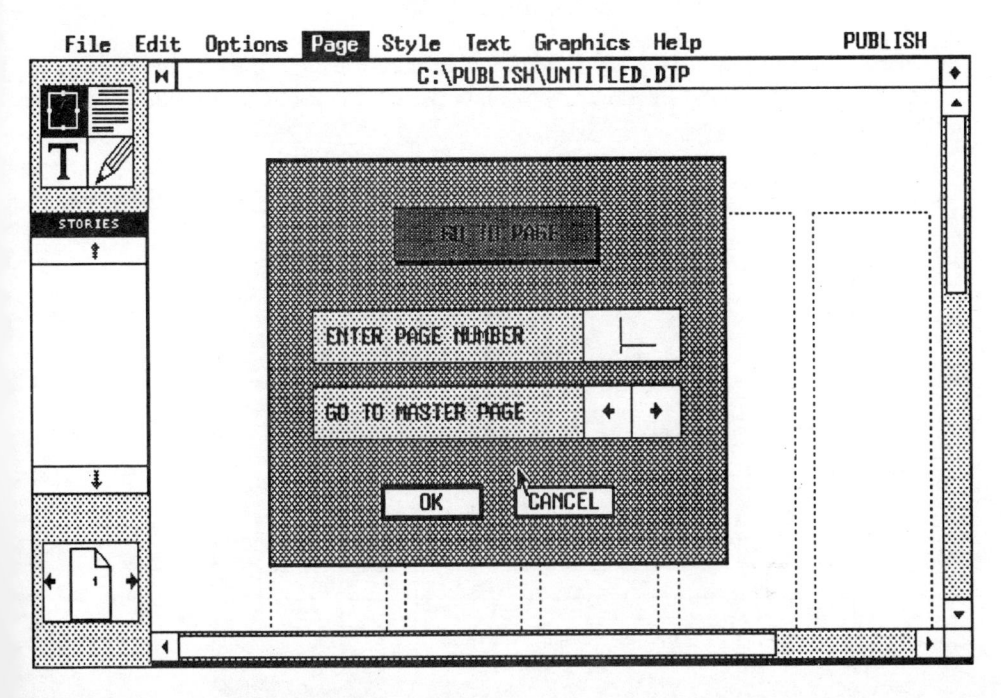

Figure 3.2 Go To Page Control Screen

We now want to choose the master page option, so click on the left facing arrow, which will bring up the left hand master page. We can now switch between the left and right master pages by using the arrows on either side of the page icon. As we do this we will see that the only difference, in the default style, is the position of the wider margin on the page, which moves from left to right hand side as we switch pages.

When we are setting up master pages for any document we should bear in mind all the elements of text and layout that may be required. In particular, we will have to define the left and right margins for the pages, and the top and bottom margins, always remembering to leave room for any headers and footers that may be specified. The number of column guides used has no impact on these major dimensions, as columns are always made to be of equal size and spacing, and fitting inside the overall page layout. They are only appropriate where the page is to be divided into columns or sections, and to give some guide to the construction of these on a consistent pattern.

Fig 1.3 (in Chapter 1) illustrated the various elements of the page layout which should be considered at this stage.

Any changes we make to the master pages will reflect on any new pages that we create in our document. However, we can modify any later page in the document, in any way we choose, without affecting the master pages.

The margin settings, and the overall page layout controls are linked to the control of the column guides. To see the controls available select the [Set column guides] option in the {OPTIONS} menu.

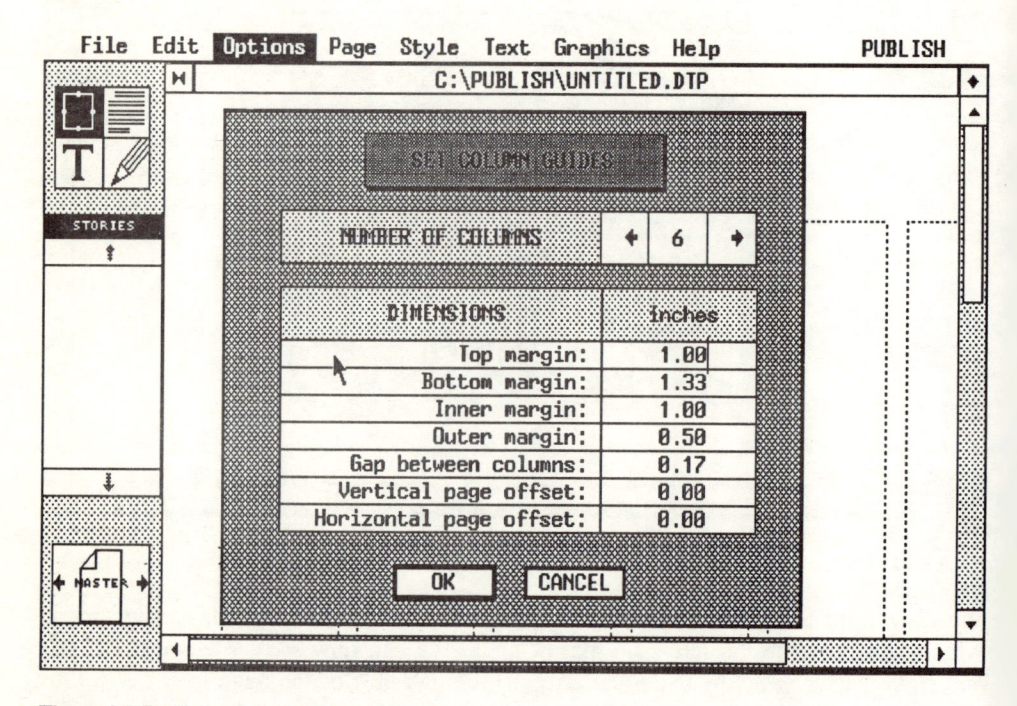

```
File  Edit  Options  Page  Style  Text  Graphics  Help          PUBLISH
                          C:\PUBLISH\UNTITLED.DTP

                              SET COLUMN GUIDES

                          NUMBER OF COLUMNS      ←  6  →

                              DIMENSIONS          inches
                              Top margin:          1.00
                              Bottom margin:       1.33
                              Inner margin:        1.00
                              Outer margin:        0.50
                              Gap between columns: 0.17
                              Vertical page offset: 0.00
                              Horizontal page offset: 0.00

                                  OK     CANCEL
```

Figure 3.3 Set Column Guides Control Screen

We can change the number of columns by clicking on the left or right arrows in the 'NUMBER OF COLUMNS' box, selecting any number between 1 and 9. These will always be assumed to be equal sized, and equally spaced columns. Control is available over all the page margins, so that these can be set up as desired. Note the terminology relating to the side margins, which refer to the *inner margin* (which is the binding side) and the *outer margin*. The inner margin will include the measurement for the normal text margin, and the additional gutter margin, to allow for binding of the document.

Any changes that are made will reflect on both master pages, so that it is not possible to have different column arrangements on different master pages. It is important to remember that these column guides are just that, guides to indicate positions on the paper. We can use or ignore them as we please in subsequent pages.

The vertical and horizontal page offset controls are necessary to compensate for the way that different printers accommodate their paper, and in the section on printing we note how to adjust these for your own particular hardware set-up.

We are not restricted just to defining master pages in terms of columns and margins. We can add anything we like to a master page, that can subsequently be used in a document. This will be seen in operation in some of the practical illustrations later. This could be a company logo, address block, publication title, etc., or merely a fixed arrangement of frames to define certain parameters of the various pages. All the editing features of Timeworks Publisher can be used on the master pages, to enhance them in any way we require.

Once the master pages have been defined, we would switch back to the normal document pages for any further work. From the Page menu select the GO TO PAGE option, and enter the appropriate page number in the space indicated. If you are starting a new document, then the normal choice will be page 1, which will always be a right-hand page. We can now start adding the features to each page as required.

As we use up each page of the document, from the page menu we can select to:

Add Page	Appends a page to the document end.
Insert Page	Adds a new page at current position.
Delete Page	Deletes the current page

When we save the document all pages, including the master pages, are saved for future use.

You have total control over the layout of the master pages. The final results are a matter of good design, which is something we will touch on briefly later. However, good design, like beauty, is very much in the eye of the beholder, and does depend more than anything else on your own particular skills and perception.

When a master page has been created, we would normally wish to save it for future use, as a separate entity from the document which it controls. The master page definition is just one element of a 'style sheet', which will be explored a little later. To save a master page definition, however, it must be saved as if it was a full Style Sheet.

This is available as the [Save style sheet...] option in the {FILE} menu. You will be asked to give a name for the Style Sheet, which will always require to have a .STY extension. There is a DEFAULT.STY Style Sheet on the program disks which defines the normal opening page, and other parameters, so unless we wish to alter this we would select a different file name at this point, and a different directory if required.

Frame Manipulations

In chapter 2 we made use of some basic frame manipulations. This was a very simple view of their function. Frames, and their use in DTP applications, are extremely powerful, as we shall see.

A number of individual characteristics can be assigned to frames, and we will be looking at the following functions:

OPTIONS Menu:
Show Rulers
Ruler spacing
Frame Borders
Frame Tints
Repel Text
Size and Position

PAGE Menu:
Bring to front
Send to back

Column guides, set up in the master pages, are used to provide general alignment of frames. For most purposes these will be quite adequate. However, to give further assistance, Timeworks Publisher is supplied with a set of rulers. In the {OPTIONS} menu we can use the [Show rulers] function to toggle on and off the ruler display. We may also choose the units, using the Ruler spacing controls, that will be used on the rulers from the following options:

Picas and Points
Centimetres
Inches and Tenths (Decimal)
Inches and Eighths (Decimal)

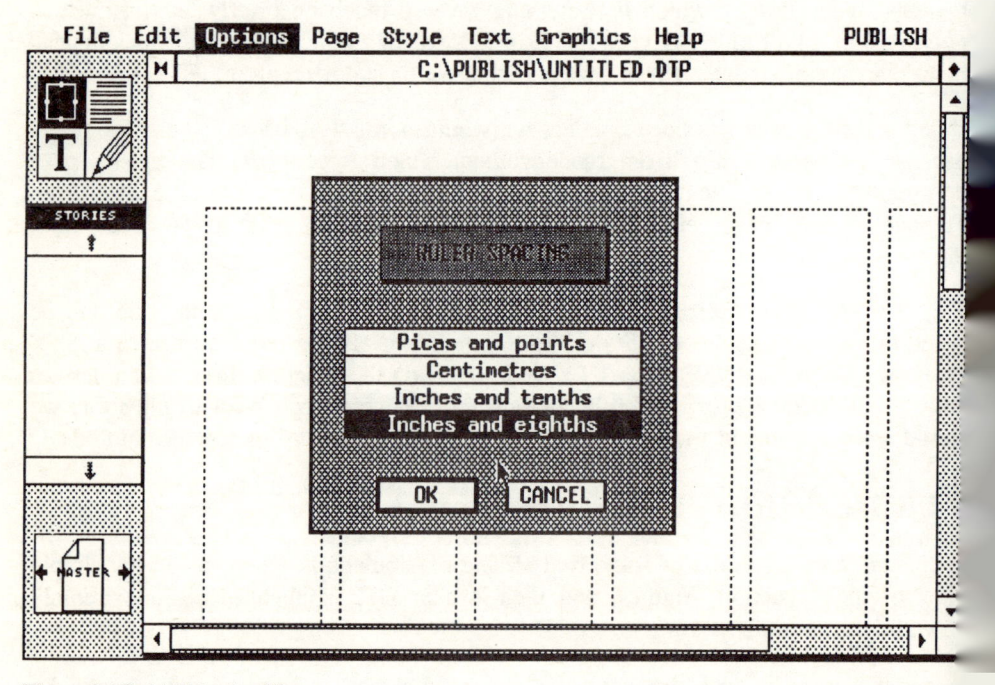

Figure 3.4 Ruler Selection Menu

The default option is inches and eighths, although the measurements are always expressed as decimals. Remember that neither the inch nor the centimetre measurements will relate very comfortably with the point measurements always used for text spacing, etc., and the metric form is the least compatible. (If it helps at all, one eight of an inch is equal to 9 points, in typographic measurement, so there is some correlation there). If we show the rulers, then any changes we make to the units selection will be carried out in view. The rulers use the top left hand corner of the page as the 0,0 reference point, and this cannot be offset. Once we change the rulers many of the measurements used within the system are adjusted accordingly.

For our present purposes, select the [Ruler spacing] control in the {OPTIONS} menu to set the ruler units in centimetres, as we are not going to make use of any text measurement options, and then select the [Show rulers] option.

With the rulers showing, a Hairline cursor moves over the ruler lines as we move the page cursor. This enables us to track the cursor position quite accurately. If we are to make full use of this feature then we may need to turn off the [Snap to guides] feature within the {OPTIONS} menu, as this prevents very fine positioning adjustments in some cases.

When we have placed a frame on a page, and we wish to check the accuracy of the position and size that we have chosen, we can select the [Size and position] option from the {OPTIONS} menu when the frame is active.

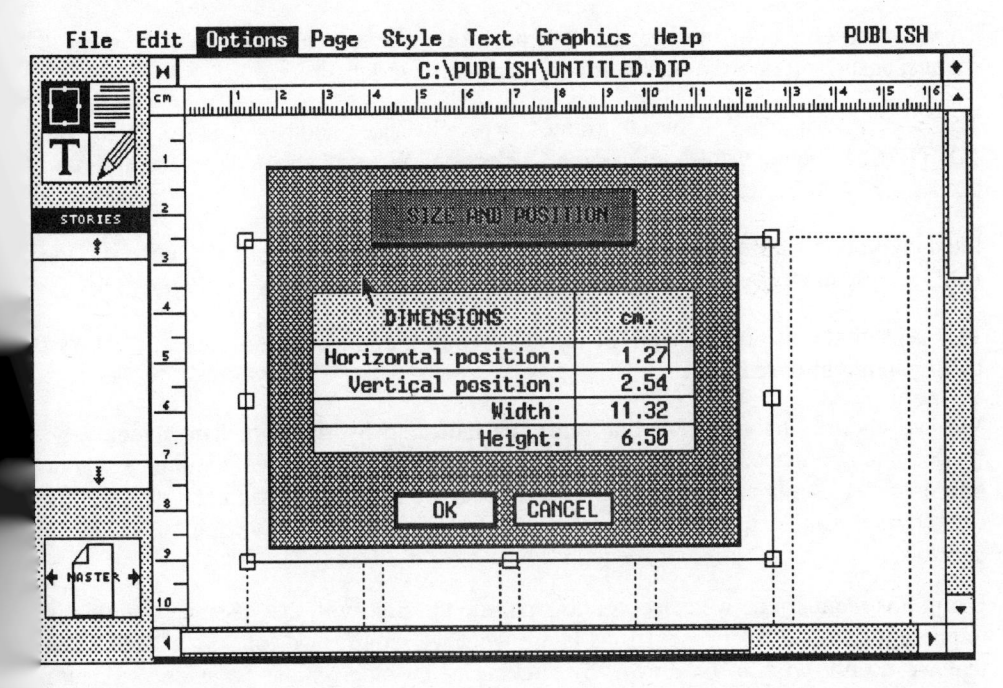

Figure 3.5 Size and Position Menu

This displays precise information in the ruler units chosen. We can change any of these parameters by using the mouse to position the cursor, delete the current value, and insert a new value. Once accepted, these changes will be reflected on the display. Using this facility we can get extremely good control of frame position on the page (Down to .01cm precision). Positions set using this feature will override the [Snap to guides] feature.

We can also access this menu by *double clicking* in the appropriate frame, as there is not an [ALT] Key combination for this.

When we view a page of our document we see a two dimensional view; that is, we have width and height, but no depth. Although our earlier exercises did not demonstrate this feature, frames are actually created using a 3-dimensional page. Each frame, in effect, occupies a different layer on the page. The layer occupied is directly related to the sequence in which the frames are created.

If we consider the first frame created to sit on the basic page level, then each successive frame will sit at a higher level. When frames are made to lie side by side on the page this has no particular significance. However, in many applications, including the TIMEWORKS.DTP document that we looked at earlier, different frames will overlap into the same space. Where this happens, later frames will sit over, and may obscure earlier frames. The hierarchy is strictly related to the sequence in which the frames are created.

To view the effects of this, get a blank page on your screen, and create three small frames, ensuring that they do not, for the moment, overlap.

To help discriminate between frames we will use another feature from the {OPTIONS} menu, the [Frame border] selection. We will create a different frame border for each frame.

Make any one of the frames active and select the [Frame border] option in the {OPTIONS} menu. A further selection menu is presented, as shown in Figure 3.6.

This represents the current state of the active frame border, i.e. no border, as shown by the highlight over NONE.

We can choose any one of 4 line types, as indicated by the right hand block. The border can be placed on any or all sides of the frame, as we require. For our purposes, let us select the ALL AROUND choice, and use a different line type for each frame. Create a border around each of the three frames to suit, using these controls.

Using this menu, once we select a line type, the program will then assume that this is required all around the frame. If this is not what we require, we can turn off the sides that we do not wish to be drawn, by clicking at the appropriate point on the menu screen. It is not possible to mix line types in a single frame, although a similar effect may be achieved using graphic controls which we will meet later.

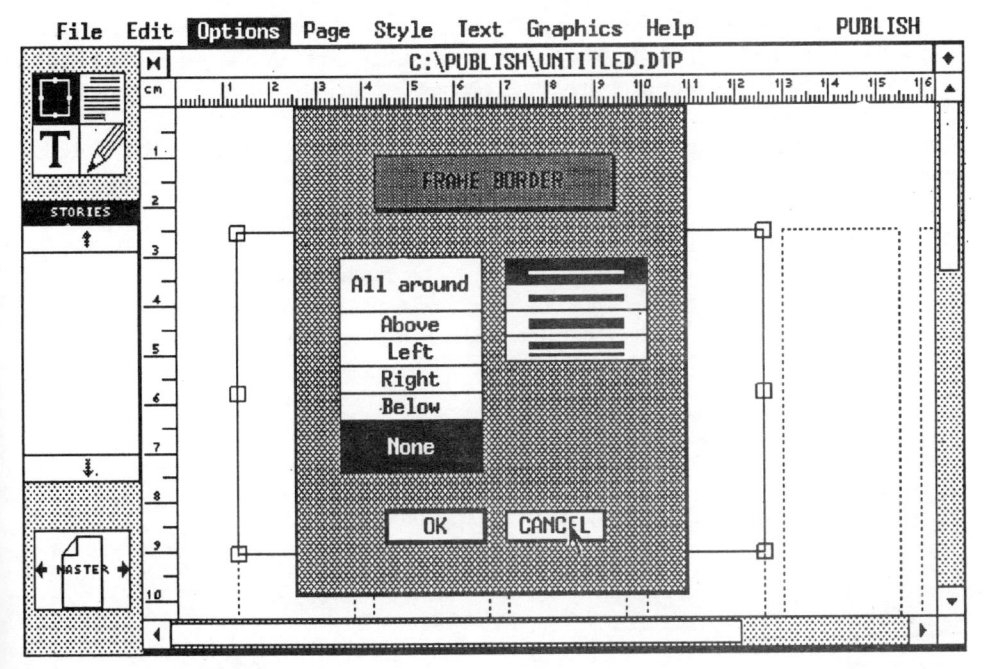

Figure 3.6 Frame Border Controls

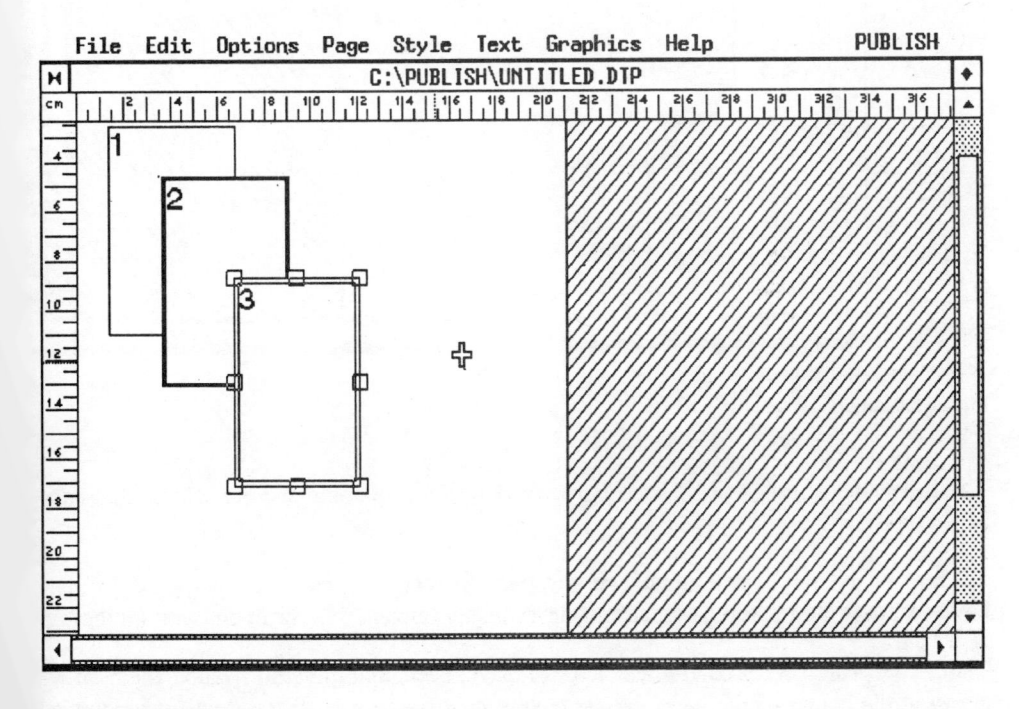

Figure 3.7 Frame Hierarchy 1

Now move the frames around to any position on the screen, allowing them to overlap, and we will see that each will always occupy the same layer on the page. That is, the later, or higher number frames will always obscure the lower frames. See Figure 3.7.

However, we do have the facility to control this aspect using options in the {PAGE} menu. Place the frames in such a position that each is clearly visible, but partly overlapping each of the others. Now make the highest level frame the active frame, and go to the {PAGE} menu. Select the [Send to back] option, and you will see the active frame move behind all the others. Now, no matter how we move the frames, this new hierarchy will apply. If we now select this same frame, and use the [Bring to front] option in the page menu, then the original hierarchy will be restored. We can use this feature freely to shuffle frames about on the page, and control their level.

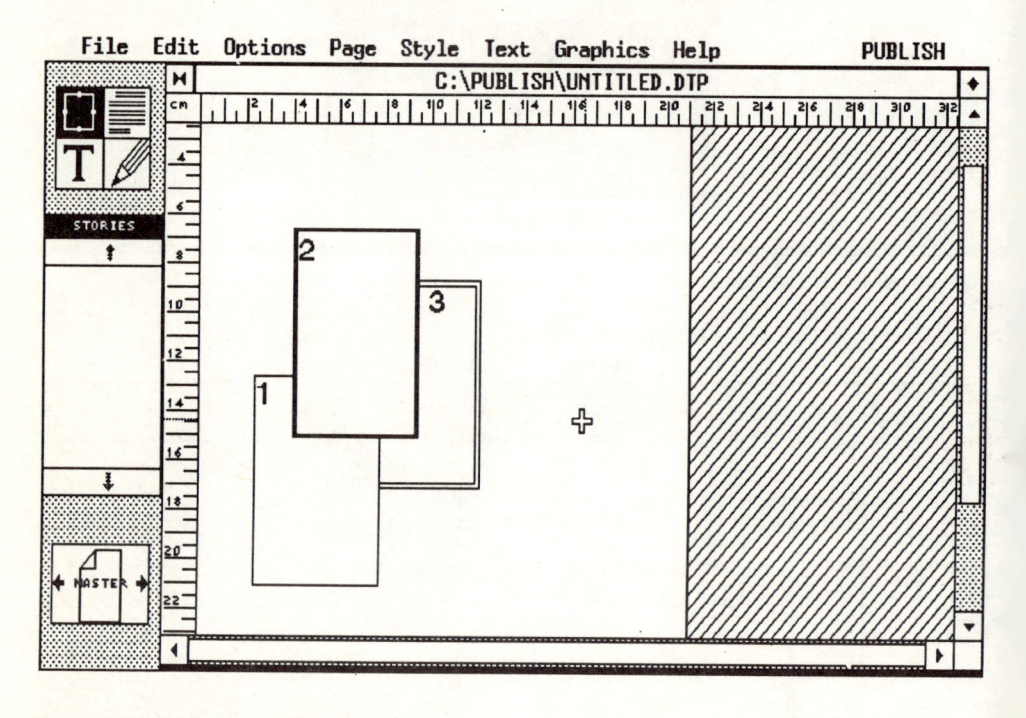

Figure 3.8 Adjusted Frame Hierarchy

The full value of this will be seen later when we look at some special effects that can be incorporated.

So far we have always created frames as distinct entities on a page. There is, however, nothing to stop us creating frames inside one another, or even over another.

Using the group of three frames that we have been manipulating, place them in a group in the centre of the page. Now create a new frame such that it totally surrounds the three smaller frames. When we do this the original frames will disappear from view entirely, and we cannot access them at all. However, if we use the [Send to back] instruction on the new frame, the other three re-appear and we have full control again.

As mentioned earlier, this feature is quite powerful, and can be used to good effect. However, too much fiddling might cause a frame to disappear from view entirely, and it may take a fair degree of shuffling to restore it. This is unlikely to be a major problem in practice, but you do need to be aware of the possibilities for trouble.

Although we have been manipulating basically empty frames, these same functions can be used on any filled frame.

For our next exercises we will need some filled frames on the screen, so abandon all current work, or simply cut all existing frames to start afresh.

We want to create one frame to hold some graphics, and another to hold some text. For the former we will import our PC.GEM file, and for the latter the EXAMPLE.DOC file we used earlier. Import these files now. Create a small frame for the graphics image, about 8cm square, and a larger frame for the text file. Initially create these so that they do not overlap, and load the files into the appropriate frames. Ensure that the graphics frame is created first, so that the hierarchy is known.

The text content of the frame above is not significant in any way, so you can call in any suitable text files that you have available, in the acceptable formats.

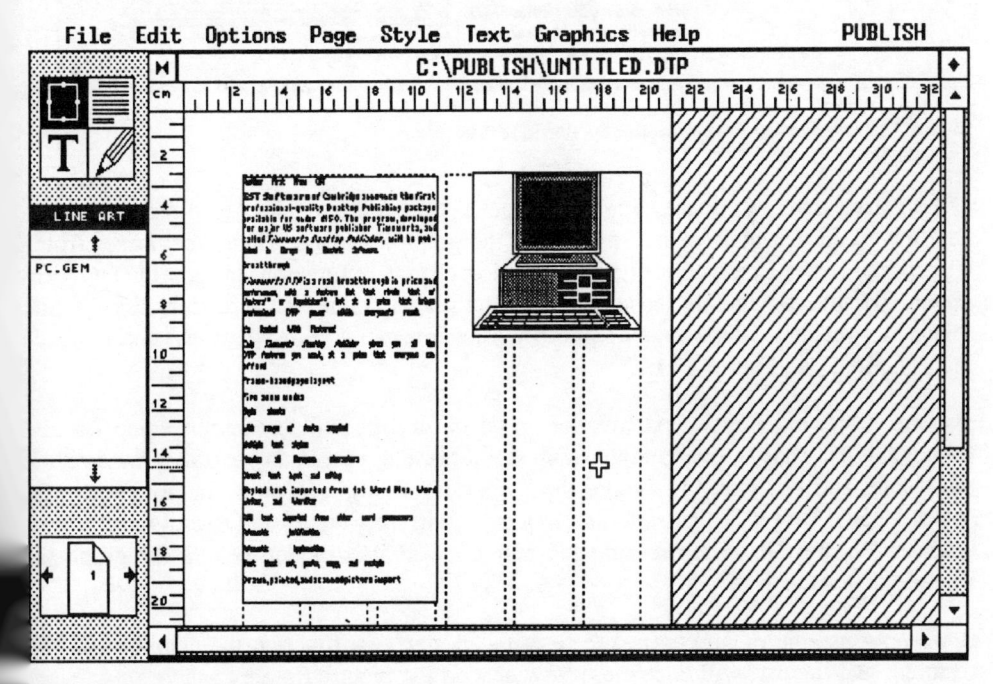

Figure 3.9 Basic Test Frame Layout

Move the smaller frame so that it overlaps the larger. As this frame is lower in the hierarchy, it will move in behind the text frame, and be obscured by it, but have no other effect. Now use the {PAGE} controls to bring the graphics frame to the front, and choose a larger scale view so that we can examine the effects where the frames overlap.

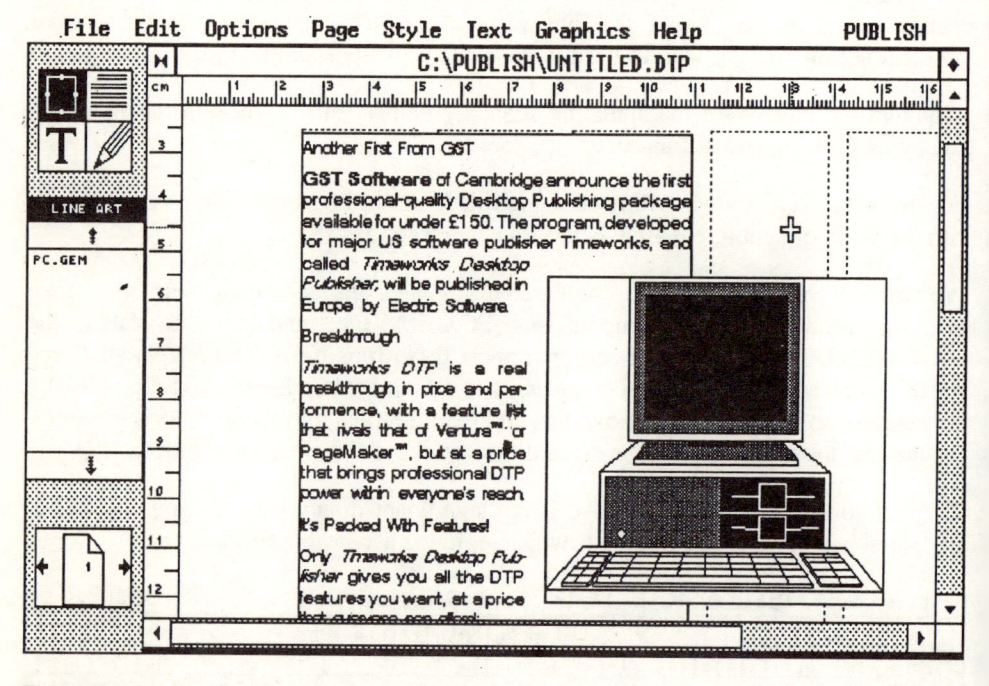

Figure 3.10 Overlapping Frames Illustrating Repel Text Feature.

We will see that, where the graphics frame has moved over the text frame, the text has flowed so that none of it is hidden by the graphics image. This effect arises from a property of the frame controlled by the [Repel text...] function, in the {OPTIONS} menu. To investigate this, ensure that the graphics frame is the active frame, and select this feature. This brings up another selection menu with which we can control this function. See Figure 3.11.

We can select the Repel Text function to be on or off, and the default value for all frames is ON. That is, overlapping frames will normally force any text to flow around the frame, and not under it. Ignore the "Frame Padding" controls for now and just select Repel Text OFF; accept this, and we will see the display re-drawn. Now, however, the text has been re-arranged and some of it is hidden behind the graphics frame. See Figure 3.12.

If we now use the menu controls to reset the Repel Text function the display will be restored, and the text will once more flow around the picture frame.

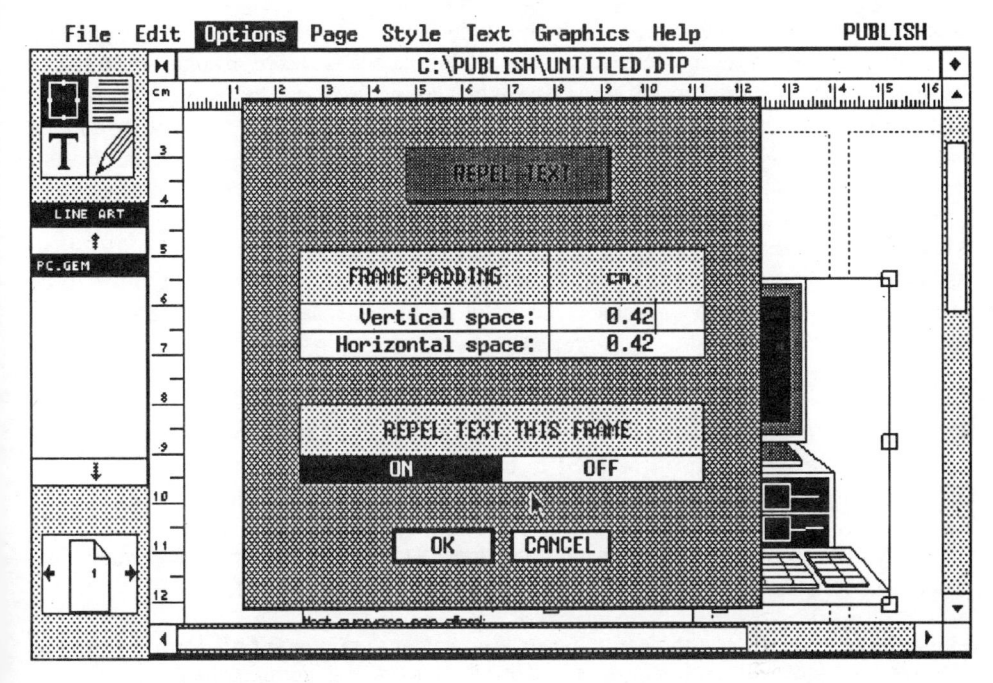

Figure 3.11 Repel Text Controls

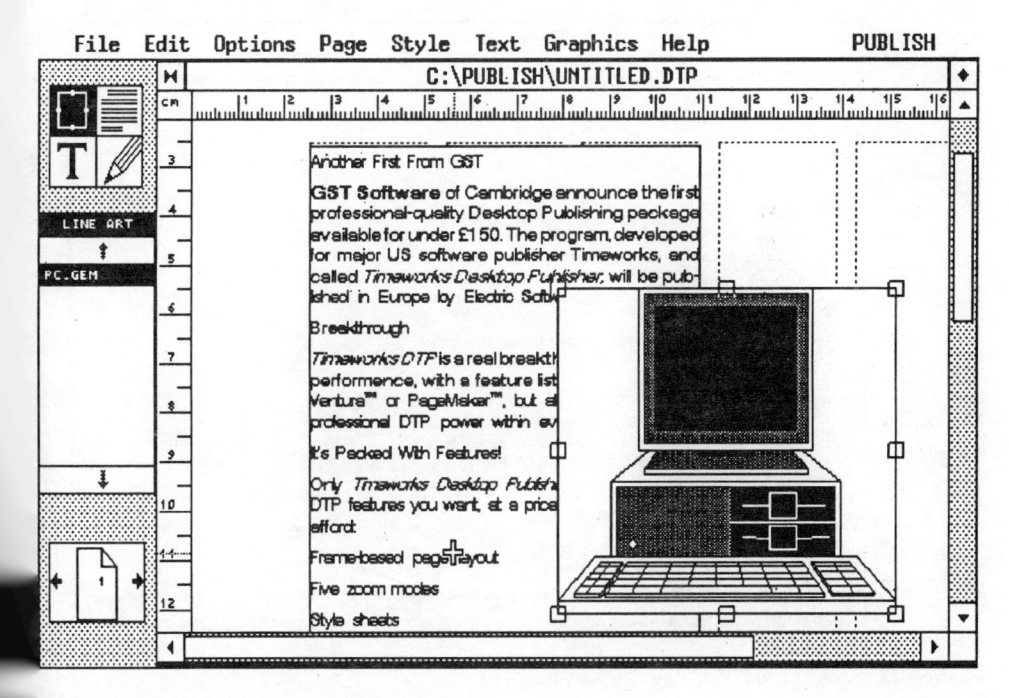

Figure 3.12 Illustrate Repel Text OFF Feature

If we bring up the [Repel text] function again we can look at the frame padding control. This allows us to define how much white space to leave around the graphics image, and we can set this to any value we require, from zero upwards. Try a zero value, and some other values, to view the effect. Also remember that you will often have a better image if you turn off the frames and columns display, using the feature in the {OPTIONS} menu.

Move the graphics frame to different positions within the text frame and notice that, no matter where you place the graphics frame, it is not possible to have the text flow around both sides of the graphics. To achieve this effect it is necessary to have separate text frames, with the graphics image bridging both. We did see this demonstrated in our earlier example.

By using this feature, however, we can create the effect of text flowing around a full graphics image, and this can be used to create interesting page designs. The [Frame padding] control can be used to adjust the white space to suit our requirements.

So far we have only created plain white frames. There is, in addition, a [Frame tint] control, once again in the {OPTIONS} Menu, which can be utilised.

Make the graphics frame the active frame, and select the [Frame tint] control from the {OPTIONS} bar, and we are presented with the appropriate menu screen.

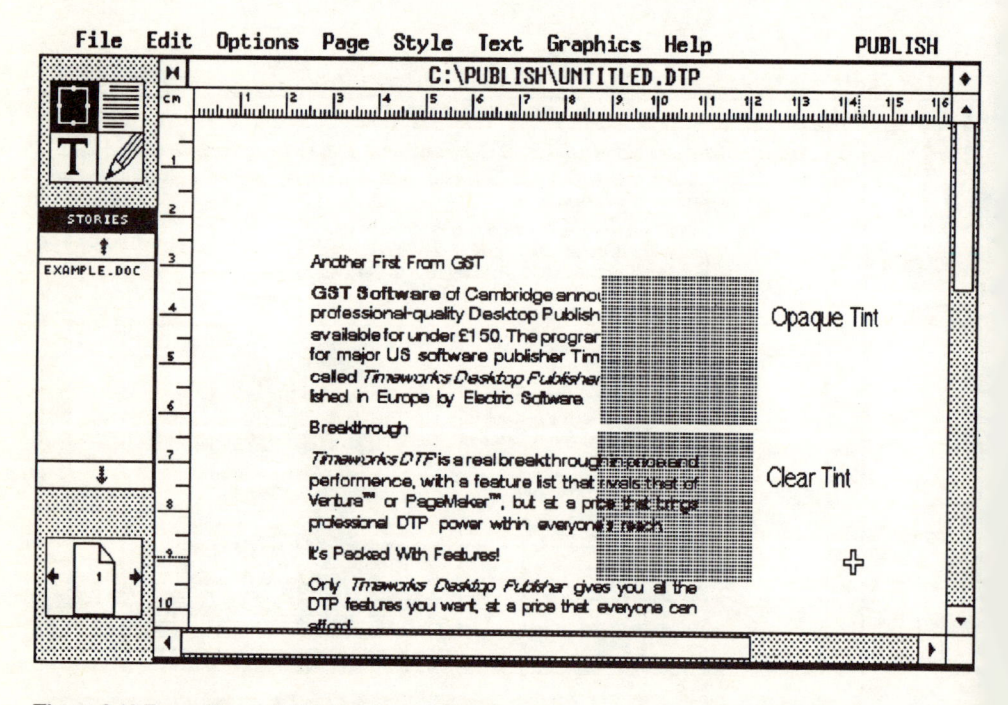

Figure 3.13 Frame Tint and Visibility Control Features

We can control the 'VISIBILITY', which we will look at shortly, or we can select from a range of 'tints', which are structured to produce a *grey scale* when printed.

Selecting any one of the tints available will result in the change being reflected in the background of the graphics frame. (This will not happen with *dot image* frames which are represented differently on screen)

To look more closely at the 'visibility' function create another frame of about 3 or 4 cms square. Switch OFF the repel text feature, and fill the frame with a light tint. Move the frame over a section of text, and we will see that this becomes obscured. If, keeping this frame active, we now select the CLEAR option in the FRAME TINT screen we can see that the text will show through this frame. Although easy to control, this feature can again be used to good effect in creating design options on the finished page.

In the above, we have seen the use of all the controls available for the manipulation of frames. Timeworks Publisher does not discriminate between empty or full frames, or between graphics and text frames, and each can be manipulated in the same way.

Use the above to 'play' with the frames options, and to explore these features and consider some of the design effects that may be achieved. We will return later to look at some special effects, and some further points about frame manipulation as they become relevant to later chapters in the book.

One feature to pay particular attention to is the REPEL TEXT feature, as this can give rise to some unexpected results if you do not keep its operation in mind. The problem is most acute when working with small text frames, or large text sizes. As you manipulate frames to bring them close together, to achieve particular design objectives, the automatic selection of the repel text feature on all frames can cause some elements of text to disappear when such frames are close together. This can be a little disconcerting when it is not expected. This can usually be recovered, or avoided, by switching off the repel text feature as you move frames around the page. This function can be restored once the frame is correctly positioned.

4

Text Manipulation

Within Timeworks Publisher, text can be entered into the document in one of two ways:

>By direct entry into a frame, from the keyboard;

>*or*

>By 'import' of a text file produced in a word processor.

The first system is of use mainly for short documents, and for special text, such as headlines, etc. The latter is the most usual method for longer documents.

Timeworks Publisher has a number of quite powerful text handling features, and is, in terms of its printed output, more versatile than most word processors. However, because it is basically a graphics orientated system, and because it is continually re-formatting the screen display as text is entered, text entry becomes slow as the amount of text builds up. (This is a common feature of all DTP packages).

This is not a problem with most word processors which are specifically designed for fast and efficient text entry. As many word processors are now also equipped with spell checkers, and other associated enhancements, they are especially useful for preparing text for publication. (This text is being prepared on Microsoft Word 4 for eventual inclusion in a DTP package).

The *text* function, in many ways, appears to overlap the *paragraph* functions that we will be looking at later. As defined earlier, the term paragraph has a particular meaning within this application, and always consists of an identifiable block of text. This block may be of any size from a single character, up to any number of lines of text, but is uniquely isolated by the use of the carriage return codes at each end of the block. In particular, we will be taking a long look at the concept of *style* and *style sheets* and these are specifically related to paragraph functions.

To effect text manipulations we will be making use of the following menu features in Timeworks Publisher:

STYLE Menu:
Font/Size
Normal
Bold
Underlined
Italic
Light
Outlined (not on PC version)
White
Superscript
Subscript

TEXT Menu:
Search
Search & Replace
Search Again
Soft Hyphen
Kern
Headers and Footers
Header on this Page (Toggle)
Footer on this Page (Toggle)

FILE Menu:
Import Text

EDIT Menu:
Cut
Copy
Paste

By the end of this chapter we will have demonstrated most of these commands, and have a basic understanding of their functions. We will also be looking at some of the features, and difficulties, of importing text files.

The {STYLE} menu gives us the basic control over the way that the text will appear on the printed page. From this we will define the shape (Typeface) of the characters that we will use, and any enhancements (Typestyle) that we may wish to make. The use of the term *style* here differs slightly from the way that we will be using it later in the context of style sheets, and it will be important to be able to accept both usages of the word. However, this is just one of the areas of popular typography where the terminology has become a bit loose.

Before we enter any text, however, we must first create a frame to contain it. Using the [Actual Size] page display option, create a frame that just fills the visible area. This will be of suitable size to be able to see the effects of our text entry.

Within this application we can set the type and style we require before we enter the characters, or by editing them after they have been entered on the page. To enter text mode we must click on the text icon 'T' in the Toolkit, and notice the cursor change to the 'I' bar, when the pointer is within the working screen. We will also notice that the browser changes to show the text styles available.

When the program is initially loaded certain default parameters are set. We have already seen this in terms of page size, etc.

For text, the basic default is to use 10 point Swiss, normal font. Unless we issue instructions to the contrary all text entered to the document will adopt this style.(We will see later how this default setting may be changed, using style sheet controls)

To enter our first text we just click with the text cursor within the frame.This will place a separate line cursor at the correct position for the next (in this case the first) text character. From this point on we can use the normal keyboard controls for any text entry, but notice that cursor movement keys will have no effect until we have entered some text. The [TAB] keys will also not have the usual effect, and can only be used at appropriate times, which we will see later.

If we now type in any short line of text, for example:

'This is the default text in Swiss 10 point'

we will see it appear in the default style.

With a low resolution monitor, using the double size display mode will help give a better image with this small size of text.

Press [RETURN] at the end of the line, and the line cursor will move to the appropriate place, making full allowance for the size of text in use, and any other parameters set. It is possible to continue typing as much as you like, to become familiar with the procedure.

Note that the normal text wrap function operates, as you reach the end of each line on the screen, and it is not necessary to press the [RETURN] key to move to a new line.(In fact, as mentioned above, pressing the [RETURN] key specifically terminates a paragraph)

To enter text in a different style, place the text cursor at a suitable point, open the

{STYLE} menu and select the [FONT SIZE] option, or press [ALT]-T on the keyboard. This brings down the {FONT and POINT SIZE} sub-menu, and we can make our selection using the mouse. For now, just increase the point size to 24, for example, and then enter the next line of text:

'This is now in 24 point'

As soon as we start to enter the new sized text the line cursor will change to a bigger size, and the new sized characters will appear as we type. Typing [RETURN] at the end of the line causes the cursor to move down the appropriate distance for the size of text. You can carry on typing in the new size for as long necessary, or until the frame fills up.

Experiment with this feature by selecting different font and size options through the style menu, to get used to the appearance on screen.

As you work through the above exercise you will become aware of two factors that will require some consideration.

Firstly, if you attempt to enter text into a frame which is too small to hold it, the text simply will not appear, and it becomes necessary to increase the frame size to hold the text.

When working with small frames, for example, to isolate headline text, the minimum frame dimension needs to be bigger than the point size of the text in use. For example, using 36 point text, the smallest acceptable dimension of the frame height is about 40 points. This may need to be a little larger where a frame border is specified.

The second point relates specifically to more recent versions of the program, where an extended range of font sizes has been made available. Unfortunately, fonts files occupy quite a lot of disk and memory space. To minimise the amount of space used on disk, particularly for floppy-based systems, some of the screen display fonts are not fully reproduced. That is, some of the fonts listed in the font/size selector actually use the same screen fonts for a range of nominal text sizes. (For example, 12 and 14 point text does use the same size display characters). They appear on screen somewhat differently, and usually smaller, than you would expect. However, the screen spacing is correct for the size of font, even where the character size is not. This means that, although the screen may look a little strange, the printed output is normally correct. This does cause some minor difficulties in layout. In practice it was observed that when a page was viewed in full page mode, it was usually closer to the finished, printed, document than when viewed in one of the expanded modes, for affected font sizes.

For advanced users, where this is perceived as a real problem, font generation programs can be used to create the necessary display and print fonts, to overcome this. The only practical restriction lies in the amount of storage required to hold the selected fonts. We will look a bit further into these programs later in the book.

The illustrations in Figures 4.1(a) and (b) show the printed output for the range of sizes available, along with the screen representation of these. In general, this represents no major problem, though some difficulties may arise when trying to integrate graphics elements with the larger text sizes.

In the above exercises we have selected the text characteristics before the text was entered onto the screen. It is, of course, equally practicable to make changes to text after it is displayed. This is particularly appropriate where text files have been imported into the program, without any enhancement features. To change the characteristics of any block of text it is first necessary to *select*, or *highlighl*I, that text. To do this, move the cursor to the start of the section of text, and *drag* it across the text. A single word of text, with the space following it, may be selected by double-clicking with the cursor within that word.

As we do this the selected text will appear in reverse on the screen. Once the text is selected we can use the style functions to modify it. Select any block of text entered in the previous exercise, and use the {STYLE} menu to choose a different size. The changes will take place immediately, and notice that even the line spacing will change to cater for any new text size. We can revert to normal size, or make any changes we require using this simple process.

Please note that the {STYLE} menu is only available if there is a highlighted block of text on the screen, or if there is an active text line cursor in the frame.

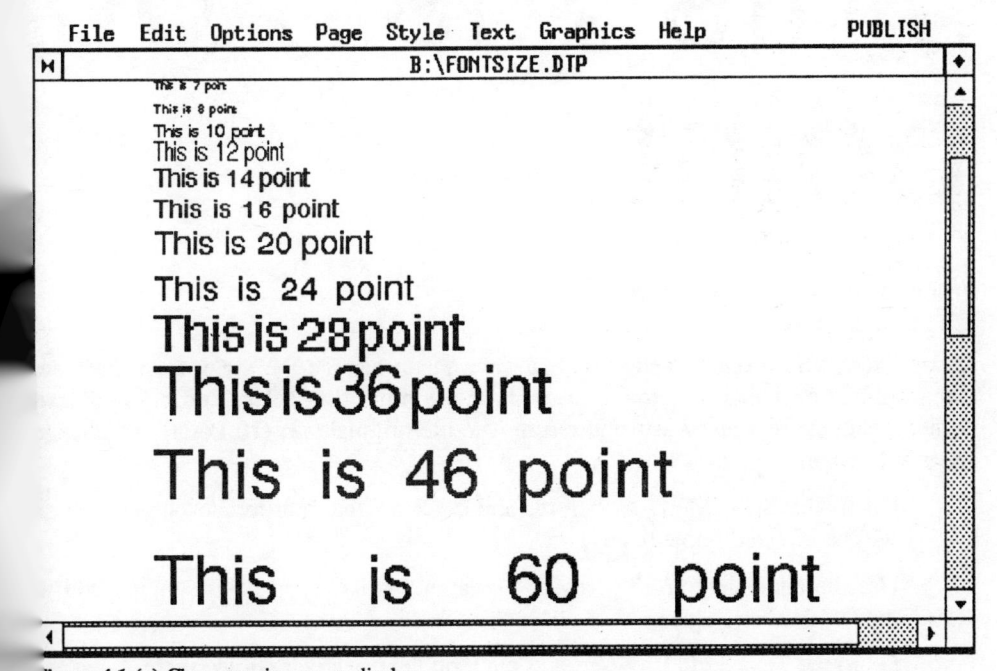

| File | Edit | Options | Page | Style | Text | Graphics | Help | PUBLISH |

B:\FONTSIZE.DTP

This is 7 poin
This is 8 point
This is 10 point
This is 12 point
This is 14 point
This is 16 point
This is 20 point
This is 24 point
This is 28 point
This is 36 point
This is 46 point
This is 60 point

Figure 4.1 (a) Character size screen display.

This is 7 point

This is 8 point

This is 10 point

This is 12 point

This is 14 point

This is 16 point

This is 20 point

This is 24 point

This is 28 point

This is 36 point

This is 46 point

This is 60 point

Figure 4.1 (b) Print out of Figure 4.1(a)

If the size of the text is acceptable, but we want to change the style, then there are three options available, but for each of these we must first select the required text. Select a suitable section of text and return it to the original size (10 Point). To change the style we can:

> Go to the Style Menu as before, and click on the appropriate choice, which will be effected immediately, *or*
>
> Use the equivalent [ALT] Key combination, as indicated on the menu, and in the table in Fig 4.4, *or*
>
> Go to the Text Style Browser, and click on the particular choice there.

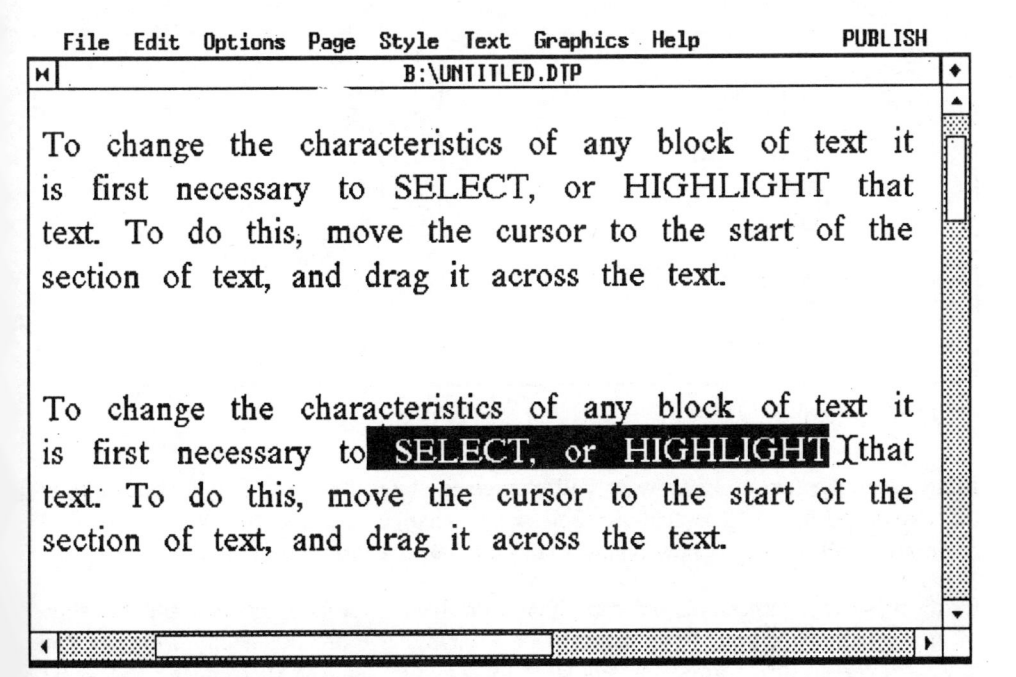

```
File  Edit  Options  Page  Style  Text  Graphics  Help        PUBLISH
```
```
⌧                       B:\UNTITLED.DTP                        ♦
```

To change the characteristics of any block of text it
is first necessary to SELECT, or HIGHLIGHT that
text. To do this, move the cursor to the start of the
section of text, and drag it across the text.

To change the characteristics of any block of text it
is first necessary to **SELECT, or HIGHLIGHT** (that
text. To do this, move the cursor to the start of the
section of text, and drag it across the text.

Figure 4.2 Text Highlight Selection

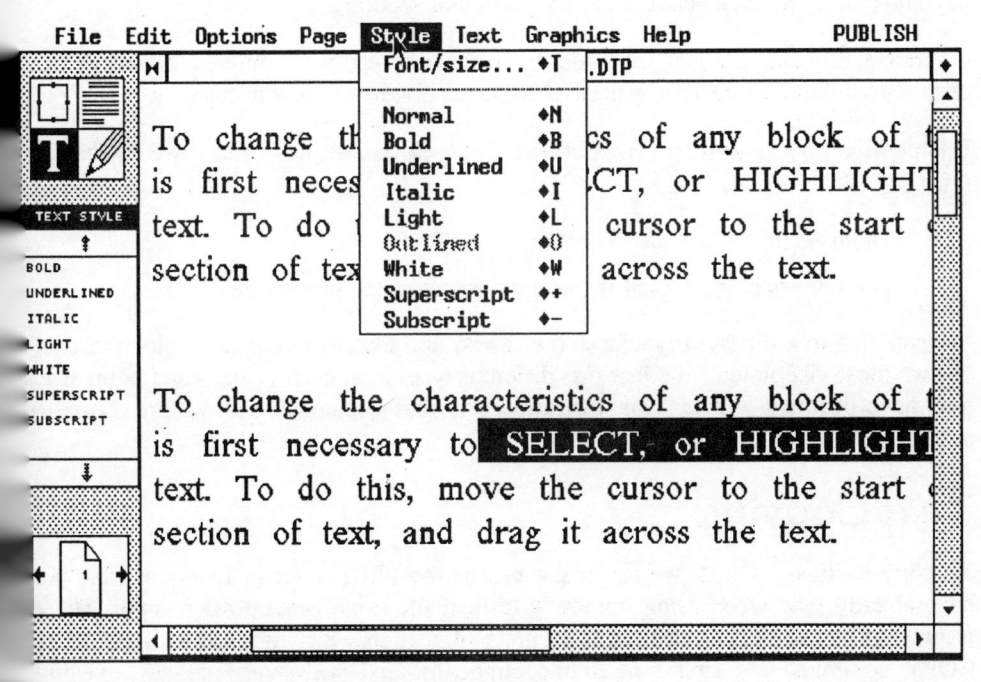

```
File  Edit  Options  Page  Style  Text  Graphics  Help        PUBLISH
```
```
                        Font/size...  ♦T    .DTP
                        Normal        ♦N
                        Bold          ♦B
                        Underlined    ♦U
                        Italic        ♦I
                        Light         ♦L
                        Outlined      ♦O
                        White         ♦W
                        Superscript   ♦+
                        Subscript     ♦−
```

To change the characteristics of any block of t
is first necessary to **SELECT, or HIGHLIGHT**
text. To do this, move the cursor to the start
section of text, and drag it across the text.

Figure 4.3 Screen Display for Text Style Controls

Normal	[ALT]–N
Bold	[ALT]–B
Underlined	[ALT]–U
Italic	[ALT]–I
Light	[ALT]–L
Outlined	Not available on the PC
White	[ALT]–W
Superscript	[ALT]–[+]
Subscript	[ALT]–[–]

Figure 4.4 Text Style [ALT] Keys

In all cases the text style browser will change to show the current style condition, at the cursor position. Note that as each single change is made the whole screen is re-drawn to allow for the new features, and this takes a little time.

Using these simple controls we can change the basic typeface, the size and the style of any selection of text. If we have made a change we are not happy with, we can always revert to the 'normal' default style by selecting NORMAL from the {STYLE} menu, or pressing [ALT] N, when the text is selected. Note that this option is not available in the browser. The program will make all the necessary adjustments to the page layout, as we make changes to the particular sections.

Of course, any changes that are made do not have to apply to complete lines. We can change individual characters, groups of characters, words or any group of words.

It is possible to mix different sizes of text on the same line, however, if we do this we must note that:

> The base line for the text is common; and

> The line spacing adopted is that appropriate to the larger size of text.

We can also mix different typefaces (i.e. Swiss and Dutch) in the same block of text, but we must take note of the fact that different typefaces, even of the same point size, may have different widths. This may affect any text alignments that we are trying to achieve, and needs to be used carefully.

Text Copying

To copy sections of text, we can make use of the {EDIT} menu functions, that we have already seen when using frames. With text the same general rules apply. There is only one clipboard for text, and sections of text to which we apply the CUT or COPY command are first sent to the clipboard, and will overwrite any existing contents. This will not, however, have any effect on any frame stored on the frames clipboard, which is regarded as quite a separate entity.

To copy, or move, a section of text we must first select it, using the text highlight controls. Select one of the lines of text that you have created, and activate the [Copy] option from the {EDIT} menu. As before, nothing much seems to have happened. However, this section is now stored in the clipboard. Now de-select the text by clicking anywhere else on the page, and move the cursor to the point where you wish the text to appear.

If you have only a few lines of text on the page, the cursor will only move to the next available character position. In this case you can move it further down the frame using the [RETURN] key to insert blank lines, and the [SPACE] bar to move across the screen.

With the cursor in the required position, click on [Paste] in the {EDIT} menu, and the copy will appear. There is a need for a some caution in this exercise, where you are copying different fonts or styles within the same page. To demonstrate this we need to work through a short exercise.

Clear the current frame, or put a new empty frame on your screen. Type in a short line of text in the default text selection, and press [RETURN] to start a new line.

Use the text cursor control to highlight the line entered, and select [Copy] from the {EDIT} menu, to copy it to the clipboard. De-select the line, by clicking outside of the highlighted section, and click once again to place the text cursor. Now select the [Paste] function from the {EDIT} menu, and the copy line will be placed, just as we would expect, with the text cursor at the end of the new line.

Press [RETURN] once more to start another new line. Now open the {STYLE} menu, and select a new, significantly larger, point size. Type in a short line at the new size, and then press [RETURN] to start a new line again.

The clipboard still contains a copy of our original line of text, so we can open the {EDIT} menu and [Paste] the line in the new position.

Note, however, (and this is the point of the exercise) that the copied text has adopted the size of the last line typed, and not that of the original text.

This may or may not be acceptable, depending on what you are trying to achieve. It did, however, lead to some surprises when the copy process was first used and needs to be carefully observed.

The problem, where it is such, can be overcome in one of two ways:

> Modifying the text style after the copy has been placed to adopt the appropriate characteristics; *or*
>
> Ensure that the text setting at the cursor position is correct. This can be done by setting the appropriate style, and then typing and deleting a space. This sets the current type characteristics without entering text onto the page.

There is another slight anomaly which may be observed which appears to operate in reverse to that above.

For example, text is entered onto the page in point size 14, and then subsequently edited to a different size. If we now wish to copy this new block of text, using the procedures above, we will find that the copy is created using the *original* specified text size, and not that which may actually appear on the screen.

As with all such occurrences, these are easy to control when you are aware that the problem may exist.

In most applications you will be manipulating blocks of the normal text format, and these problems should not arise too frequently. Special caution will be necessary where you are working with text sizes which are not easily distinguishable on the display, and which will not show up until the final printout.

So far we have been manipulating text in short sections. However, this is not a necessary element of the Timeworks Publisher package. Although I have said that entering text is relatively slow in this type of application, nevertheless it is not a major problem for amounts up to perhaps a page or so of text, in different frames.

To allow such text entry Timeworks Publisher does have the basic word processing functions. That is, there is *word wrap* at the end of lines, and all the normal text entry keys, the delete controls, and the cursor movement keys function as you would expect. You also have some of the more advanced features for use on larger text blocks, such as SEARCH and REPLACE, which are best demonstrated in a later section. Hyphenation can be controlled effectively within Timeworks Publisher as this is quite an important element in aligning text to maintain a good appearance.

Before we go on to look at these functions there is one further element that we can demonstrate at this point.

Kerning is the ability to control the spacing between individual letters in a word. In most normal, that is small sized, text applications it does not have tremendous application. However, as we will almost inevitably be using larger size headlines, etc., then it can become quite valuable.

Clear any work that you may currently have on screen, and create a new blank frame. The desired effect is more noticeable if we use the 60 point size, where available, even though this is not properly presented on screen, due to the display font limitations discussed earlier. Type in the word ATTIC in this size, three times down the page, (that is, type [RETURN] between each). If we look at that word, as it appears in this text, it looks fine. If we look at it on the screen, it appears a little unbalanced. This demonstration really requires that we look at the printed result as well, which we have illustrated. See Figure 4.5 overleaf.

The main problem with the balance is in the amount of space between the 'A' and the

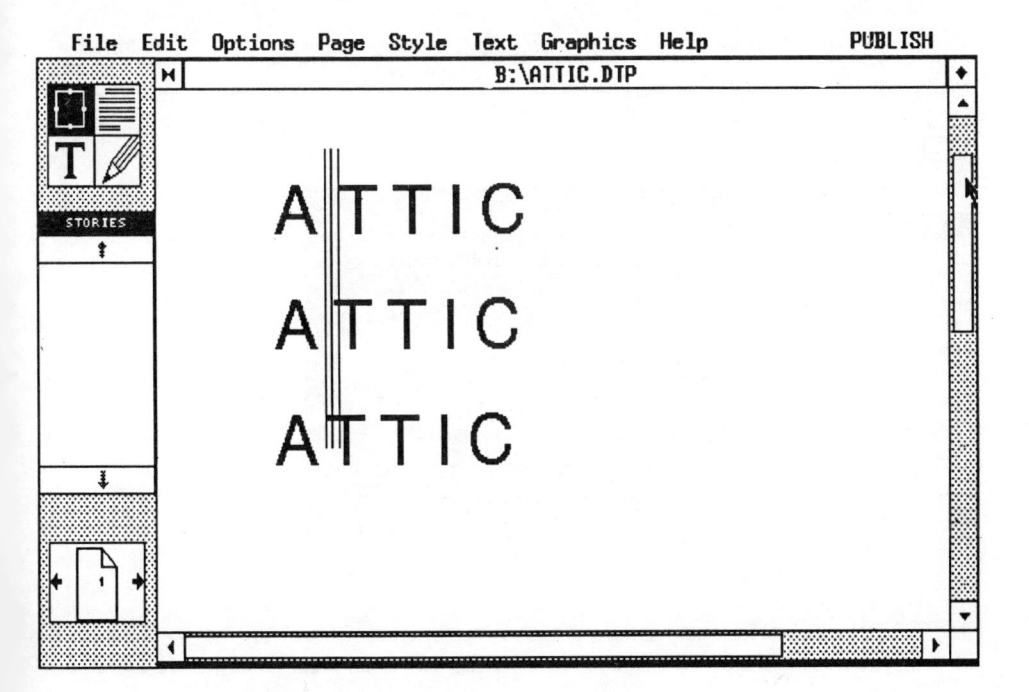

Figure 4.5 Kerning Example; Top: Screen Display; Bottom: Printout from screen display

first 'T', and possibly also between the 'I' and the 'C'. (This is a matter of personal judgement). With three copies on the screen, we will leave the first copy as a reference.

Place the cursor between the 'A' and 'T' of the second copy. Open the {TEXT} menu, and select the [KERN] option, to get the KERN TWO CHARACTER display.

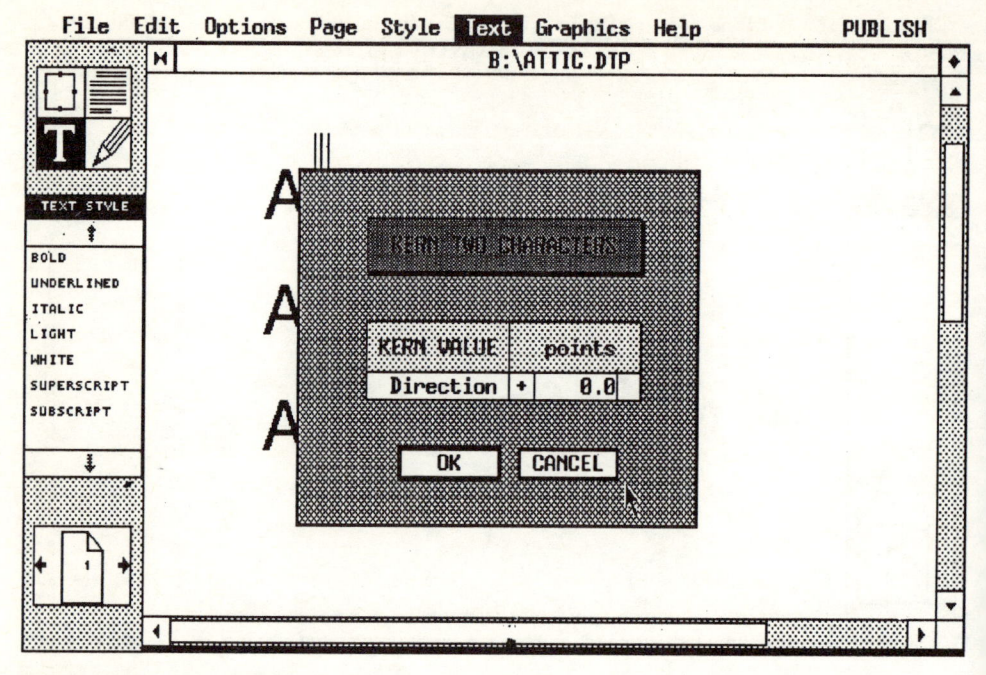

Figure 4.6 Kern Control Screen

As we want to move the letters closer together, we will require a (-) direction. Point to the (+) box on the screen and click to change it to (-). Place the cursor on the 0.0 number, delete this and enter the value 4.0 (i.e. 4 points), and accept. The screen display will show the changes, which are noticeable. Now repeat this sequence for the third copy, but increase the kerning to -8.0 points. It is now possible to compare the three separate examples. It is really a matter of visual judgement as to which offers the best appearance, and this will only be finally determined by viewing the printout.

Repeat this example using other character combinations. For example, the user manual recommends the word AWAY, as a case where kerning may be of benefit.

Remember that kerning can be used to move characters closer together or further apart, depending on the particular requirement. There is a key combination which can be used in this process. [ALT] K causes a 0.5 point *decrease* in the distance between the two characters concerned, and may be used repeatedly. However, such a small increment will not show up clearly on the screen, and will need to be judged on the basis of a printout.

Text Files

For most serious applications, text will be entered into the DTP program by IMPORT from a word processor file. Timeworks Publisher (PC version) lists eight text file formats with which it will work:

Wordprocessor	Filename Extension
ASCII	(.ASC)
Word Perfect (Version not specified)	(.*)
WordStar (Version not specified)	(.DOC)
Microsoft Word 4	(.DOC)
1st Word Plus	(.DOC)
Word Writer PC	(.)
Quintet	(.*)
Beyond Words	(.)

During the preparation of this book opportunities have arisen to use the first five of these options, and any comments must apply in detail only to these. However, it is likely that the general observations will cover most word processor packages.

Problems arise when trying to take text files from other programs because of the different file structures and, more particularly, the different print codes used within the files to specify various print options. For example, all of the above word processors use different codes and methods of indicating bold text, italic text, underlined text, etc. The more advanced programs, Microsoft Word 4, Word Perfect 5.0 and WordStar Professional 5, for example, also have functions to change the size of the text, involving additional code structures.

The ASCII file structure is different, in that it is stripped of all such codes, and retains just the basic text information, without any enhancements.

To overcome any problems, Timeworks Publisher will generally ignore any special codes, and such text enhancements are not included in the IMPORT files. 1st Word Plus, which in any event comes from the same stable as Timeworks Publisher (GST), and which operates under GEM, is one exception to this rule, and many of the text enhancement features are imported intact. WordStar files, too (although the different versions may respond differently), will import some basic text enhancements. One problem that has been observed with WordStar is that early versions did not support the underlining of spaces between words. To overcome this in normal text applications it is necessary to type the underline character between words. In the translation into Timeworks Publisher this gives rise to a double underline at these points, which needs subsequent editing.

As it is not possible to cover all the different word processor options that you may be using, the only way to check this situation out is to create a file on your present word processor, import it, and check the result. In general expect to lose all text enhancement controls, and be particularly careful to check the imported text for odd characters that may appear. If you have many problems, then you should use the option to save your word processor documents as ASCII files, which will strip out all the odd codes, and leave you with a clean text file. All the necessary enhancements can be added after the text is imported. Importing text documents which contain tables also creates some problems, due to the different ways in which some word processors, and Timeworks Publisher, handle tab settings. This is covered at the end of the chapter on paragraph styles, as it is necessary to understand those techniques to achieve a satisfactory result with tabular text.

Another area where some problems have been experienced is with the import of files containing the extended character set. With Microsoft Word 4, for example, many character codes above 127, when imported, were either ignored or incorrectly interpreted. Even if the import is not successful, Timeworks Publisher does employ an extended character set, which is in fact the GEM International character set, which can be used within documents. They are entered in the normal fashion by holding the [ALT] key, and entering the numeric code, using the number key block. The character will appear only when the [ALT] key is released. The character set available with version 1B12 is illustrated in the diagram (Figure 4.7). The table shows the results when printed out on a laser printer. This differs from that produced using the 24 pin dot matrix in that codes from 218 to 255, did not produce the characters shown here. Instead all unrecognised characters were represented in the text as a question mark (?). As with many things, a short test will be required to check the operation of your particular system.

128	Ç	129	ü	130	é	131	â	132	ä
133	à	134	å	135	ç	136	ê	137	ë
138	è	139	ï	140	î	141	ì	142	Ä
143	Å	144	É	145	æ	146	Æ	147	ô
148	ö	149	ò	150	û	151	ù	152	ÿ
153	Ö	154	Ü	155	ø	156	£	157	Ø
158	¤	159	ƒ	160	á	161	í	162	ó
163	ú	164	ñ	165	Ñ	166	ª	167	º
168	¿	169	–	170	"	180	œ	181	Œ
182	À	183	Ã	184	Õ	185	§	186	‡
187	†	188	¶	189	©	190	®	191	™
192	„	193	…	194	‰	195	•	196	–
197	—	198	°	199	Á	200	Â	201	È
202	Ê	203	Ë	204	Ì	205	Í	206	Î
207	Ï	208	Ò	209	Ó	210	Ô	211	Š
212	š	213	Ù	214	Ú	215	Û	216	Ÿ
217	ß	218		219		220		221	
222		223		224		225	ß	226	
227	ª	228		229		230		231	
232	Ł	233	`	234	´	235	ˆ	236	~
237	¯	238	˘	239	˙	240	¨	241	˚
242	¸	243	ˇ	244		245	₁	246	
247		248	ł	249	ø	250	œ	251	ß
252		253		254		255			

Figure 4.7 Timeworks Publisher Character Set

Transfer of documents between different applications is often a problem, and all DTP programs have the same basic limitations in importing text, and will work satisfactorily only with a limited range of text file types. Some word processors include conversion programmes to convert between different file types, and you may be able to make use of these if you have particular problems.

When importing text files, Timeworks Publisher is very fussy about the filename extensions used. If these do not match those expected by the program, which are not necessarily the normal word processor default extensions, then the file will not load. The disk action will appear as if a file is loading, but after all the action no text will appear.

The extensions to use are listed alongside the word processors in the list above.

A potentially powerful aspect of the program, however, is an un-documented feature of Timeworks Publisher, which helps to overcome many of these restrictions. We will be returning to this after we have looked at styles in the next chapter.

The safest general assumption to make, however, is that very little of the text enhancement features of the original file will survive the import directly, and that such enhancements will have to be added after the file is imported. We have already covered the techniques for changing the features of text characters earlier in this chapter, and these techniques can be applied to the text within Timeworks Publisher. There is some additional information on this point in the user manual supplied.

Once the text is imported into Timeworks Publisher the original file remains untouched, and changes to the text are only saved within the Timeworks Publisher document. If there are any catastrophes in modifying files, within the program, it then becomes a simple matter to retrieve the original files.

The import text procedure has been covered earlier, and is easily accessed from the file menu. Make the appropriate menu selection, and identify the correct Directory and File, and Timeworks Publisher will import the text file.

The file will only appear on the page if there is an active frame available to contain it, and then will flow to fill up that frame. The file will be listed in the browser, when the program is in frame mode.

If you wish to get information on the current status of the file, or to delete a file from the stories browser, then point to the file in the Browser, and double click. This will bring up the file status screen which gives various items of information. This is quite self explanatory, and requires no detailed discussion. The [DELETE] function available from this screen will delete the file from the DTP package, and remove it from the browser, but does not affect the original file.

To load a long section of text into a Timeworks Publisher document, you will need to do this one frame, or page, at a time. The current version of Timeworks Publisher has no provision for the automatic import of text over a number of pages.

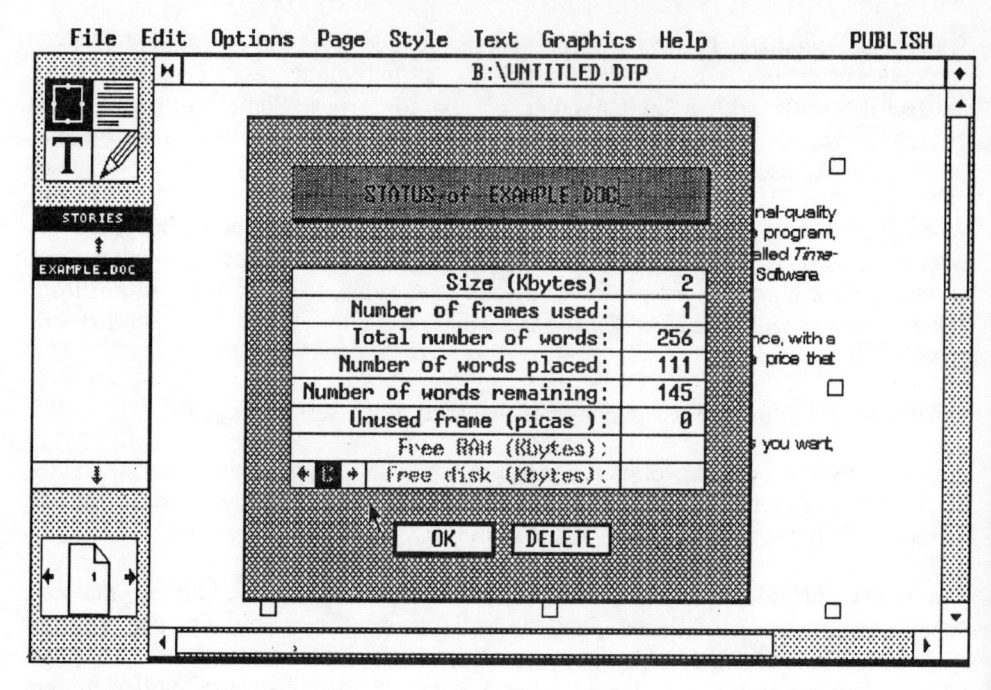

Figure 4.8 File Status Screen

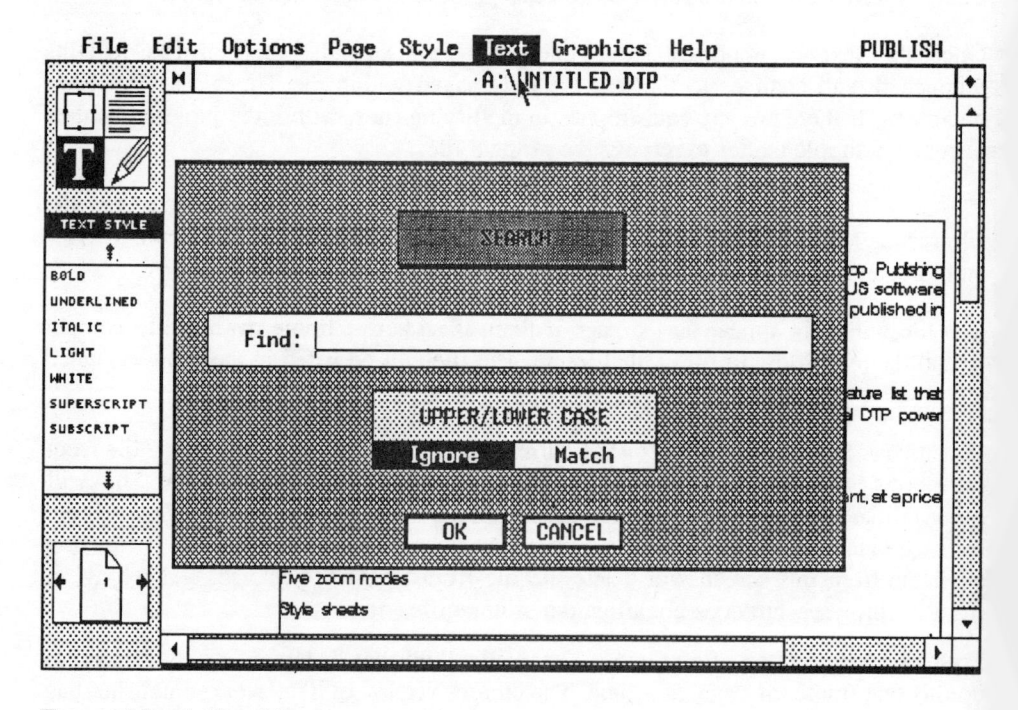

Figure 4.9 Search Control Screen

To assist in editing text, and to provide some additional features, Timeworks Publisher has a number of other word processor operations which can be used. These functions, available only when in text mode, are found within the {TEXT} menu.

One such function is the ability to locate particular words, or groups of characters, within a file, in order to manipulate them. This basic function, termed *search*, can be initiated by clicking on this option in the text menu, or by using [ALT] F from the keyboard, when the text cursor is active in the block.

This will bring up the Search screen, into which you can enter the character string that you are seeking. You can choose to make this sensitive to upper or lower case characters. For example, if you are searching for headlines which may have been entered as capitals, and to avoid finding the same word within the text, you would enter the text string exactly as required, and select the [MATCH] option.

This function will only search for text forwards from the text cursor position, so be sure that you have this set correctly for the earliest possible occurrence of the text string. If it fails to find the text it will issue an error message which, when acknowledged, returns you to the text screen. Once you have entered the search parameters these are retained in memory until the next search is executed. This avoids having to re-enter the same information if you decide to repeat the search.

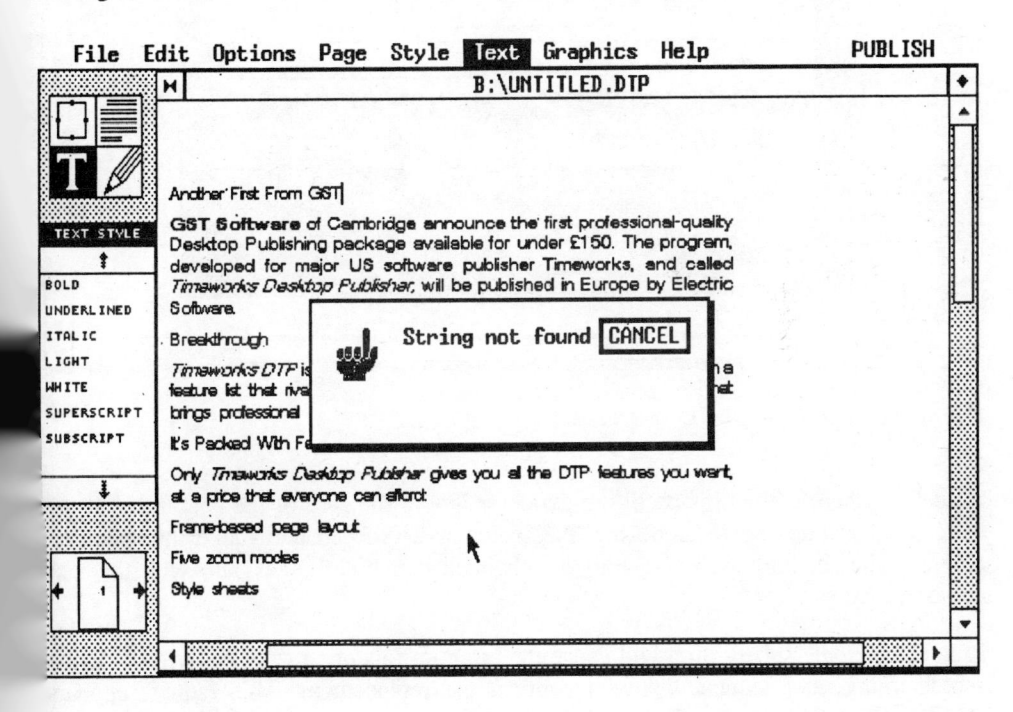

Figure 4.10 Search Error Screen

The search function is used to get to a particular point in the text, and then to perform some manipulation. In many applications we require to change the text in some particular way, usually by changing words, spelling or other information. Where it is likely that this will be repetitive it can be speeded up using the *search and replace* function, also in the Text menu, or use [ALT] R. This calls up the appropriate screen, with two additional options:

To specify a second string to be used to replace the search text; and

The opportunity to specify single, multiple or total replacement of the search string.

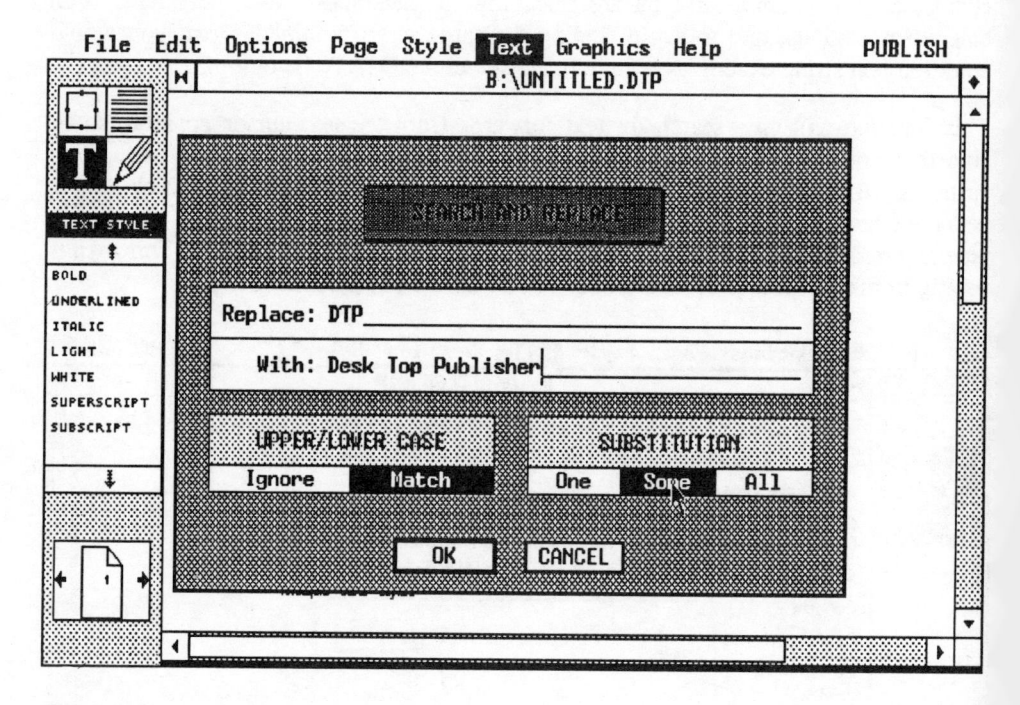

Figure 4.11 Search and Replace Control Screen

As before, there is the opportunity to match or ignore the case of the characters. If we have selected one substitution, then the search will proceed and make the specified change. The function will end with the changed text highlighted, and with the text cursor at that position.

Requesting *some* substitution will cause the program to stop at each occurrence of the search string, and request that you confirm the replacement. This request appears along the top line of the display and requires a 'Y' response to replace, or an 'N' response to leave the current selection and move on to the next occurrence. Pressing the [ESC] key will end the function completely.

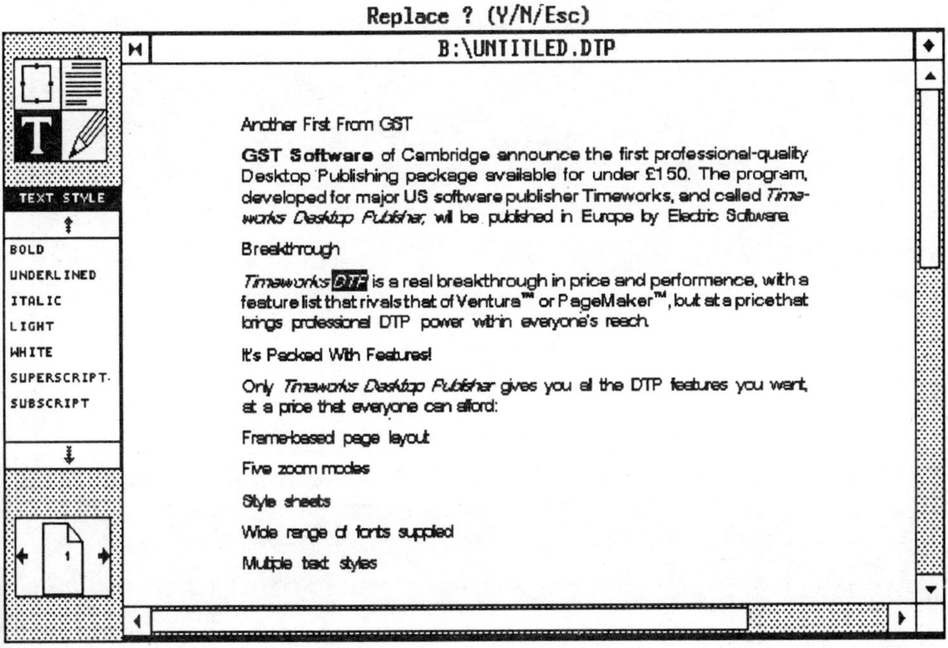

Figure 4.12 Confirm Replace Request Screen

The third option is to select ALL occurrences, and this will zip through the text making changes as specified, without asking whether or not to proceed.

During this process the program will assign the correct text characteristics to the modified words, etc., detecting these at each separate occurrence.

Headers and Footers

When creating longer documents, such as books or reports, it is quite usual to have certain lines of text repeated along the top (headers) or bottom (footers) of each page. This would include details such as book or report titles, chapter or section titles, page numbers, etc.

By creating these lines of text as Headers and Footers the program can keep track of them automatically, placing them in the appropriate position on the left and right pages as required.

Headers and footers can be created in any of the operating modes, by selecting the [HEADERS AND FOOTERS] option from the {TEXT} menu. This will display the appropriate control screen.

As can be seen from Figure 4.13, headers and footers are created using exactly the same process, just by selecting the appropriate choice within the control screen.

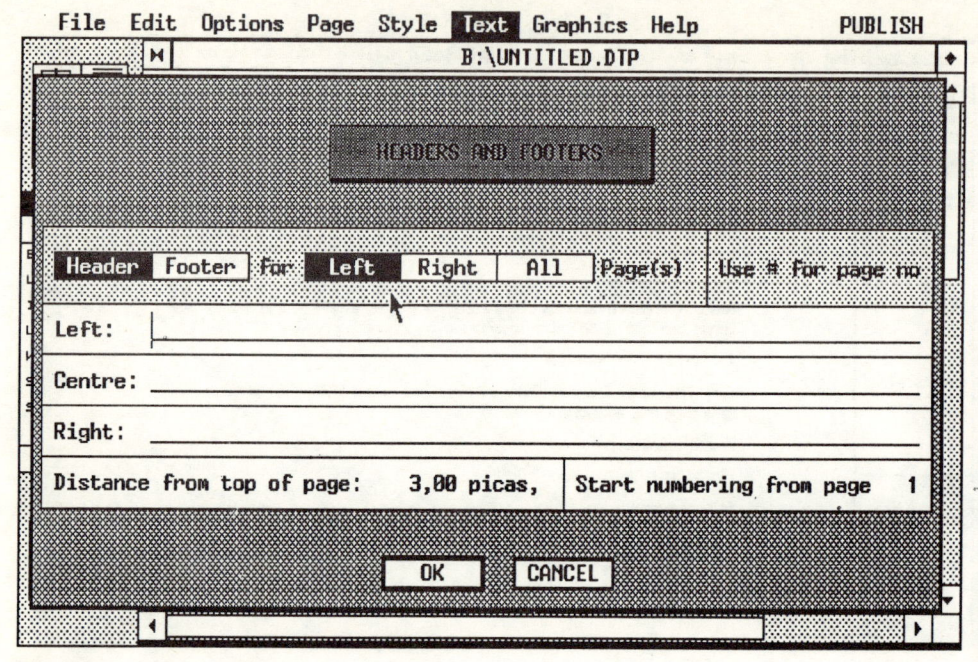

Figure 4.13 Headers and Footers Control Screen

Different text may be specified for left and right pages if necessary, but only where these have been selected when the program was initiated.

It is possible to select different elements of text for different sections of the header or footer line, though it would be a little unusual to occupy all three possible locations. To specify the text simply type it into the location desired. To place a page number just type [#] in the relevant section of the display, and the correct page number will be allocated by the program, as each page is printed.

Headers are located at the top of the page between the physical top of the page, and the top margin. It is, therefore, necessary to specify a distance from the top of the page which is less than the normal top margin. This same applies to footer positions. We have referred to this earlier when discussing the general page layout principles.

As it is normal to have to define new headers and footers, for example, for each chapter of a book, it is sometimes necessary to change the first page number specified within the headers/footers by altering the 'Start numbering from page' value. Once the appropriate details have been added to the display screen, and accepted, the program will automatically place the appropriate text on each page.

The {TEXT} menu gives the option to include or exclude headers and footers on any particular page. For example, it is quite usual to omit a header from the first page of a chapter or section, as is the case with this particular book.

To set the text type and style to be used in the headers and footers we need to jump forward to the definition of paragraph styles. However, for now take it for granted that these aspects are controlled by specific paragraph styles, labelled HEADER and FOOTER, automatically created when we select this function. We will see in the next chapter how we can modify these to suit our requirements.

5

Paragraph and Style

The one reason above all others that you will have decided to use a DTP package must be the desire to give your documents some additional visual impact. You can do this by controlling the format of the text, and general page layout, and by including illustrations as a part of this. Another important feature of DTP software is to help adopt a consistent appearance in all our documents, and to promote the concept of a 'House style'. When handled properly, this can help the readers of these documents to identify with the source, and to feel comfortable with the document.

Where we have adopted this approach we are really starting to use 'style' in the way it was originally defined within Typography.

In the previous chapter we saw how to manipulate various features of our text, to change the size and appearance of words and characters in order to bring out certain characteristics, or merely to separate out headings, titles, etc. If we are working on a long document, and we need to go through the whole thing, changing the characteristics of each section of text individually, then this will take a long time. A further danger of this approach is that consistency is difficult to maintain. Given that with the current version of Timeworks Publisher, using dot matrix printers, there is a total of 24 fonts, each of which can be assigned one of six different styles, and with all the other layout options that are available, it is easy to predict some confusion.

The concept of *style* and the use of *style sheets* is introduced to help eliminate these problems.

We have earlier made a point of defining a *paragraph* as a quite distinct block of text, and this remains important. Furthermore, we do not put any particular restriction on the size of this block, and it can be anything from one character to very many. We must recall that the particular feature that defines the paragraph is that it is marked at beginning and end by a [Carriage Return] code. In practice this means, as we would expect, that a paragraph will begin on a new line, and will terminate when the next new line is created.

The concept of style that we are going to discuss is applied to text in terms of defined *paragraph* blocks. That is, the style we specify will be applied only to one paragraph at a time, and will not, with one exception, extend across paragraph boundaries.

To begin with a relatively simple example, if we are creating a report we will probably define some clear text divisions within the report, which would probably include:

Major headings at the beginning, and maybe at various points within the report;

Sub-headings to identify the various sub-sections of the report;

A particular text layout for the general content of the report; and

A special text layout to emphasise certain points in the report.

Now we would normally wish for these sections to be applied consistently throughout the report, and frequently would want these to be consistent from one report to another.

This same approach is just as relevant to any form of regular publication, be it a restaurant menu, a product data sheet, a price list or a club Newsletter.

In order to ensure that we can achieve this consistency we will identify these particular components of the document, and we will assign a specific *style* to them.

Timeworks Publisher enables us to create a series of defined styles, and to name them in a sensible fashion so that they can easily be recalled, and applied.

In the brief exercise in chapter 2, we saw this in action, without any explanation of what we were doing. We will now repeat this exercise, but with a more detailed look at the procedures involved.

Start up the program, or use the {FILE} menu to start a new document. In the latter case you will be asked if you wish to load a stylesheet. As we saw earlier, a style sheet is used to contain the basic master page layout. In addition to this the style sheet will also include *paragraph style* definitions. The Timeworks Publisher program comes with a default style sheet, stored, logically, in a file called DEFAULT.STY which is loaded automatically with the program. If we respond [NO] to the request to load a style sheet, then the program will assume that we wish to retain use of the default style. This is satisfactory for present purposes, so click on the appropriate box to proceed. We are then asked to select a page format, which displays with the default selection highlighted. Again, this is adequate for our present purposes, and we can accept this.

We are then presented with the normal blank page, representing page one of our document. If we click on the paragraph icon in the Toolkit column, we will see the browser change to display the four default paragraph style options available.

Switch to full page view, and select the frame tool to define a single frame occupying the full page length, and four columns wide. Import the text file, EXAMPLE.DOC as we have done before, and make sure that it flows into the frame. (Make the frame active, and click on the file name in the browser - you haven't forgotten that!). Set the display to show actual size, so that we can see the effects of any changes immediately.

Now select paragraph mode from the Toolkit. If we move the paragraph cursor into the frame, and click on any text, we see that it will cause the whole of that paragraph to be highlighted. This is, of course, the first distinguishing feature of operation in this mode.

Also take a look at the browser, which has now changed once again, and shows a listing of PARAGRAPH STYLES. This shows four options, labelled:

```
BODY STYLE (Now Highlighted)
BULLET
HEADLINE
SUBHEAD
```

These are *style labels* of the type that we will be creating for our own documents. For now, however, we will see how they can be applied to this test file.

When a paragraph is selected in the document, the browser will always indicate the current paragraph style that is active. Body Text is the style that defines the basic characteristics of the bulk of any document. This is the style adopted whenever we type directly onto the screen, unless we specifically change our selection. It is an important style in that, uniquely, every style sheet we produce must have a body text definition. If we do not create one, using that name, then the program will always adopt the default body text style.

The file when first displayed, in fact, always adopts the body text style, which here has the characteristics:

```
SWISS FONT
10 POINT TEXT SIZE
JUSTIFIED TEXT (Even Margins)
```

Some additional enhancements to individual words within the file are also apparent, but these are simple style variations on the basic body text.

Move the cursor to the first line of text, 'Another First From GST' and click. This will highlight this section of text, i.e. paragraph. Now move the cursor to the browser, and click on the HEADLINE option. We will see the screen change, and this line will now have adopted a new format. If we look at this we will see that it has the following obvious characteristics:

> DUTCH FONT
> 36 POINT TEXT SIZE
> CENTRED IN THE FRAME

There are some other characteristics applied, but these are not so apparent at this point.

Now move down to the word 'Breakthrough', and click. The word is highlighted, and the browser highlight moves back to BODY TEXT. With 'Breakthrough' highlighted, click on SUBHEAD in the browser, and this will change to the appropriate configuration, which is:

> SWISS FONT
> 20 POINT TEXT SIZE
> LEFT JUSTIFIED

We can work through the text as much as we like, applying these styles as required to look at the effect.

To see a slightly different option, move down the text display, to the point which lists some of the Timeworks Publisher features, beginning with 'Frame Based Page Layout'. Highlight this option, and click on BULLETS in the browser. Repeat this for 4 or 5 lines of this text and we will see the paragraph format change again. This time a special character (the bullet) has been added, and the paragraph spacing has been varied to highlight the points listed, and to indent the text. The basic text, however, has remained in the body text format

As we can see above, each Paragraph Style has three easily identified parameters: typeface, size and justification, plus others not so apparent. Using the paragraph controls, and the style sheet approach, it is very easy to assign these aspects consistently throughout a document. Remember that in any sensible document layout you will only be using a limited number of such style options, so that specifying and applying them will be quite straightforward. If you have finished messing around we will now see how to achieve this, using the four options that were identified earlier, which will be simple variations on the above themes.

We will continue to make use of the same file for our demonstrations, unless you have created a file of your own that you would like to work on. So that we start at the same point, restore the original appearance of the file, or abandon the document and load it again.

The most straightforward way to create a style sheet is to modify an existing one, and then to save it under another name when completed. We will do this here, and make small changes to the current style sheet definitions.

The first step in creating a style is to think of a suitable name for it. Be logical in the choice, so that the name has some easy relationship with the function. For our example the name HEADING would be suitable for the first option. In fact, as we are going to save our style sheet under a different name entirely, there may be no need to change the individual style names at all.

With the operation mode set to paragraph mode, and with any paragraph highlighted, we can start to create our own style. We can enter the style creation sequence by choosing the Paragraph Style option from the Text menu, or we can double click on one of the styles listed in the browser. In either case, this will bring up the paragraph style master control form, which shows the various choices we will have to make. This will currently contain the settings for whichever of the paragraph styles that we have selected.

For this exercise double click on the HEADLINE style in the browser, which will display the basic style control screen:

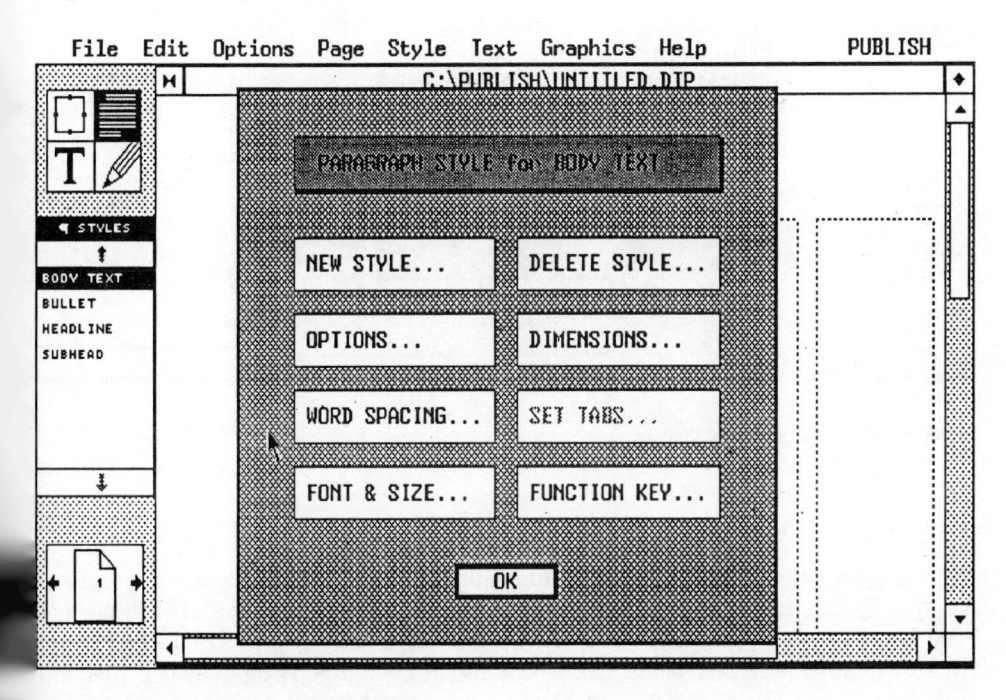

Figure 5.1 Paragraph Style Control Screen

We now have the choice either to modify, or delete, the existing style, or to create an entirely new style.

Before we proceed with defining a new style, we will look in detail at the eight different functions available through the control screen menu.

NEW STYLE...

When we click on this option we are presented with the *Paragraph Style Name* screen. This shows the name of the currently selected paragraph style. A text cursor is located at the end of this name, so we have the ability to delete the name, and enter a new one as required.

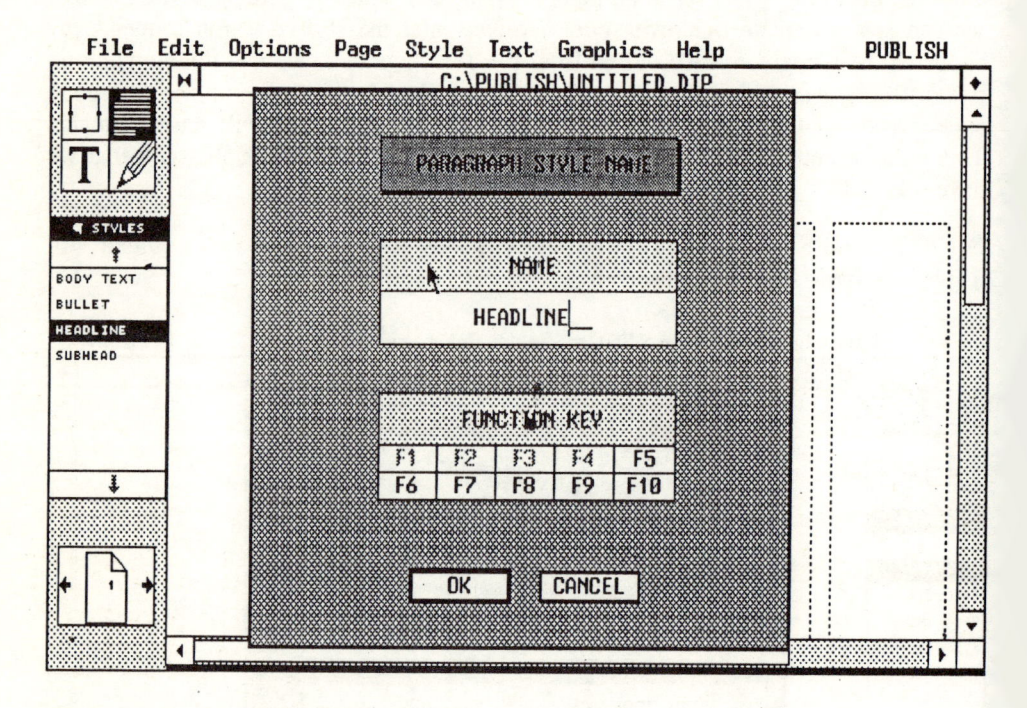

Figure 5.2 Style Name Control Screen

The function key block shows us the function key status. Those shown in grey text are already allocated to a particular style, although which is allocated to each current style is not shown on this display. If we are creating a new style to add to the current list we would enter a new name, and select one of the currently un-allocated function keys. If we then click on [OK] the changes are recorded. Click on [CANCEL], for now, to leave present definitions undisturbed.

OPTIONS...

Open the OPTIONS screen by clicking on the appropriate box, and we are presented with a further range of choices relating to various aspects of the text layout.

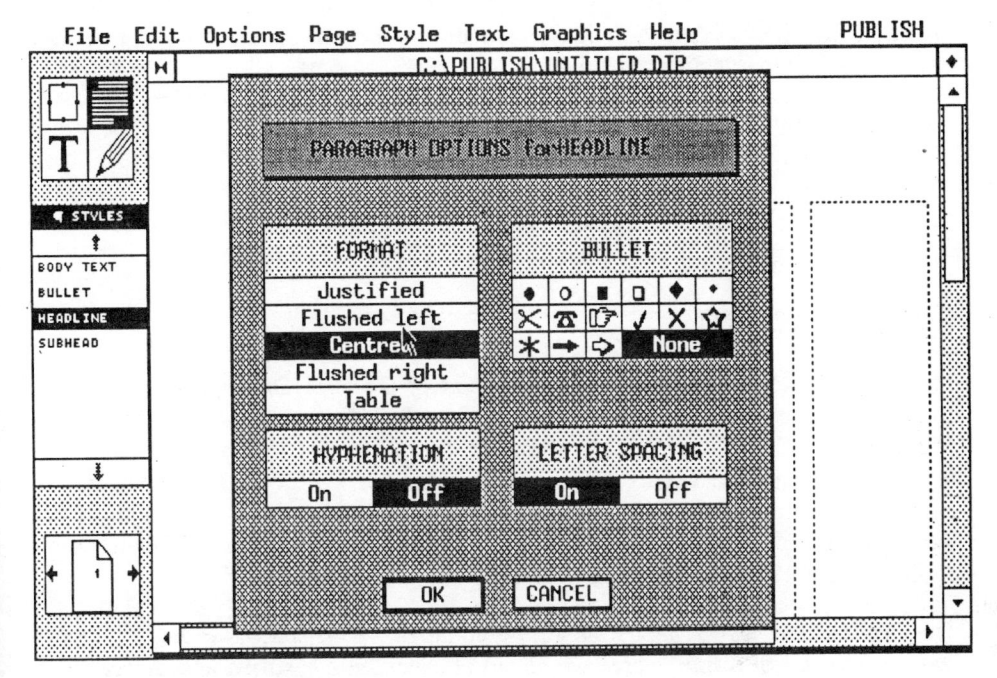

Figure 5.3 Style Options Screen

In the format box we have four choices relating to the position of the text with respect to the frame in which it is created. The current selection for the HEADLINE style is highlighted, but this can be modified by simply clicking the mouse on the required selection. The fifth choice in this list, TABLE, is used where we wish to create columns of text. The [TAB] key functions in the normal way only where a TABLE format is selected from this menu. We will be looking at this particular aspect in more detail later.

The BULLET table allows us to select a display character used to emphasise a listing of discrete points. No bullet is selected for the HEADLINE style definition.

The HYPHENATION box enables us to choose whether or not to allow the text hyphenation controls to function within the particular paragraph definition. This would not normally be on for large size text selections, as used in headings, etc., but would be usual in normal body text definitions.

Letter Spacing controls are used to assist in the process of line justification, where even right and left margins are required. We can set limits to the amount of space the program will allow between separate words to achieve justification. Where this will not allow the program to achieve full justification Timeworks Publisher can insert additional space between the letters in each word, to help achieve a more even appearance. In this screen we can decide whether or not this is to be allowed. It is necessary to experiment with different options to see the effects of this selection in any particular case.

We can identify from this particular screen all the relevant parameters for the current HEADLINE style selection:

Format	Centred
Bullet	None
Hyphenation	Off
Letter Spacing	On

WORD SPACING

This is the function, mentioned in the context of the OPTIONS menu, which gives control over the word spacing within a paragraph definition. Here we note that the control measurements are "ems" which we defined in the first chapter, and this is irrespective of any other units of measure we have chosen for the document. In most cases the selection shown will be adequate. We would only wish to modify this where we are trying to achieve a precise fit of text into a particular frame, where normal editing does not achieve the required result.

The *hyphenation hot zone* defines the amount of blank space we are prepared to leave at the end of a line, where we have not specified a justified appearance. If the space left by moving a whole word to the next line exceeds this parameter, then the program will insert a hyphen in the word to improve the alignment. Of course, this will not happen if we turn hyphenation OFF in the options menu control.

In short lines, such as used for headlines, which would not normally be justified, these options are not too significant. However, to be complete we will note the current settings for the HEADLINE style:

Min Space between words	0.3 ems
Max space between words	0.9 ems
Hyphenation Hot zone	5.0 ems

FONT and SIZE

This brings up a duplicate of the menu that we have previously used in the context of text styles, and we can make our choice as before. The chosen style is then attached to the whole of the paragraph. This does not prevent us from making any changes we like to individual words within a given paragraph.

The options selected for the current headline style are:

Font	Dutch
Size	36 point

DIMENSIONS

This allows us to set the main format characteristics of full paragraphs. It is of limited application in single line paragraphs, such as headings, etc., and of greater significance in larger text blocks. It is particularly important, for example, in the definition of the body text style, which we will look at later.

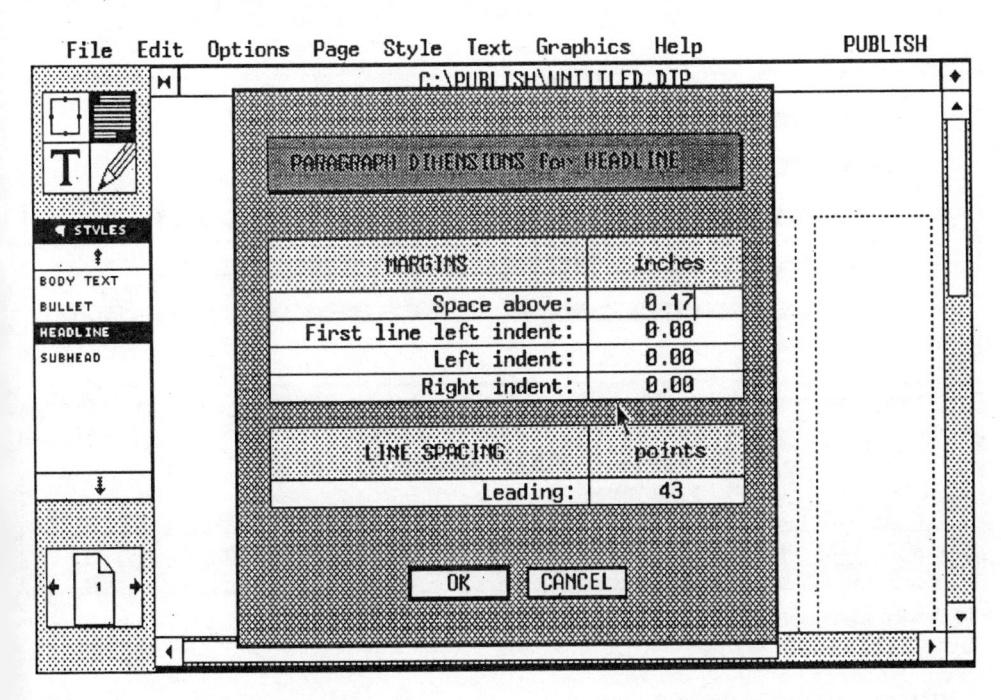

Figure 5.5 Dimension Control Screen

The margins control allow us to specify:

SPACE ABOVE This controls the amount of white space above the paragraph, measured from the baseline of any preceding text. This value is added to the normal leading value to give the spacing between the two base lines, across a paragraph boundary. This value is ignored if the first line of the paragraph is the first line in the frame, so that the base line of the first line of text is at the normal leading value from the top of the frame. (During some exercises this value was actually measured as 1 point greater than the leading, but this is unlikely to be significant)

FIRST LINE LEFT INDENT This allows us to have the first line of text in the paragraph aligned differently from the main body of the text. This is defined in terms of the distance from the edge of the frame. This may be inset from the rest of the text if this value is greater than the normal Left Indent value. Alternatively the first line may be set the opposite way, being closer to the left margin than the rest of the text, using a value that is less than the normal left indent. (This is called a *hanging indent*)

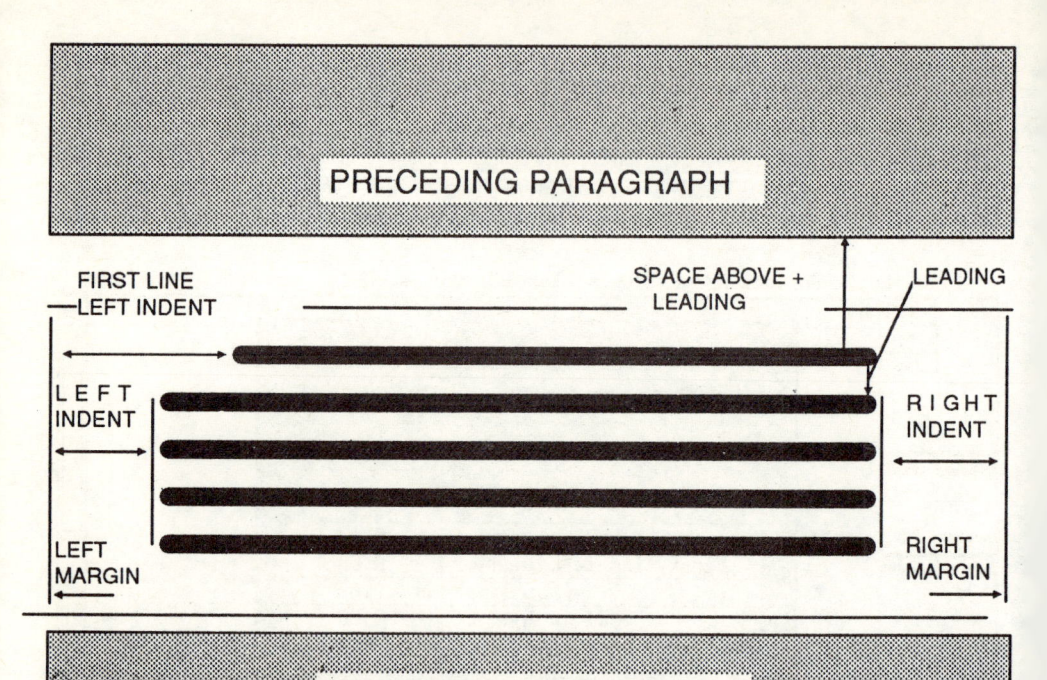

Figure 5.6 Paragraph Dimension Definitions

LEFT INDENT This sets the space between the frame edge and the start of the normal line of text within the paragraph, but does not affect the first line parameters set above.

RIGHT INDENT This allows us to modify the right margin setting to move the text away from the normal right hand frame margin.

LINE SPACING This allows us to set the leading, which was defined earlier. The program has a default setting for each text size, which will be shown on screen. We can modify this if required, but as with word spacing we should have a particular aim in mind, as large changes in this may look odd.

Once again, for the headline style the following parameters have been set:

Space above	0.17 inches
First Line left indent	0.00 inches
Left indent	0.00 inches
Right indent	0.00 inches
Line spacing	43 points (Default)

Notice again here that, although all other dimensions are quoted in inches, the leading is defined as points. Frequently it will pay to look at all the measurements in terms of points when working closely with text spacing.

FUNCTION KEY

This presents a duplicate of the paragraph style name screen, but identifies the particular function key associated with the style, and allows this to be changed. The current selection shows that key [F2] is assigned to the headline style.

SET TABS...

The SET TABS menu is only be available if we have selected TABLE FORMAT in the OPTIONS menu. We will look at this particular function separately later on.

TEXT STYLE

There is no function within the Paragraph Style menu which allows control of the text style (i.e. Bold, etc.) in the same manner as the other parameters. To set a particular style characteristic it is necessary to leave the Paragraph Style control screen, when all other parameters are set.

Then, while the style name is still highlighted in the browser, open the normal {STYLE} menu and select the appropriate characteristics. This can be any sensible combination of the selection available, and these will be fully assigned to the selected paragraph style.

From this you can see that the controls available on the screen presentation, and the subsequent printed output, are very comprehensive. Although the choices available may seem overpowering, in practice they are applied in such a well controlled sequence that few problems actually arise.

In many cases, where you are building up on a current style sheet, only a small number of selections need to be adjusted. The default values, particularly relating to word spacing, leading, etc. are usually adequate for most normal applications.

Once the paragraph styles have been assigned they can, of course, be incorporated within the document. If we modify any of the styles while working in a document these will change all occurrences of that style within the document immediately, but will not have any impact on the saved style sheets. The changes, however, will be saved with the document, for use next time the document needs to be edited.

A complete style sheet description consists of the master page definition *and* the paragraph style definitions. To link these two together, to save as a style sheet, we should have the Master Page on screen when we make the paragraph style definitions. It is possible, with later versions of the program, to modify and save the style sheet definition at any point in the document development. This was not the case with all of the earlier versions, where the style sheet definition was strictly related to the master pages. Remember, however, that to modify any permanent feature of the master page, this needs to be done with the master page on screen.

Using and Modifying Paragraph Styles

Now that we have reviewed all the parameters required to set the paragraph styles we should practice this, by modifying the default styles supplied with the program, as this will enable us to judge the effect immediately, and to practice with different options.

Get the example file on screen, and use the default settings to set some examples of each of the paragraph styles available.

Another First From GST

GST Software of Cambridge announce the first professional-quality Desktop Publishing package available for under £150. The program, developed for major US software publisher Timeworks, and called *Timeworks Desktop Publisher,* will be published in Europe by Electric Software.

Breakthrough

Timeworks DTP is a real breakthrough in price and performance, with a feature list that rivals that of Ventura™or PageMaker™,but at a price that brings professional DTP power within everyone's reach.

It's Packed With Features!

Only *Timeworks Desktop Publisher* gives you all the DTP features you want, at a price that everyone can afford:
- Frame-based page layout
- Five zoom modes
- Style sheets
- Wide range of fonts supplied
- Multiple text styles
- Handles all European characters
- Direct text input and editing
- Styled text imported from 1st Word Plus, Word Writer, and WordStar
- ASCII text imported from other word processors
- Automatic justification
- Automatic hyphenation
- Text block cut, paste, copy, and restyle
- Drawn, painted, and scanned picture import
- Picture scaling and cropping
- Automatic text runaround

Figure 5.7 Paragraph Styles Applied to EXAMPLES.DOC

Ensure that you are in paragraph mode for this exercise, and double click on the HEADLINE style in the browser, to open the style control screen. As we are only going to modify the current style we will not need to use the NEW STYLE... option, and can select the Options menu directly.

Change the current Format setting to Flushed right, and then click on [OK] on this and the following screen. When the control menu is removed we can see the new format in effect on the page.

While the HEADLINE style is highlighted in the browser, open the {STYLE} menu, and select Italic AND Light in succession, again to see the results displayed immediately. If we were now to use the HEADLINE style anywhere else in the document this new setting would be adopted.

One point that you may have noted is that if you are using a small frame size and switch to Italic text, part of the extreme right hand characters of the headline seem to have disappeared across the frame boundary. This is a small problem with the text representation on screen, and will not affect the printed output.

You should try a few variations on this theme before moving on to some other paragraph style selections.

Use your own initiative to make some variations on the SUBHEAD style in a similar fashion, using a selection of the options available.

Heading and Subheadings would normally consist of an amount of text, less than a full line long. Normal text paragraph will occupy more space, and need some further parameters set. To examine this we will modify the current Body Text style.

Open the BODY TEXT style menu by double clicking on this in the browser, and immediately select the OPTIONS menu. Just to demonstrate the change we can choose the FLUSHED LEFT format. Leave the bullet at NONE and letter spacing ON. The default values of word spacing are adequate for most applications, and we will not change these here.

From the FONT & SIZE menu select DUTCH 12 Point, and then move on to the DIMENSIONS WINDOW, which now has more relevance.

For the purposes of this exercise, then, we will set FIRST LINE LEFT INDENT at 1 inch, LEFT INDENT at 0.5 inches, and RIGHT INDENT at 0.5 inches. We will not change the default LEADING, which is set at 14 points for our new 12 point text size.

Once we have completed this process and installed a new BODY TEXT style the whole document will change to accept this new style at every point at which it was specified .

This will happen any time we modify an existing style. It is an extremely powerful feature allowing major changes in document style and layout, with very little effort. However, as with all such powerful tools it has to be used carefully. Be sure that, when you do modify an existing style, it is your intention to do so for the whole document.

As you make various changes throughout the document be sure that the changes do not result in an inconsistent appearance across the whole document. For example, it is usually better to have the whole document justified to the same pattern, if you use different margin settings (i.e. the whole document should be justified, or left aligned, etc., and the two options should only be mixed with care).

The fourth style available, BULLETS, is used to provide some means of emphasising certain points in the text. While we can create emphasis by changing the style, as we have done above, such bulleted lists are a common means of providing such emphasis. These use graphics symbols (often referred to as DINGBATS), coupled with line indents to bring out certain text. This can, of course, be accompanied by other text changes if required.

We create bullet paragraphs following the same general sequence as above. We will make some small changes to the BULLET STYLE in the program to demonstrate this. Double click on BULLET in the browser, and open the options screen. This already shows a selection for Flushed left text, which you should change to Flushed right. Select one of the alternative bullet symbols, and exit from this function to check the results on screen. With PostScript printers there is no bullet selection available.

Use the controls that we have learned to make the following additional changes to the bullet style definition:

Font	Dutch
Size	12 point
First line left indent	0.5 inches
Left indent	1.0 inches
Right indent	0.5 inches

None of the changes that we have made will have any impact on the original style sheet. If we save the document as a DTP file, however, all the changes that we have incorporated will be saved, as we would hope.

These are then available for use any time we work on this particular document.

Remember that to allocate a paragraph style we can do this either by clicking on that style in the browser, or by pressing the appropriate function key, as assigned when creating the styles.

From the above you will see how simple it is to create different styles and appearances from the same basic text file, even just using simple modifications to the DEFAULT.STY definition file supplied with the program.

Creating a Style Sheet

In the above exercise we have just made modifications to the default Style Sheet supplied as part of the Timeworks Publisher program. Once you have become familiar with the basic workings of the program, you will probably wish to have your own style sheets, or even to substitute your own default style.

A Style Sheet will consist of two major elements:

>Your Master Page Layout; *and*

>Specifications for your paragraph styles.

Once these are set you can save them under a suitable name for future recall.

Remember that it is quite practicable to have any number of Style Sheets, and that these may, for example, have a common page layout, and differ only in the paragraph styles. Alternatively, you may want to work on different sizes of paper, but use the same basic paragraph styles etc.

The easiest way to create a Style Sheet is to modify an existing one, and the one that is available immediately is the Default Style Sheet from Timeworks Publisher. This is stored on disk under the name DEFAULT.STY, and is accessed every time we start up the program. To find the appropriate directory use the file menu to select a NEW application. When asked 'Do you want to load a Stylesheet', indicate [YES], and the directory will be searched for the appropriate file. There is only one Style Sheet at the moment, and this will be listed in the GEM Item Selector. If we accept this it will be loaded into the document. During this we will see the Paragraph Styles appearing for a short time in the browser, as they are loaded.

Creating our own Style Sheet will effectively be a process of editing the default Style Sheet.

The first step, of course, is to establish some idea of how we wish our documents to appear. We will be looking at some approaches to this in the chapter on document design, and you may wish to look at that first before proceeding. Once you have a good idea of what you are trying to achieve, then we can continue with this exercise.

The first question to determine is what size paper are we going to use, as this has a major impact on our other choices. Are we going to have single sided documents, or a multi-page document requiring two master pages? We also have to consider what format we are going to have for the presentation of the document, to make appropriate allowance for Binding Margins, or for document folding, etc. A knowledge of the physical margins, in relation to the mechanics of your printer is also important. Some aspects of this are also discussed later, in the appropriate section. Before we start this exercise, then, we must be sure that you have made these preliminary decisions.

Let us assume, though, that all these factors have been considered, and we have come up with the basic definition of our document as follows:

A4 PAPER SIZE
PORTRAIT ORIENTATION
MULTI-PAGE DOCUMENT
1.00 INCH TOP MARGIN
1.00 INCH BOTTOM MARGIN
0.75 INCH OUTER MARGIN
1.25 INCH INNER MARGIN
BASIC 3 COLUMN GUIDE STRUCTURE
FIXED INFORMATION AT PAGE BOTTOM

From the file menu call up a NEW document, and indicate NO to the request to load a style sheet. On the PAGE FORMAT screen select the following options:

A4: 210 x 297 mm
LEFT & RIGHT MASTER PAGES
PORTRAIT ORIENTATION

From the basic screen, type [ALT] G, or open the PAGE MENU and select 'go to page'. Choose the Left Master page using the left pointing arrow. From the OPTIONS MENU select the SET COLUMN GUIDES function, to bring up the required screen.

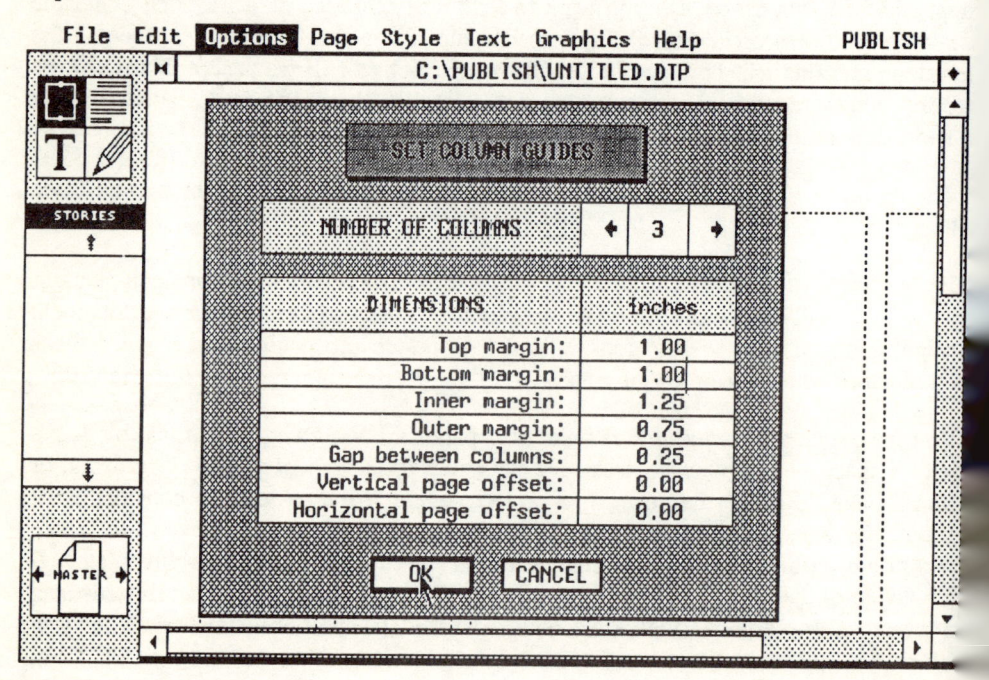

Figure 5.8 Set Column Guides

Click on the left pointing arrow to reduce the number of columns to three. Set the other parameters as per the specification above, but add a GAP BETWEEN COLUMNS of 0.25 inches. Leave the page offset values at zero, for now, until you have had a look at the printer options later.

Once these have been entered, and accepted, we can see the effect on screen immediately, and select FULL PAGE view to see this more clearly. Now turn to the other master page, by clicking on the right pointing arrow, beside the Master Page icon, in the Toolkit. These new parameters are reflected in the second master page.

Let us now add some information, for example the publishers address, at the bottom of each page. We will need to create a frame, across the bottom of the current Master Page, aligned with the column limits and *below* the bottom margin. It will be easier to achieve the final positioning if we switch off the 'SNAP TO GUIDES' function ({OPTIONS} Menu), which will try to keep this frame within the guide layout. Enter text mode, and activate the cursor in the frame. Using the default text style enter your address in this frame. We want this to sit centrally across the page, with a single line separating it from the basic text. With the frame active select the FRAME BORDER option, and choose the second single line thickness, positioned *above* the frame.

To make the address sit centrally within the frame we will actually have to create a Paragraph Style to control this. Switch to paragraph mode, and select the Address block, then call down the Paragraph Style control screen from the {TEXT} menu, or by clicking twice on one of the styles in the browser. We will specify a new style, called ADDRESS.

From the OPTIONS screen select the CENTRED format, leaving all others as the default value. Set the FONT and SIZE to 10 point Dutch, and exit the menu. Use the {STYLE} menu to select bold text for this line. This completes the definition so we can exit by clicking on [OK] in the main menu screen. The style ADDRESS, is now listed in the browser, and the address line has changed to adopt this format. View the page in both ACTUAL and FULL size views to check the appearance. If the address appears a little close to the frame border you will need to adjust this by inserting a blank line above the address, but ensuring that the frame size is big enough to hold the blank line, and the text line.

We want this same information to appear on the other master page, also, so to save us from having to create this all over again, switch to frame mode, and COPY the frame to the clipboard using the functions in the {EDIT} menu. Switch to the other master page, using the arrows beside the page icon. Select PASTE from the EDIT menu, or use [ALT] V, and place the frame in the correct position.

To ensure that the frames are in the same relative position on the page, select the SIZE and POSITION controls from the OPTIONS menu, or double click on the frame. The horizontal position should match our set margin position (0.75 or 1.25, depending on which master page we are viewing), and the vertical position should be the same on each page.

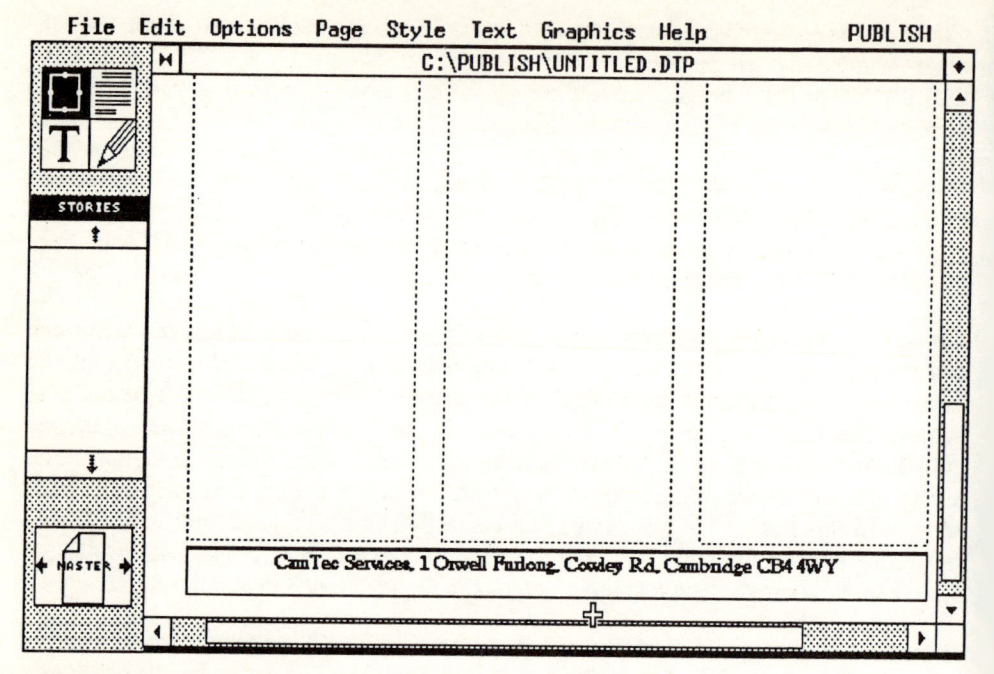

Figure 5.9 Master Page Format

If all this is satisfactory we have completed the basic page definition. If we now use the GO TO PAGE control ([ALT] G), and specify Page 1, in the response screen, we will see the appropriate master page duplicated on screen, for any future work.

Now we have to create our paragraph formats, and for the purposes of this exercise we will limit ourselves to three options, basically similar to those used in the previous exercise.

As we already have the default styles on display we will work by editing, or even accepting, those for our own Style Sheet. We have already created the ADDRESS style, so now we will move on to create a HEADLINE style. As we will be saving this information in a separate Style Sheet we can keep the same names, even if we change the specification.

Return to displaying the master pages, and again choose the left master page, for consistency. Double click on HEADLINE in the Browser to bring up the Style control menu. As we are not going to change the name we do not need to specify a new style. We can go directly to the options menu, and select the appropriate parameters. The current choice would seem appropriate, so we will accept those (although you can change them if you have some other scheme in mind). Next select the FONT and SIZE menu and make the appropriate choices. Modify the text style from the {STYLE} menu if required. As before, unless there is a particular need we can accept the DIMENSION defaults, and by looking at the FUNCTION KEY screen we can see that F2 is currently assigned to this style. Click on [OK] until our working screen is restored, and the style is now set.

Repeat the process, using the first example above to specify a new SUBHEAD style, and a new Body Text style. If required, create additional style types if you are keen enough at this stage. Any style types that we do not require can be deleted. This will delete them only from the current sheet, and will not affect the stored Style Sheet, unless we choose to overwrite this. (The delete style option is available from the main Paragraph Style control screen).

There is one notable exception to this above action. The Body Text style *cannot* be deleted. The program will follow all the normal processes, as if following the instruction. When complete, however, the Body Text style will remain listed in the browser.

It is, therefore, necessary to have a specified Body Text in all your Style Sheets, as without it Timeworks Publisher will insert its default Body Text style, Swiss 10 Point, which may not suit the application.

If you have created your own Body Text style, and try to delete it, the program will substitute the default style in its place. Remember that all text which does not have a specific style attached to it will automatically use the Body Text style.

Now that we have created our own Style Sheet we will wish to save it. From the FILE menu call up the 'SAVE STYLE SHEET' option, and we will be presented with the GEM Item Selector, with the current style directory displayed. We can, if we wish, overwrite the default sheet, but for now let us use an alternative name, FIRST.STY, and save that.

The naming convention for Style Sheets is consistent with the general rules. The first part of the name should be selected to have some meaning to yourself, and to be no longer than eight characters. The extension, however, must always be .STY, so that Timeworks Publisher can recognise this.

To ensure that all is well, now select the NEW option from the file menu, and abandon the current work. When asked if you wish to select a new Style Sheet select [YES], and the program will automatically load in the default style, before presenting the GEM Item Selector. Accept the default style, just to ensure that all traces of your own creation have disappeared.

Now select NEW file again, and repeat the sequence, but this time specify the new Style Sheet and, Hooray!, there it is on screen.

Provided that you have followed all the various steps discussed above this is quite a painless process. With no previous experience of this type of program, the author's first attempt worked exactly, so you should also have no problems.

If the Style Sheet does not appear to have been saved, first of all make sure that you have identified the correct directory, but also make sure that you did have the master pages active when the Style Sheet was saved.

The next step is to test the Style Sheet to see if it meets your requirements.

To do this effectively, you will need to create a short text file into which you can incorporate the styles defined. If you have not yet been fired with enough enthusiasm to create your own text files then cheat!. Pick one of your favourite magazines, newspapers or books (how about this one?), and copy a short section, including headlines, etc.

As the file need not be very long it can be entered directly to the screen. There is also no reason why you should not use your word processor to test its compatibility.

It will soon become apparent how easy it is to achieve some quite attractive layouts. In some of the later sections we will be looking at how to mix some of the effects that we have already seen to provide additional enhancements.

We create our basic Style Sheet, working with the master page definition. We can modify any of the styles created while working on a document. Changes that we make to the Style Sheet, within the document, will not be reflected in the stored Style Sheet. It would appear that even if we attempt to save the modified Style Sheet, using the FILE menu, this will *not* in practice over-write the existing file, but will just remain attached to the document.

To create a modified Style Sheet we need to go back to the editing associated with the master page definition. This feature is quite useful, as it ensures that you have the control associated with the use of Style Sheets, but retain the flexibility to amend individual documents.

Importing Style Sheets

In the previous chapter we noted that there was a method of overcoming some of the limitations on importing text styles from other word processor packages. Now that we are more familiar with the concept of STYLE, as applied here, we can look a little closer at this.

This feature is not actually documented by the publishers of Timeworks Publisher, at the time of writing, but can be an extremely useful feature, and is very simple to use.

In our example Style Sheet, we created some paragraph styles which we called HEADLINE, SUBHEAD and BODY TEXT. To make use of these we loaded a file into our document, and applied the styles to each relevant paragraph.

Using this new feature we can now apply these styles *before* the file is imported, and using *any* word processor.

To achieve this, as we prepare our file on the word processor, we simply precede the appropriate text with the style name enclosed in < and > symbols.

For example, to create a HEADLINE in the word processor, for use in the DTP document, we would type:

THIS IS A <HEADLINE> When imported into the document, the initial <HEADLINE>, sets the style, but does not appear in the document. The text "THIS IS A HEADLINE", however, will appear in the correct format.

This feature has strict limits in its operation, but not sufficiently to provide any major problems. To use it fully the following rules must be followed:

> The style name, enclosed between < >, must be EXACTLY the same as that used in the Style Sheet;
>
> The style name MUST be the first entry on the text line, and must have no preceding spaces;
>
> The style name must not contain any blanks;
>
> The style characteristics can only be applied to a COMPLETE paragraph;
>
> Any occurrences of <text> at any point in the document other than the beginning of a paragraph, will be treated as normal text, and be printed, including the < and > characters;
>
> The style assignment will remain active only for a single paragraph, that, is until the first [CARRIAGE RETURN] character is found; and
>
> In the absence of any alternative instruction the text will adopt the Body Text style.

Provided that we stick to the above rules, then we can make full use of this facility.

The last one of the above rules means that no code need be inserted for the Body Text, as this is the default text style used in the absence of any specific instructions to the contrary. Text in the document will automatically revert to this style at the end of each paragraph, unless it meets another style code.

As we have mentioned earlier, various word processors use a wide variety of codes for their internal functions. If it appears that these codes are causing problems, then use the option to save your document in ASCII format. All the style instructions will be preserved, and carried through into Timeworks Publisher.

It is not possible, using this technique, to attach style to single words, or groups within a paragraph. Such changes will need to be made within the document in Timeworks Publisher.

If, within the word processor, you use a style name which does not match any set up within the DTP program, a new style will be created by Timeworks Publisher, using that name, but adopting the style of the default Body Text This means that you can deliberately introduce a new style when working in the word processor, and then edit the definition when it is imported into the Timeworks Publisher document.

This ability to import style controls within the document is extremely useful. Most modern word processors are able to store preset text blocks which can be called up using simple two-key combinations. This can be used to define the style codings, including the < and > symbols which can readily be incorporated into the document without the need for long repeated text entry operations. This function operates under a variety of names in different word processors, including Keyboard Macros, Glossary, Concordance, etc.

Tabular Paragraph Styles

In an earlier section we expressed some reservations about the successful import of tables, etc., from external documents. The main problems arise in relating the table and tab settings within the imported document, to those which can be achieved within Timeworks Publisher. With care, however, this can be achieved with most word processors with little difficulty.

When creating a paragraph style, one of the choices in the {OPTIONS} menu is to select a 'Table' format. Where this is selected we are given the additional ability to set up a maximum of nine tab stops across a frame. The tab positions are fixed by measurement from the left hand frame edge, and will be set using the units of measure current for the particular document.

One area of confusion arises with some word processors where tabs are set in relation to character positions, and these do not necessarily relate directly to the system within Timeworks Publisher, where you have much greater control over character size and spacing.

Also, when using a word processor there is a tendency to use multiple presses of the tab keys, using the program default tab settings, to locate text in particular columns, rather than set up specially defined tabs for each different table. When Timeworks Publisher imports a text file, it will count each individual tab character, and attempt to relate this to the settings within the paragraph style.

Documents will only import successfully where the tab settings within the document relate directly to those set up using the controls within Timeworks Publisher. In this case, when the paragraph style is applied to the appropriate section of text within the Timeworks Publisher document the correct alignment will be achieved.

Thus, to achieve the easiest conversion of tables for use within Timeworks Publisher you must either:

Use the tab controls within your word processor to set up tabs that will correspond exactly with those to be used within Timeworks Publisher;

or

Separate each column of text within the basic document using a *single* tab character, even if this does not give the correct alignment on screen. Within the Timeworks Publisher document the alignment will be restored correctly.

For example, using Microsoft WORD 4, with the normal default tab settings, the following table was created using a single tab character between each item, on each line. In this document the alignment is clearly not acceptable for normal use.

When the document is imported into Timeworks Publisher, and assigned to a frame, using the normal body text settings, even the tab spacings will disappear.

To create a table within Timeworks Publisher it will be necessary to create a paragraph style, TABLE1, which contains the necessary information.

Use your word processor to create a copy of the table below, and import it with a suitable name into a blank Timeworks Publisher document.

```
City Qtr 1      Qtr 2       Qtr 3

Bristol 1250 1450 2340
Leeds 2450 120 4500
Birmingham 3600 4800 5400
London 3260 5250 4750
```

To create a new style, we use the normal process of modifying an existing style, and giving it a new name.

Select the paragraph tool to list the current paragraph styles in the browser, and double click on the body text style to activate the style control menu. Select NEW STYLE, and assign a name TABLE1 to this. From the options menu select the Table Format. Use the dimensions control to set a left margin inset of 0.5 inches, setting both left margin and first line left margin at this value.

The selection of a TABLE format enables the Tab Setting menu, and this should be selected next. Allow the first column, headed CITY, to align with the normal left margin, and create tab positions for the remaining columns.

Select the [SET TABS] control to activate the appropriate screen. The number 1 is highlighted in the control panel, but no [TAB TYPE] or [TAB POSITION] information is yet displayed. The tab type is selected by clicking on the appropriate box on the menu, and for this exercise select the 'Centre' type, which will cause all text to centre itself automatically on the tab position. Once a tab type is specified, then the tab position control is activated. Enter a value of 3.00 inches for the first tab position.

Now click on TAB NUMBER 2, and set a centre tab at position 4.00 inches, and TAB NUMBER 3 at 5.00 inches.

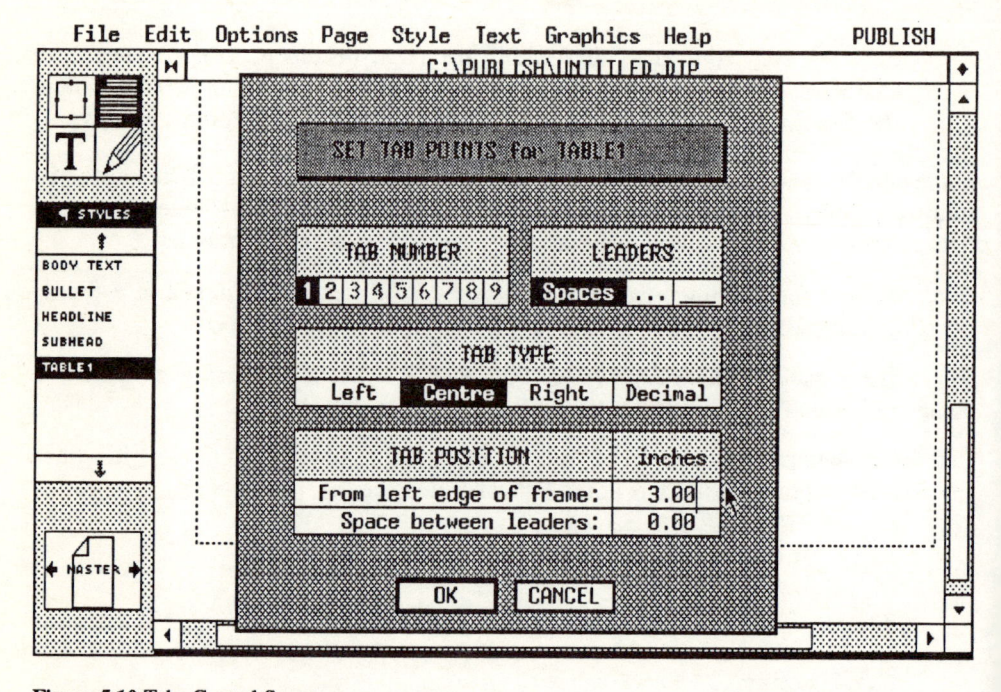

Figure 5.10 Tabs Control Screen

For this demonstration we do not require to specify leaders, and the relevant parts of the control can be ignored.

Now exit from the Style Control screen by pressing on the [OK] boxes, and note the new style listed in the browser.

This paragraph style can then be assigned to the imported text, and the appropriate table constructed.

The appearance of the table may then be improved by the addition of graphics and text enhancements using the normal processes.

One other point which was noted in this exercise in relation to the import of Microsoft WORD 4 files, and which will occur with other word processors, is that additional lines inserted between paragraphs, by pressing the [RETURN] key, are ignored when the text is imported.

To overcome this, where it represents a problem, a tab character should be inserted in any "empty" line before the [RETURN] key is pressed. This will then cause the

City	Qtr 1	Qtr 2	Qtr 3
Bristol	1234	1456	2340
Leeds	2450	120	4500
Birmingham	3600	4800	5400
London	3260	5250	4750

City	Qtr 1	Qtr 2	Qtr 3
Bristol	1234	1456	2340
Leeds	2450	120	4500
Birmingham	3600	4800	5400
London	3260	5250	4750

Figure 5.11 Imported Table Plus Graphics Enhancements.

required empty line to appear in the imported document. This technique was used to generate the appropriate space between the table headings and the contents, which would otherwise have closed up.

This particular feature is not a bug in the program, but is necessary to allow the correct operation of the assigned paragraph styles, which incorporate this in the 'SPACE BEFORE' setting, to achieve paragraph separation. The additional space will only occasionally be required in special cases, such as the table example here.

When defining table settings, in any given paragraph we can specify up to nine separate tab positions. These have to be defined in numeric sequence, by first clicking on the TAB NUMBER, and then completing the definition. The tab type option allows for four different alignments around the tab position, to suit the given application.

Left: The text will begin at the tab position, and progress in the normal fashion across the page.

Right: The text will be arranged so that the right hand end of the text will align with the tab position.

Centre: Text will be centred on the defined tab position.

Decimal: Used to align the decimal point for tables of numbers etc.

Once the tab type has been defined, its position on the page, with reference to the left hand frame edge, can be set.

Leaders are symbols, usually dots or underline characters, which lead up to the TAB position, to define a link between elements of the table. Unless specifically selected otherwise, these would be spaces, and would show as blanks on the screen.

Leaders are usually used to provide a link between items in a list, or merely to provide an enhanced appearance of text, as in:

> Chapter 1 ....Introduction
> Chapter 2 ....Getting Started

The leader character is assigned to the second tab position, i.e. the tab locating the words 'Introduction' and 'Getting Started' above.

The SET TABS screen allows you to control both the type of leader required, and the space between each dot or underline symbol.(This spacing will have no impact if the leader character is a space)

Again this is an area where some experimentation is required to see the results of particular choices, but in practice the use is quite straightforward.

Bullet Paragraph Style

This style is most usually employed to create a list of emphasised points. A graphics character, the BULLET, is used to highlight each item of text.

A bullet style is created using exactly the same procedures as for any other style, usually by modifications to an existing definition.

The dimensions controls need some careful consideration, as they do not have quite the same effect as with other paragraph styles.

One point is that the 'First line left indent' control is used to position the bullet character in relation to the left margin. The 'Left indent:' figure is used to determine the start position of the related text. Any text which is longer than a single line will wrap around to start its new line at the left indent margin. In that way bulleted lists do not have to be just single line items.

The 'space above:' control may well normally be set to zero to prevent the appearance of too much white space between each item. This can, of course, be set as required for any particular application.

Bullet style text format may be set to any of the standard options. However, the position of the bullet on the page is not affected by this selection. In this case flushed left, justified and flushed right may be used equally well, but the centred format should be used with care. Note here that text is only justified where it exceeds a full line in length, and that the program will not attempt to stretch short lines to fill the available space.

a	●
b	○
c	■
d	□
e	◆
f	•
g	✄
h	☎
i	☞
j	✓
k	✗
l	☆
m	✱
n	→
o	⇨

Figure 5.12 Bullet Symbols

For direct entry of a bulleted list within a Timeworks Publisher document just type in the first line required, and assign the appropriate paragraph style. Any further text entered will automatically adopt the bullet style set for the original text.

To terminate the direct entry of the list, however, you will need to press the [RETURN] key after the last line. This will place a bullet character on the next line, in preparation for any following text. Click the paragraph marker onto this final bullet, although there will be no screen response to this, and then select the BODY TEXT style, or another alternative, to de-activate the bullet style.

As with all other text imports the bulleted style can be assigned to imported text as appropriate in the conventional way.

The available bullets can be printed directly by activating the text cursor, and selecting the bullet font from the style menu. The bullets characters can be entered using the lower case letter keys 'a' to 'o', to give the sequence shown in Figure 5.12. All other keys pressed will give the 'a' character.

Header and Footer Paragraph Styles

In the previous chapter we mentioned that when the Header and Footer options are selected, then a paragraph style is created for each. Initially this will adopt the characteristics of the body text style.

To modify these we simply double click on the appropriate style in the browser, and step through the various control options selecting the particular attributes required. No special procedures are required.

Modifying the default document style.

When we first use the Timeworks Publisher program we are presented with a default Style Sheet which contains the definition for the basic page layout. This consists of a master page layout with the following parameters, as shown by the set column guides display:

Top Margin	1.00 inch
Bottom Margin	1.33 inch
Left Margin	1.00 inch
Right Margin	0.50 inch
Gap between columns	0.17 inch
Vertical Page Offset	0.00 inch
Horizontal Page Offset	0.00 inch
Number of columns	6

Also included are four separate paragraph styles:

Body text;
Bullet;
Headline; and
Subhead.

In chapter 8 we discuss how to ensure that your printer output aligns up with your on-screen documents, and this may involve changing the vertical and horizontal printer offsets. Rather than make this change for every document we would want to incorporate this permanently into our default Style Sheet.

It is also probable that after a little experience you would wish to use different, and perhaps more, basic paragraph style definitions.

To modify the default Style Sheet, we use the same basic processes discussed earlier.

Start up the program in the normal way, and allow the default Style Sheet to load. Switch to the master page, and make the required changes to your column layout, and to your selected paragraph styles.

Note that if you are anticipating using left and right pages, which is required for printing on both sides of the page, then the left and right margins become termed the "Inner" and "Outer" margins, to allow for the different settings on the left and right pages.

Whilst still displaying the master page, select the [Save style sheet] option from the file menu.

You will be asked to confirm that you wish to overwrite the existing definition, and once this is accepted the modified Style Sheet will be stored. All future use of the program will now adopt the new default style.

6

Graphics Functions

In this chapter we will review the fourth of the possible modes of operation within Timeworks Publisher, the Graphics mode. This feature is quite comprehensive, and we have a number of options to consider. When you have finished this chapter we will have the opportunity to look at ways of linking all the functions that have been discussed, to create some interesting documents.

As with the text option, we have two alternatives here. Certain graphics functions are available within the Timeworks Publisher package, but we also have the ability to import graphics from external sources. We will look at these two elements quite independently.

Timeworks Publisher Internal Graphics Functions

As before, we should begin this chapter with a clean sheet on the screen. Create a single frame to occupy the whole screen, and operate in actual size page view, to give finer control over your actions.

To enter graphics mode we click on the pencil icon in the Toolkit, and we will see the browser change to show the graphics controls available. This allows us to use seven basic modes of graphics construction:

      STRAIGHT LINE
      BOX
      ROUNDED BOX
      CIRCLE
      ELLIPSE
      LINKED STRAIGHT LINES
      FREEHAND LINES

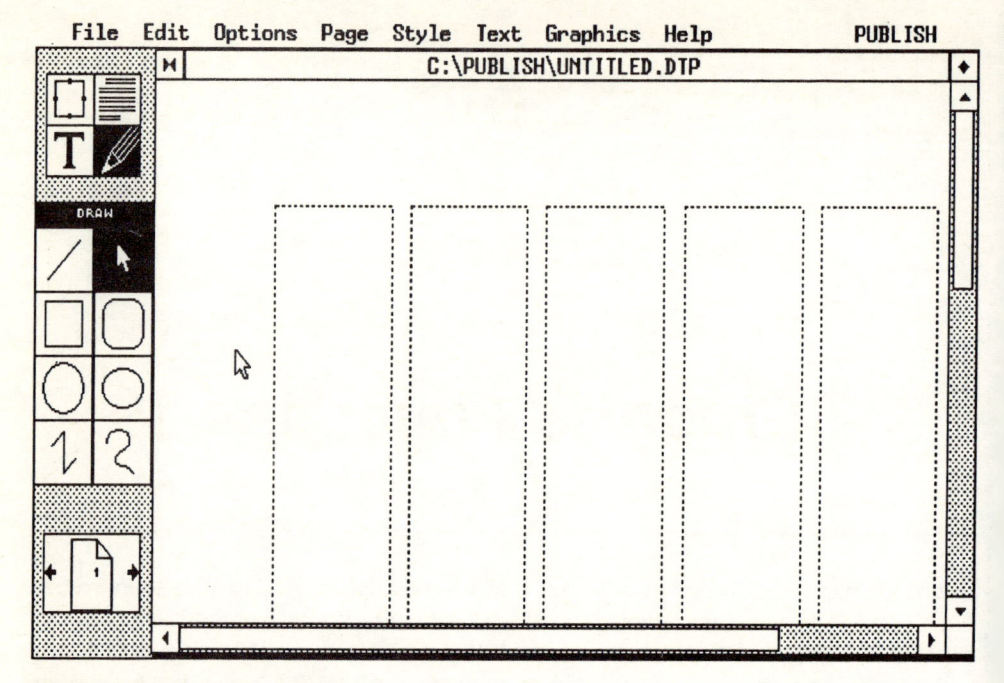

Figure 6.1 Graphics Toolbox Display

All the enclosed shapes, boxes, circles etc., can be filled with a range of shades and patterns. The arrow symbol, within the Toolkit, allows cursor control without any drawing functions attached, for movement of the drawn images.

When we enter graphics mode, and click in the frame, a grid will appear. This, however, is so lightly presented that it may be quite difficult to see. The grid will adopt the measure of the selected ruler spacing. When first selected, also, the [Snap to grid] function is set, and this may be turned off from the {GRAPHICS} menu. The display of the grid may be disabled, but as this is not intrusive on the display, unlike the frame surround presentation, there is little need to do this.

To create a graphics element select the appropriate tool, the straight line for our first exercise. The cursor will change to a fine cross hair when it is within the working screen. Place the cursor at the start position required, press and hold the left hand mouse button and drag the cursor to the required end position. The graphics has a 'rubber band' display so the line can be seen as it is extended. When the button is released the line is dropped onto the display and a graphics FRAME is displayed around the element. Once the graphics is displayed in this fashion it becomes a discrete unit. It is not possible, for example, to edit the graphic to add additional lines or other features to form a more complex single graphic.

If we click anywhere on the blank screen the graphics frame will disappear, but can be restored by clicking on the object drawn. While the frame is visible the graphics can be further manipulated. For example, by clicking and holding in the graphics

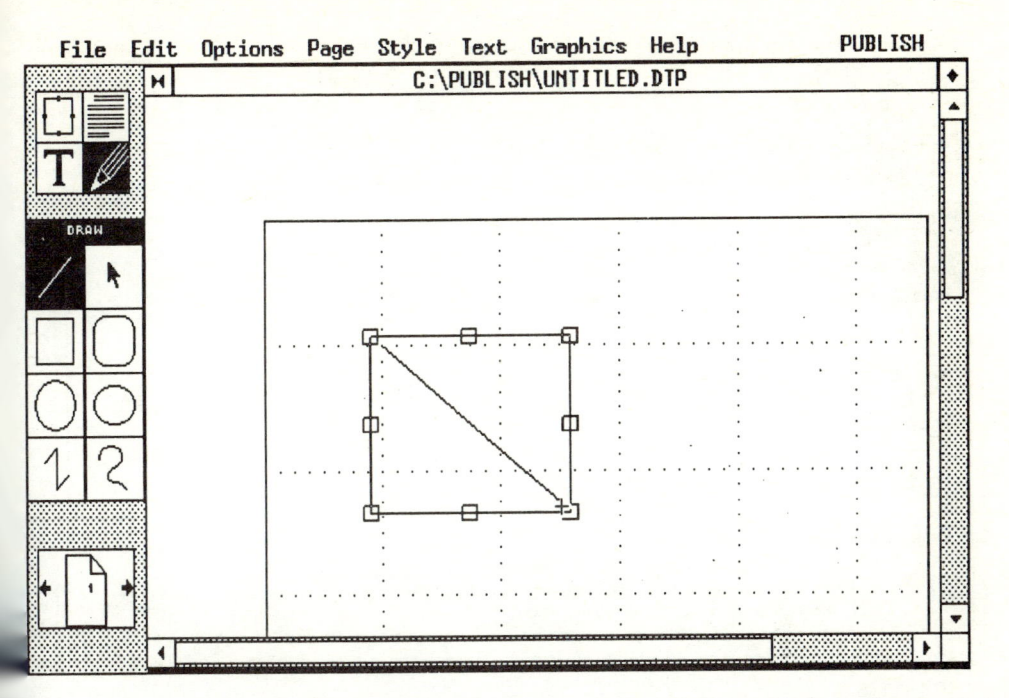

Figure 6.2 Basic Graphics Element with Frame

frame, and by dragging the mouse, the graphics can be moved to any point on the screen. By clicking on one of the frame handles, and dragging, the graphics may be re-sized. The frame may be made longer or shorter, or can be stretched diagonally. Any changes to the frame make corresponding changes to the graphics in the frame. This differs from the general text frame function where changing the frame size only impacts on the amount of text contained within the frame, and not on its other characteristics.

When modifying a line graphics frame, however, care has to be taken that the resulting line does not become distorted, where you are only trying to change the length. Problems can arise because the line frame does not have an end 'handle', but only corner handles. Any movement tends to form a diagonal change, and it will take little practice to ensure that straight line stretch is achieved. When viewing the screen during this procedure it becomes necessary to try and force the frame handles together to achieve a linear stretch, (i.e. during manipulation the frame may temporarily disappear; however, the graphics will be restored when the button is released).

As an example of the difficulties here Fig 6.3(a) shows the frame extended to stretch the line, but Fig 6.3(b) shows the resulting line, which is not what we want.

In Fig 6.4 we show the required frame stretch, in which the extended frame outline is not visible (look at the position of the small hand), but this does result in a straight line stretch.

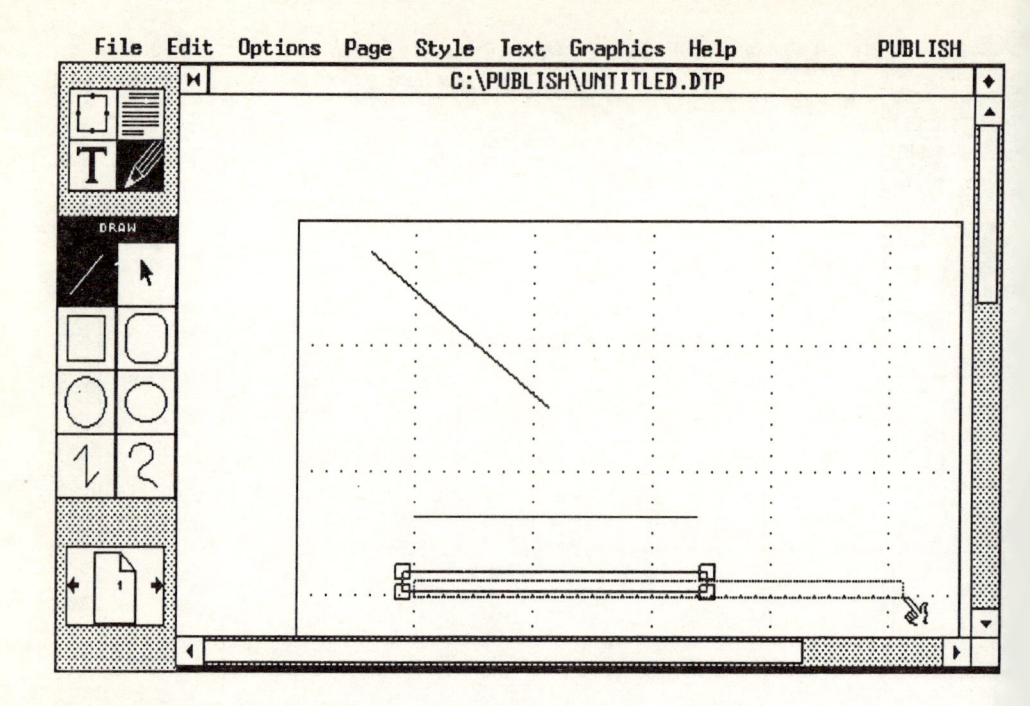

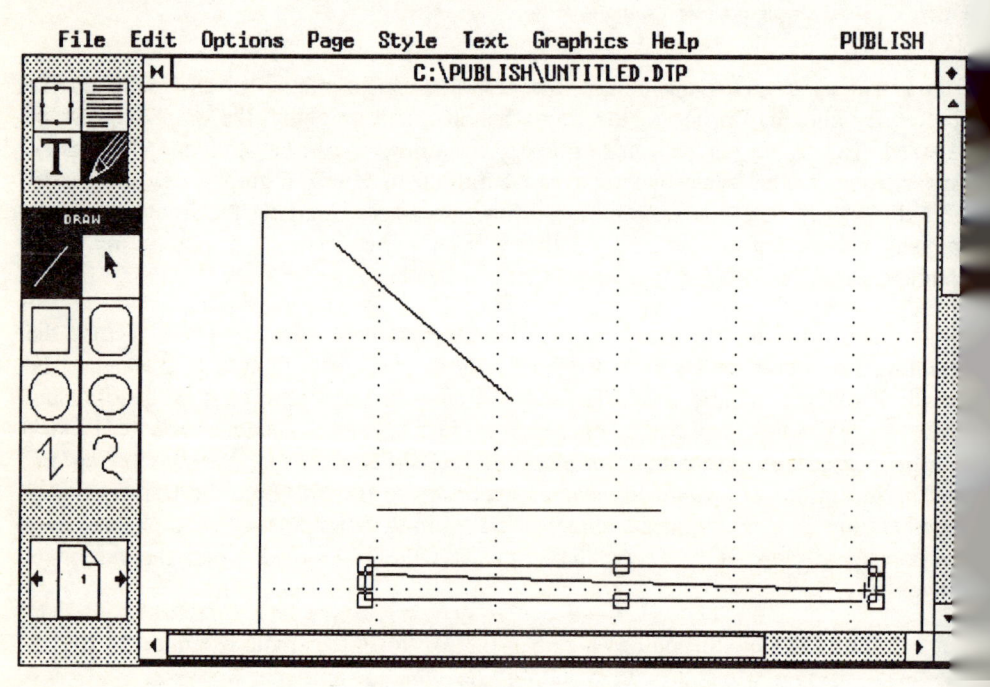

Figure 6.3 The display in the top picture produces the result shown in the bottom screen - see Figure 6.4 for the intended result.

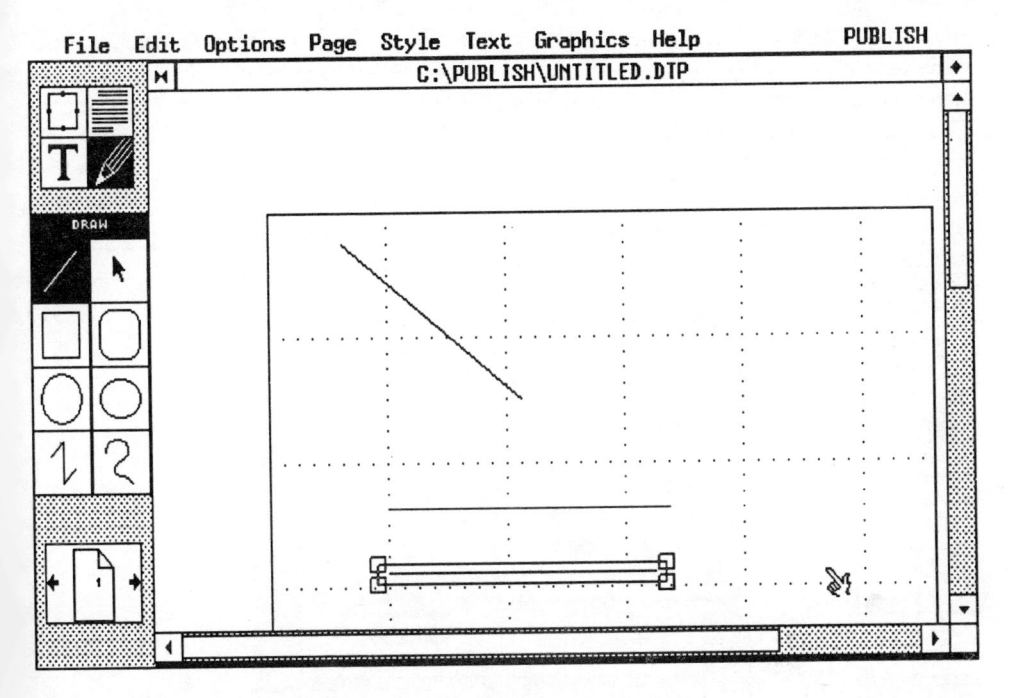

Figure 6.4 This is how it should look! Compare with Figure 6.3.

The graphics frame can be controlled in the same way as the text frame. For example the SIZE and POSITION controls in the {OPTIONS} menu will function normally. This is particularly useful as it enables you to achieve very fine control over the graphics positioning. It is also, frequently, a simpler means for achieving straightforward length adjustments. When using this option with straight line graphics it is worth remembering that the depth of a line is zero, so that setting the frame depth to zero for the line graphics will ensure that it will be absolutely even.

This becomes particularly important when trying to position graphics elements in relation to text, or other elements in the document. The computer display is not always of sufficient resolution to ensure precise positioning of the graphics, in relation to text, and in many cases it is necessary to resort to a test print to ensure the results required. As an example of the power of the built-in graphics functions, some of the illustrations for this book were produced within Timeworks Publisher (See Figs 5.6,7.1,9.2, etc.), and this has enabled extremely fine control over positioning and presentation.

Once a graphics element has been created, it can also be easily removed from the screen. Click on the object so that the frame appears, and select [Cut] from the {EDIT} menu. The graphics will be removed to the Graphics Clipboard. This offers the same facility as those in the other options. Graphics objects stored on the clipboard will be over-written by the next CUT or COPY action, but until that time may be used to paste into other parts of the document.

All of the graphics line elements, have a number of options available, which allow variations in thickness, appearance, and the use of arrowheads on the line ends. These functions are controlled from the [Line style] option in the {GRAPHICS} menu. Clicking on this option brings up the appropriate control screen, and the required selection can be made.

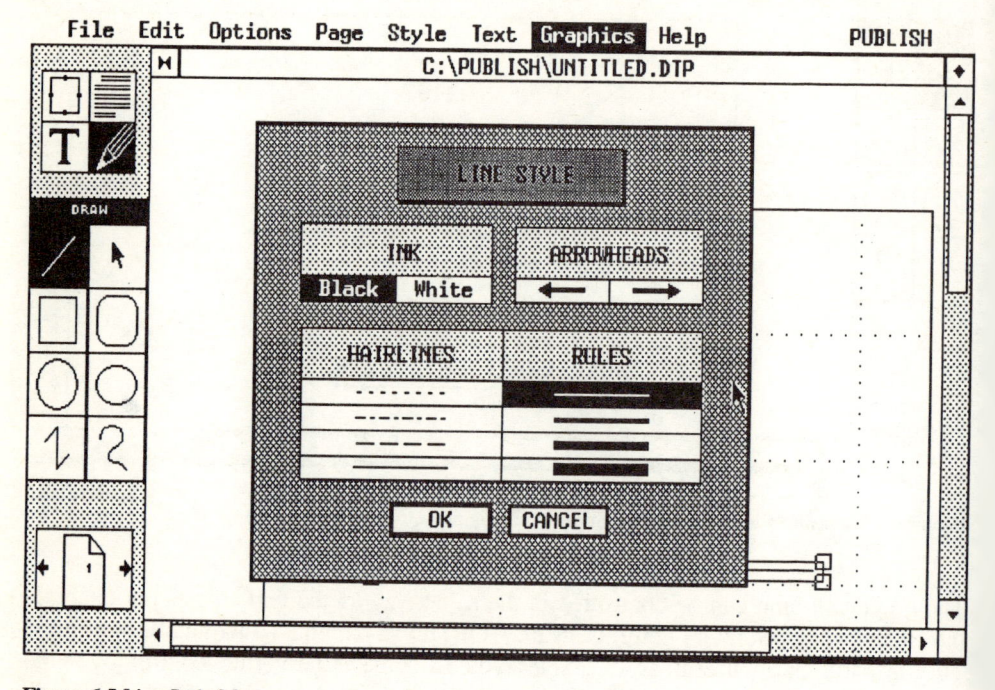

Figure 6.5 Line Style Menu

This selection will be assigned to all three of the line drawing functions, as well as the borders of the closed objects. It will affect any currently active graphic element, and any subsequently created.

To demonstrate the Linked Line function, select the appropriate tool from the browser. In this case, to draw the line we place the cursor at the start point, and click, and then move onto the next point and click again. Continue with this until the last point is placed, and then double click to terminate the line. This will cause the line to be presented in the set format, with or without arrowheads, and the graphics frame to be displayed. As before, the frame can now be moved or re-sized as required.

When moving and adjusting frames it is better to select the cursor tool (Arrow) from the browser to avoid placing spurious graphics on the screen. This will arise if you do not pick up the frame handles precisely enough, or attempt to move a frame when one of the other graphics tools is selected.

When drawing linked lines it is possible to drag the cursor, i.e. press and hold the button. However, it is still necessary to click at each end point. At the last point it is necessary to click once to fix the point, and THEN double click to terminate the line drawing function. If you fail to do this the last drawn line element will be lost.

The *freehand* drawing function is also quite straightforward, and to try this, as before, select the appropriate tool from the tools browser. This time place the cursor at the start point, and then drag it to produce the required line. Releasing the mouse button terminates the drawing procedure and fixes the line on the screen. There is, however, a limit to the complexity, and length, of the line drawn in this fashion. When this limit is reached the program simply will not draw any further. The graphic can only be extended by starting with a fresh line at the point where where the first finished off. Remember, though, that each graphic is a separate entity, and cannot be easily manipulated as a single unit.

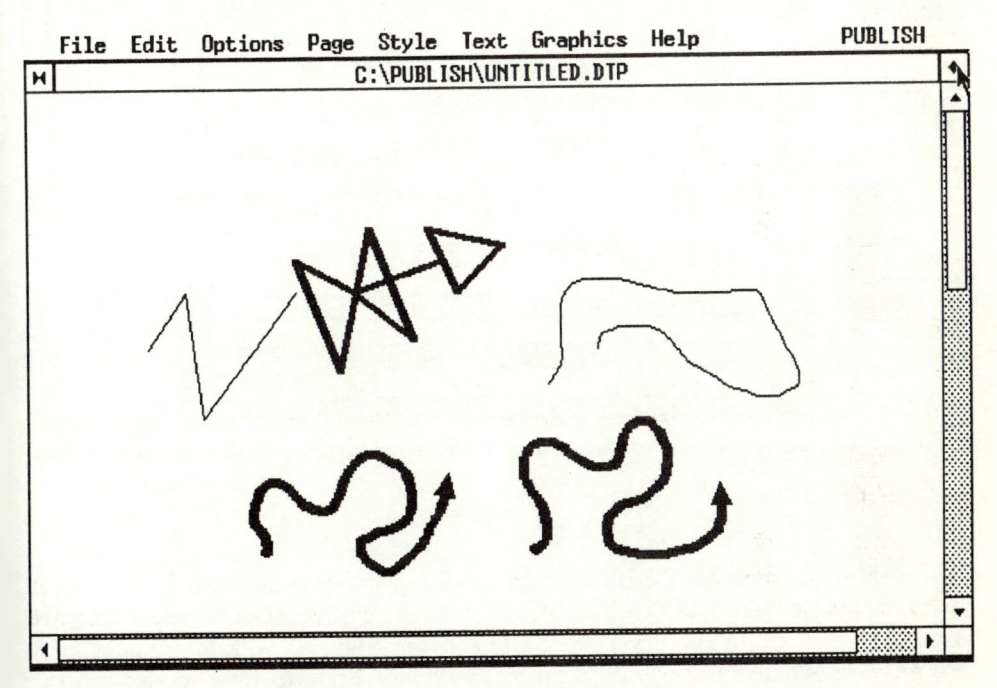

Figure 6.6 Linked Line and Freehand Line Graphics

Line graphics can be made to overlap each other, without any problems, to achieve special effects. They can also be drawn across other elements on the page, such as text, or other graphics elements. In this respect the frames are unlike the text frames, and the REPEL TEXT frame characteristic has no relevance.

Closed object drawings are used in a similar fashion. However, they differ from the line graphics in an important way. A closed object, i.e. a box or square, is always assumed to be filled, and consequently will normally obscure other graphics elements that lie behind it. It does not, however, obscure any text on the screen. This means that graphics items can easily be used to provide enhancements to the presentation of text on the page, in addition to the normal frame tint and border controls.

Closed objects can have a wide selection of *fill styles* attached, and these are selected from the [FILL STYLE] screen available through the {GRAPHICS} menu. As before, the selection is made by highlighting the appropriate choices on the control screen.

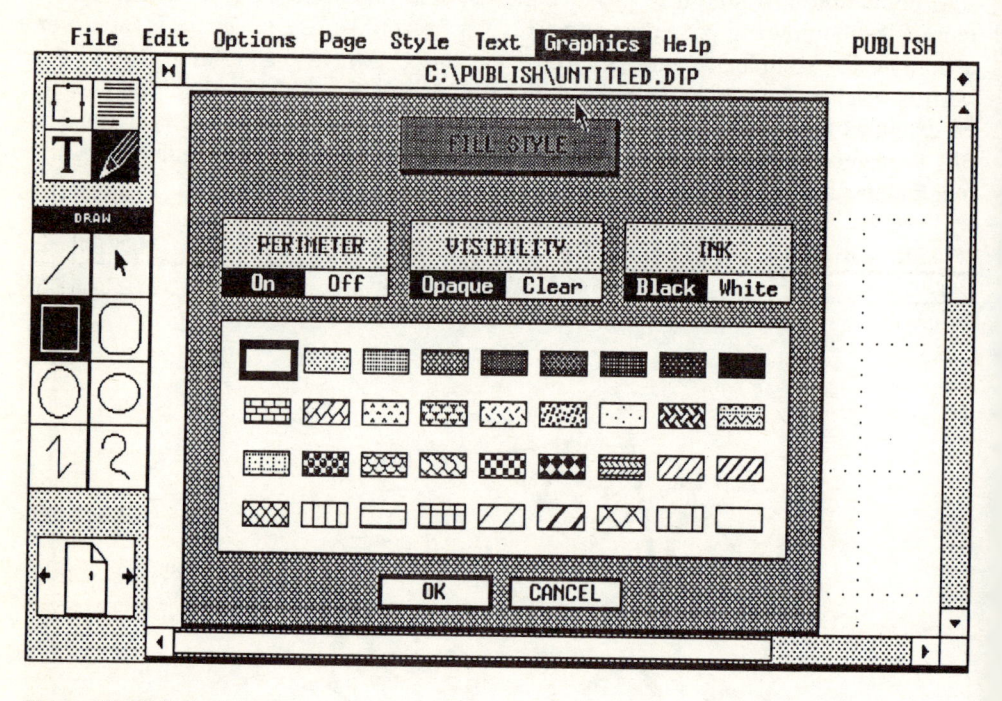

Figure 6.7 Fill Styles Menu

This enables you to select the fill style and choose whether or not to have the object perimeter drawn. Where the object obscures another, it is possible to select CLEAR visibility, which will allow lower objects to show through. As with text frames, it is also possible to make use of the [Send to back] and [Bring to front] options in the {PAGE} menu to vary the relationship between various graphics frames in the document. However, this function only works in relation to other graphics frames, and will not, for example, cause the graphic to disappear behind a text frame, as will happen in text mode.

Closed objects, which have the PERIMETER ON option set will make use of the current LINE STYLE selection, and so may have thin, thick or dotted perimeters as required. Any arrowheads will, however, be ignored.

Making use of the closed objects is perfectly straightforward, as we shall see. As usual, however, before making use of them we should set the appropriate parameters.

Select the Square Box tool from the browser, and open the FILL STYLE screen, from the {GRAPHICS} Menu. Select an appropriate fill style, set PERIMETER ON and VISIBILITY OPAQUE. Exit from this screen and select the LINE STYLE control from the {GRAPHICS} menu, and specify a suitable style.

A box is drawn by placing the cursor at one corner, and dragging to the opposite diagonal. The box image is shown on the screen in outline, and the object is placed when the mouse button is released. The box will have the characteristics specified. Once placed, it then becomes possible to move the graphics, or to re-size them as before.

One of the fill style options, is to set INK to black or white. When drawing on a white background, setting INK to white will show as a clear fill. However, if the object is placed on a coloured background, then selecting white INK, with a CLEAR FILL can produce some additional effects.

To see this in action create a black filled box, of about 1.5 inches square. Now create a smaller box, about 1 inch square, filled with a distinctive black/white pattern. Use the [Copy] and [Paste] functions in the {EDIT} menu to create a second copy of this. Using the {GRAPHICS} menu [Fill style...] function set VISIBILITY to CLEAR, INK to WHITE, and set perimeter to ON, on one of the two copies. When first created this will appear as a simple white filled square. If we now move this to partially cover the black square we can see the effects. Place the original graphic, with the normal black ink setting close to the second to make the changes more apparent. This feature may not appear to have any particular benefits at this stage, but as you use the graphics to achieve particular effects, some of these functions will become of more obvious use.

Figure 6.8 Use of White Ink in Graphics.

The use of rounded box graphics elements is exactly the same as the above, with all the same features and functions.

Using the circle and ellipse options is just as straightforward, but the cursor behaviour may not appear quite as expected. In both cases the graphics parameters can be set as before. However, to create either of these objects the cursor action needs to reproduce the action required as if we were producing the frame which is to contain these graphics, rather than the graphics themselves. This may seem a little odd until you try it in practice. It does continue to look odd, but at least it is possible to see what is happening.

Select the CIRCLE tool from the browser, and set the fill parameters as required, with the perimeter turned ON. Now place the cursor anywhere on the screen, and drag the mouse to form the required shape. You will notice that the circle is constructed across the diagonal of the graphic 'FRAME', and that when the mouse button is released, the circle is formed correctly, and the cursor is close to the frame corner. Also notice that the frame surrounding the circle only has corner handles, and that any consequent re-sizing of the object will use the frame diagonals as the principal measure. You should make various adjustments to the original graphic to become familiar with the function.

This method of constructing the circle makes precise positioning of the graphics a little difficult, when drawing, but the frame [Size and position] control can be used to good effect to make any final adjustments.

The ELLIPSE function acts in very much the same way, in that the graphic is created on the basis of a 'FRAME' which contains that element. However, once constructed, the corresponding frame does have a full set of handles, and the graphic can be re-sized diagonally, or along either axis.

In both cases, once the graphic is created they can be manipulated using the frame functions described earlier.

It is also possible to modify the fill style and line style of a finished graphic. Select the appropriate graphic element, and then adjust the fill and line style as required, using the control menus, and the changes will be carried out immediately. If the graphic is a copy, made using the edit functions the changes will *only* affect the selected graphic, and will not have any effect on other copies.

All graphics frames, as with text frames, once created become quite independent units in the document. If two or more frames are overlapped to achieve a special effect, it is not possible to 'tie' these frames together to treat them as a single object. Only single frames can be moved at any one time.

If we create a series of graphics elements, positioned in an overall frame structure, with a frame created in the frame mode, then adjustments can be made to the containing frame, which will impact on all the graphics elements in that frame.

Clear the screen of any previous work, and in frame mode, create a frame sufficient to fill the screen, using the actual size display. Switch to GRAPHICS mode and within that frame now create three or four separate graphic elements.

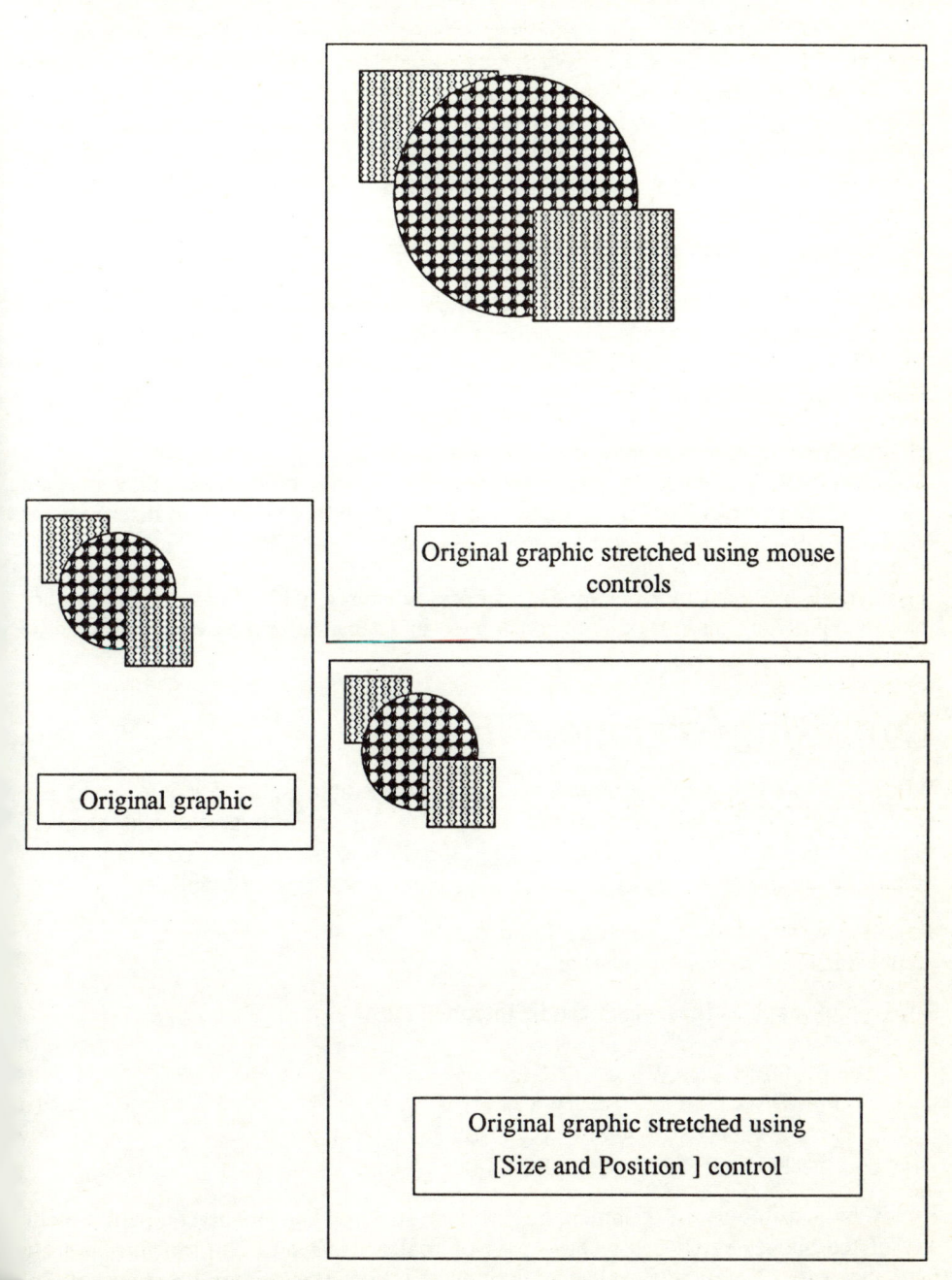

Figure 6.9 Re-sizing Graphics Frames

Now change to full page view, in frame mode, and note that moving the frame will move all the graphic elements, retaining the space and size relationships.

However, if you now try to re-size the frame the results are a little unexpected. Instead of eliminating any graphics elements which would not fit inside the frame, as happens with text, all the graphics elements are re-sized so that they occupy the same relative sizes and positions within the new frame. Again, we can demonstrate this quite easily. Using the initial frame produced, re-size this, using the mouse controls, so that it occupies a small corner of the full page view. Now make a copy, using the edit menu, and paste this onto another part of the page. Move and re-size the new frame so that it occupies the remainder of the page, and you will see how the graphics relationships have been maintained, between frames.

However, somewhat surprisingly, we get quite a different effect if we use the [Frame size and position...] controls to modify the frame size. In this case the graphics elements retain their original size and position within the frame, and are *not* changed relative to the frame size.

As before, while these graphics manipulations may have a certain amount of interest in themselves, it is only as you try to achieve special effects that they become important. The types of effects that can be achieved will be up to you to determine, as within the context of this book we will only be able to look at a few examples.

If you wish to create more complex graphics structures, which may require further joint manipulation, these should be constructed in a separate frame, which can then be moved or re-sized at will.

Importing Graphics Files

While the internal graphics functions offer considerable range for enhancing the printed page, as we will demonstrate later, they do not address the real graphics functions required of DTP packages. The reproduction of pictures, company logos, graphs, etc., requires an ability to display, and edit, more complex graphics.

To achieve this end, Timeworks Publisher has the ability to import a range of graphics images, created by other means.

The type of graphics files which can be imported are:

GEM DRAW	*.GEM Files
GEM PAINT	*.IMG Files
LOTUS	*.PIC Files
PC PAINTBRUSH	*.PCX Files

It may be possible to use different file formats, if they claim to be compatible with any of the above, but it has to be a case of trial and error to confirm this in each particular case. During the course of writing this book the author has successfully loaded files of all of the formats above. However, some files supposedly identified as

.PCX files from a particular source simply would not load into the document, presumably due to some subtle differences in format.

Timeworks Publisher distinguishes between two basic forms of picture files, and has a different ability to handle each type. *Line Art* files are produced by programs like GEM DRAW (*.GEM files), and the LOTUS 123 graphing functions (*.PIC files). These can be imported satisfactorily, but editing is limited to re-sizing the image by adjusting the size of the frame in which it is placed. The image will automatically adjust to fill the frame available to hold it.

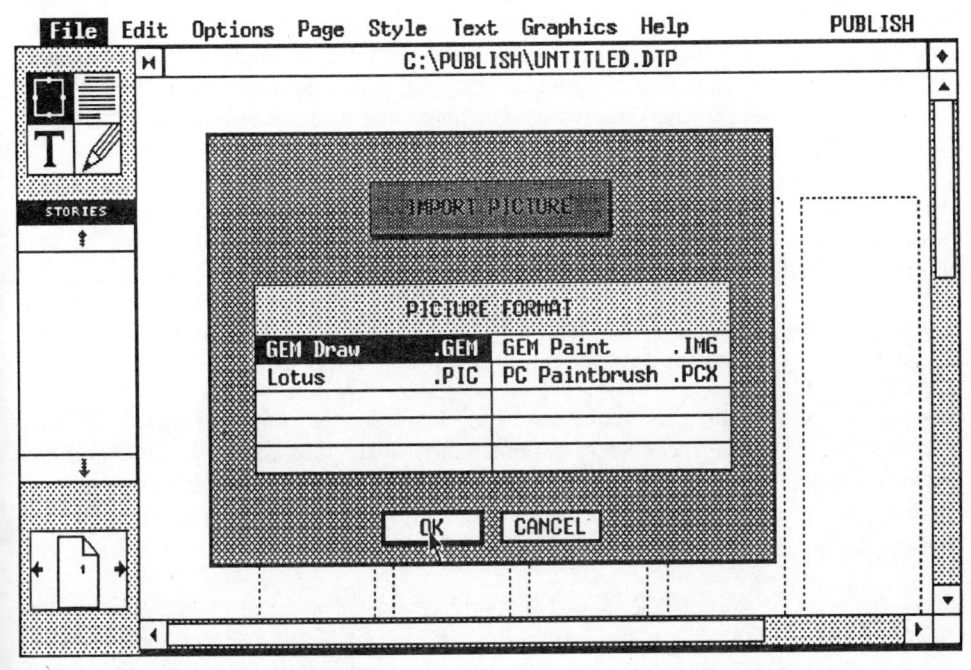

Figure 6.10 Import Picture Control Screen

The other format is the DOT IMAGE format used by paint programs, such as GEM PAINT (*.IMG files) and PC Paintbrush (*.PCX files). There are more extensive editing facilities available here, and we will look at these in some detail.

As, even with the help of the computer, my artistic ability scores about 1 out of 10, I generally have to resort to external means to acquire graphics for my own work. The principal sources of these graphics are *clip art* packages, usually designed for other programs but convertible to one of the standard formats, and by scanning printed images, and subsequent editing. How the files are produced, however, is largely irrelevant provided that the end result is formatted in one of the accepted file types.

Line Art Images

Examples of both file types are included on the Timeworks Publisher disks, and we can use these to demonstrate the appropriate graphics functions. Clear the screen of any residual work from the previous session, and select the [Import picture] option from the {FILE} menu, to bring up the IMPORT PICTURE control screen. See Figure 6.10

This shows a default selection of GEM Draw, *.GEM files, which we will accept for now. The GEM Item Selector is displayed, from which we select the PICTURES folder. This choice is preset to display only the *.GEM files. If we alter this parameter to read *.*, we will also see two other files listed, in the *.IMG format.

If you are using a twin floppy system the required pictures have not been copied to your program disks during the install procedure. They can be found on the second of the Timeworks Publisher master disks, in the appropriate directory. You should copy these files onto one of your data disks, and place this in drive A:, at the appropriate on-screen request.

Once you have located the files, and having accepted the default .GEM extension, you should select the PC.GEM image. When you have made the selection the file will be loaded, and the browser will change to show the Line Art files.

If you attempt to load the .IMG files, having specified the .GEM files, the program seems to politely ignore the request and no file will be imported.

Now you can repeat the sequence, and load in the MONALISA.IMG file, remembering to select the correct format. Once again, the file is loaded, and the browser changes to show the IMAGES files in place. You can switch the display of the browser in this mode by clicking on the title bar, which will show, in turn, the Stories, the Image files, and the Line Draw files.

Set the browser to show the PC.GEM file, and create a frame into which to load this picture. When the frame is selected, highlight the PC.GEM file in the browser, and it will flow in to fill up the available frame. This will load in extremely quickly, even if you have selected a full size frame. Editing of these files is very limited. We can change the size, and proportions of the picture using the normal frame size functions. The only other option available is to use the frame tint controls to insert a different background tint.

We can, however, switch to graphics mode, and superimpose some of the internal graphics elements on the picture. Alternatively, we could create a small text frame, sized to fit within the display screen, for example, and enter our own message onto the screen.

We can see this in action with a brief example. Expand the picture to cover about 80% of the full page view. Outside of this frame create a small text frame, slightly smaller than the screen representation in the picture, and enter some text into the frame in a size which is easily visible. Now move the frame into the screen area of the image, and the message appears as if printed on the computer screen.

Figure 6.11 Super-imposed Images

Using this and other techniques, images can be imported either to use as illustrations or, as above, to provide a frame for other text, etc.

Dot Image Files

Dot image files are imported in exactly the same way, as we have seen earlier, but there are a greater range of editing functions available.

Clear the screen of your earlier picture, or save it if you wish. Create a frame on the fresh page covering the full screen, in actual size view. Switch to the images page in the browser, and select the MONALISA.IMG file to flow into the frame. Note that the picture builds up much more slowly in this case, which is a feature of the dot image picture files. Also note that while the image is being loaded, a message appears at the top of the screen saying 'SCALING IMAGE : PLEASE WAIT'. Timeworks Publisher is restructuring the image file in order to fill the frame available to hold it, although it does not modify the original file.

When such an image is required to cover a full page there can be a considerable delay. For example, to load the MONALISA image file into a full page frame takes about 17 seconds, in full page view, and 21 seconds in actual size view. The page used later to demonstrate image scaling takes 15 seconds to load in full page view, and 39 seconds in actual page view.

Once a picture has been entered into the frame we can select one of three editing functions from within the graphics menu:

> SCALE PICTURE
> CROP PICTURE
> EDIT PICTURE

When we load the image into the original frame and every time we crop a picture, or change the size of a picture frame, the picture will flow to fill the frame as closely as possible. This often results in a distortion of the original picture, which in many cases is not acceptable. To control this, we can use the [Scale Picture] options. Selecting this from the graphics menu will bring down the SCALE PICTURE control screen, shown in Figure 6.12.

The scaling function is expressed in terms of the ASPECT RATIO of the image file. This is simply the ratio of the HEIGHT to the WIDTH of the original file, when printed.

If we wish to preserve the ratio of the original image file then we select the ASPECT RATIO PRESERVE option. If, however, we prefer to ignore this, and have the image fill the available frame then we select the IGNORE option.

Ensure that the picture frame is selected, and then open the SCALE PICTURE control screen. You will see that the IGNORE ASPECT RATIO control is set. That is, the image will be adjusted to fit the full frame, irrespective of the format of the original. If we now select PRESERVE ASPECT RATIO, the picture will be re-drawn, taking the proportions of the original file. This is likely to result in the picture changing

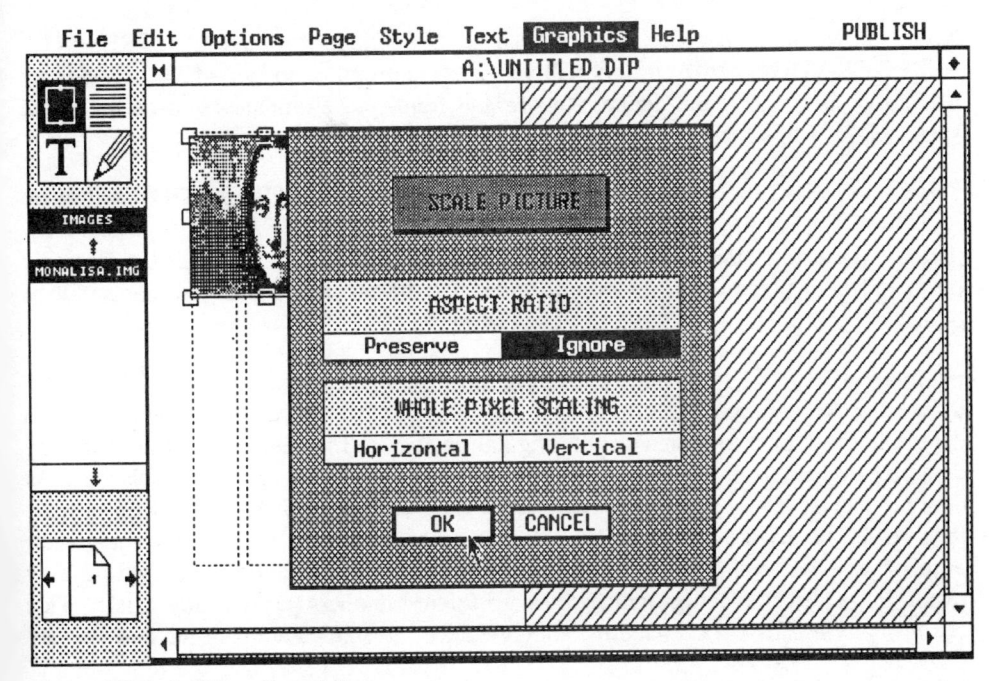

Figure 6.12 Scale Picture Control Screen

shape significantly, leaving additional white space within the frame. The frame can be re-sized to eliminate this, using the normal controls. If necessary, the program will re-scale the image for the new frame size.

Re-size the image frame, so that it is about 3 inches wide by 2 inches deep, and is placed in the top left hand corner of the page. This will be used as a reference for the various manipulations that we can use.

Now create a copy of the original frame and paste it alongside at the top of the page. We will perform our editing functions only on the copy, and compare the results each time with the original.

The crop picture function allows us to select a portion of the picture to isolate from the overall view. Call up this function, and a small scissors icon is presented. This is moved to a point to place the *top left hand corner* corner of the required area, and then dragged *down and right* to define the full area. When the button is released the selected section of the image is redrawn to fill the current frame replacing the original version.

We will use this function to isolate the head and shoulders from the general background, using the copy frame. Select the CROP PICTURE function, and move the cursor to the top left hand corner of the selected area, and press and hold the mouse button. Now drag the cursor to a point close to the bottom right hand corner of the frame, and release the button. The changes in view will occur immediately.

Now, as we had specified the original picture frame to have the PRESERVE ASPECT RATIO control set, this will apply to the cropped image, which will take up less space in the original frame. Re-size the frame, to eliminate most of the white space. COPY this frame, and PASTE it to a different part of the page.

Select the SCALE PICTURE option, and set the ASPECT RATIO control to IGNORE, but for the moment do not consider the PIXEL SCALING options. Now increase the size of the copy frame, and watch the picture expand to fill the frame. If the new frame shape is sufficiently different, the effects of the lack of scaling will be quite noticeable.

An image is built up in a frame by setting individual pixels in the display ON or OFF to create the required pattern. When an image is re-scaled the program has to determine how best to represent the original pattern, at the new scale. It does this by deciding that each pixel which is set ON in the original file, must be replaced by a new number of pixels at the new scale. That is, if the picture is to be reduced in scale then fewer pixels are available, but if it is to be increased in size, then a greater number will be available. Normally the program will make decisions which may result in set pixels being replaced by different numbers at the new scale. This occasionally results in odd patterns being generated in shaded areas of the new image.

Within the SCALE PICTURE control screen, there is the opportunity to set WHOLE PIXEL SCALING in the horizontal, vertical or both axes. This control will ensure that each pixel in the original image is replaced by a uniform number in the new image. For example, in an enlarged image each set pixel in the original may be replaced by four pixels in the new size, and all set pixels will be equally represented.

This will help prevent the build up of odd patterns, but may result in a change of aspect ratio of the picture. On some occasions, it may not be possible to apply whole pixel scaling within a particular defined frame size. In this case a warning is given, and it is possible to re-size the frame before the process is completed.

The illustration shows the variations on the basic image using all the available options, and with this example there is little to choose between the various options. Only where both vertical and horizontal scaling has been applied, in conjunction with the PRESERVE ASPECT RATIO control, can we see significant distortion of the image. In this case selecting IGNORE ASPECT RATIO will, in fact, produce a better image.

This is one of the functions where the best choice can only be determined by trial and error in each particular case. Scaling appears to be most critical where certain dot patterns are applied in the original picture. In the resulting efforts to re-scale the picture, some odd patterns may be created.

The third of the graphics functions available to us, using dot image files, is the EDIT PICTURE option. Choosing this will result in a full screen display of the selected image, greatly enlarged.

Original Picture File
Scaled to Preserve Ratio

Original File Cropped
Scaled to Preserve Ratio

Cropped Image Scaled to Ignore Ratio

Cropped Image Scaled to Preserve Ratio
Horizontal & Vertical Pixel Scaling **ON**

Cropped Image Scaled to Preserve Ratio
Vertical Pixel Scaling **ON**

Cropped Image Scaled to Preserve Ratio
Horizontal Pixel Scaling **ON**

Fig 6.13 Scale Image Examples

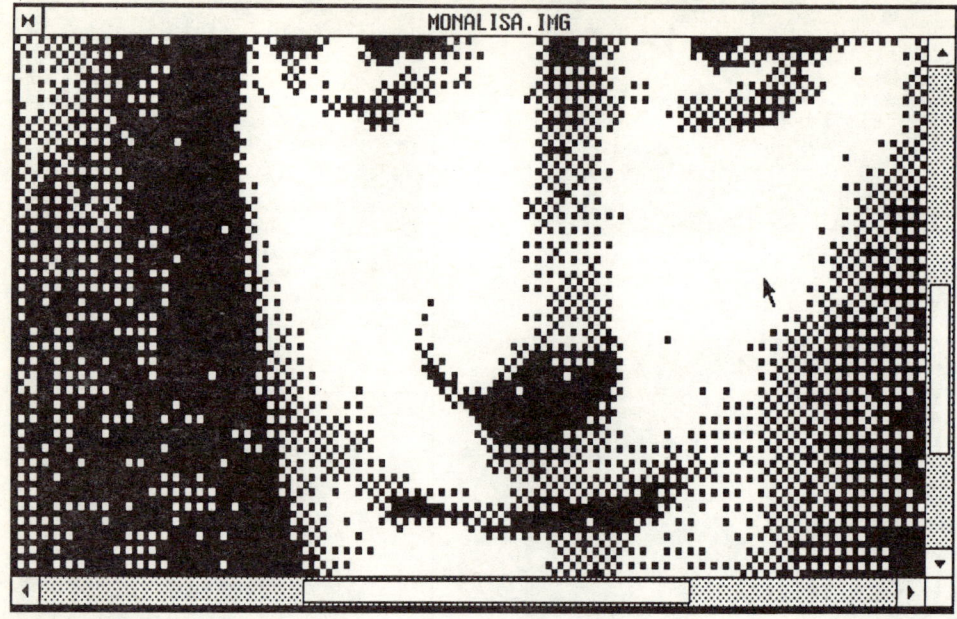

Figure 6.14 Edit Picture Screen

The scroll bars can be used to move around the image. The picture is edited by changing individual pixels using the cursor. To invert an individual pixel, point at the pixel and click once. To make larger changes point at one pixel then press and hold the button while moving the mouse. If this first pixel selected is set ON, this will be inverted (i.e Set OFF) and all pixels in the path of the mouse movement will be set OFF. Pixels which are currently switched OFF, however, will remain OFF.

If, however, the first pixel pointed to was OFF, then all pixels selected by the mouse will become set ON, and all pixels currently ON will remain so. This becomes immediately clear when tried out on the screen.

When editing is complete, the close box (top left hand corner of the screen) is used to exit the editing function. If you wish the edited image to replace the current screen image then click on [OK] in the exit screen. However, all copies of the original image will now use the modified picture. For example, in the above illustration of the different variations of MONALISA, editing any one of the picture frames will result in the changes being reflected in all the copies in the document. All references to the MONALISA file in the browser will also adopt the edited image.

The original image file stored on disk, however, is not changed by this process.

It is possible to rename a picture when loaded into a document, so that it is practicable to have slightly different versions of the same picture in one document. To change the name of a picture double click on the picture name in the browser to open the file STATUS form. It is possible, then, to edit the file name as required.

One final point about the use of graphics images, at this stage, is that they are generally slow to appear on the screen. When working on a document any change which requires a screen re-draw will, therefore, be extremely slow. To overcome this problem the {OPTIONS} menu has a selection to [Hide all pictures]. This places a marker in all picture frames, but does not require them to be redrawn at each stage in the editing process. This speeds up text and page modifications considerably. Obviously, the picture will need to be made visible again to perform any editing functions on them.

One further important difference in the two major types of picture files is the amount of memory required to store and process them. In the early chapters of the book we noted that, with floppy based systems, the ability to use graphics images is quite restricted.

In practice, however, it can be seen that a substantial number of the in-built graphics functions, could be coupled with the line art files to reproduce a significant graphics content, even on the floppy disk-based systems.

The major restriction in this area remains with any files built up using a dot image format.

7

Document Layout and Design

In the earlier sections of this book we have been looking at the technical features of the Timeworks Publisher DTP program, in relative isolation. In this chapter we will begin to see how these may be put together to achieve practical results.

One word of warning, however, is appropriate. The ability to handle the technical aspects of the program will *not* make you a good designer. It will enable you, with very few restrictions, to convert good design ideas into finished documents. Some people have a flair for design, and others do not. Unfortunately I fall firmly into the latter group, and despite the power of Timeworks Publisher, I leave the more esoteric aspects of design work to the professionals.

For work that I produce myself, which is rapidly increasing in the range of application, I apply one strict design rule:

KEEP IT SIMPLE

One of the most widespread effects of the advent of lower cost DTP, or even page design packages, was the sudden rush of, obviously home produced, advertisements. This was particularly apparent in the computer press, of which I am an avid reader.

In the examples observed, it was clear that the producers had gone overboard on the technical facilities of their particular package, and had forgotten completely about any attempt at good design. Fortunately, now things are a little more mature and some of the more glaring examples are disappearing.

Acknowledging my own weakness in this area I am going to tread carefully in discussing the design of documents, and give only the most general guidelines. We will later look at specific applications which have been developed using Timeworks Publisher, which will give some extended idea of the possibilities open to you.

For anyone wishing to take the design process further I have no hesitation in referring you to the particular book that I use to guide my own efforts (*Design for Desktop Publishing* by John Miles, Published by Gordon Fraser).

Applications

The most obvious first question is 'What can I use it for?', and the simple answer is; 'Practically anything!'. My own particular applications include:

> Production of product information leaflets;
> Production of price lists;
> Preparation of training material; and
> Preparation of simple promotional material.

I also make use of some of the features in the preparation of standard letters which I hope will have special impact.

Outside these areas the known applications include:

> Preparation of club and business newsletters;
> Preparation of advertising materials;
> Promotional materials; Business presentations;
> Forms production;
> Menu production; and
> Book publishing.

However, as mentioned earlier, the applications are principally limited only by your own imagination.

Basic Design Principles

In considering your applications, and how far you can utilise the features available, there are two major practical restrictions that you should consider.

Firstly, and this is largely determined by your budget, is the type of hardware you have available. The particular points to consider are:

1) If you do not have a hard disk, then you will not be able to make use of extensive graphics images on the page. (Using dot image files from scanners, etc.)

2) The type of printer that you have available will provide some restrictions, chiefly with respect to the range of fonts that you can use. At the lower levels, 9 pin dot matrix printers have some difficulties with the smaller point sizes (i.e. 7 and 8 point text), which makes legibility sometimes a little difficult. Some distortion may be observed on 24 pin printers when using the landscape page mode, although this would be important only for professional applications. Only wide carriage nine pin printers

will support landscape printing at all, and even these produce questionable results. Finally, even laser printers provide some restrictions in the range of fonts available, and only the most expensive Postscript printer can be thought to provide an extensive range of built-in features. (There are some ways around these restrictions which we will discuss later).

3) Your facilities for producing graphics images (where you have a hard disk) will be an obvious restriction. In preparing this book, use has been made of scanned images produced using a hand scanner with 200 dpi resolution, and some commercially available snip art images. The results using the former have been surprisingly good, particularly where the scanner has the provision to edit odd blemishes in the scanned image. Care has to be taken when scaling such images, and in considering the relative resolution of the scanner and the print out device. The snip art package used was patchy in the quality of the images available. They tended to have a very 'blocky' appearance, and are only of limited value. However, by shopping around, suitable images may be obtained. If you have any artistic abilities then one of the many excellent art packages can be used to create graphics images, provided that the file format is acceptable.

The second area of restriction is in the size of paper that can be used. In practice, because of the limitations within the program selection available, and in the ability of printers to cater for different sizes, we will normally be restricted to paper of A4 size, or one of the derivative sizes.

If we take a normal A4 sheet of paper there are basically six separate configurations that we can consider, as illustrated. These can all be used within the Timeworks Publisher package by careful selection of column guides. The basic uses of the different configurations are shown in Figure 7.1, and these are:

A4 Portrait: This is the most normal configuration, and certainly the most widely used in business applications. Multipage documents are most easily prepared using this format.

A4 Vertical Fold: This configuration is not very widely used, as the proportions of each page are not very attractive.

A4 Landscape: At one time there seemed to be a preference for this configuration in business reports, etc., with the binding normally along the top margin. Adverts and announcements frequently make use of this format.

A4 Horizontal Fold: This is quite a useful configuration for a number of applications. It effectively gives 4 A5 size pages in this format. It is particularly useful for short newsletters, as it makes it possible to produce a more attractive, and varied, layout.

A4 Gate & Concertina Fold: These are very similar, and have the particular attraction that this fold fits easily into the standard DL envelope. These are frequently used for information leaflets, etc., which are to be posted. When used with a heavier

A4 Portrait

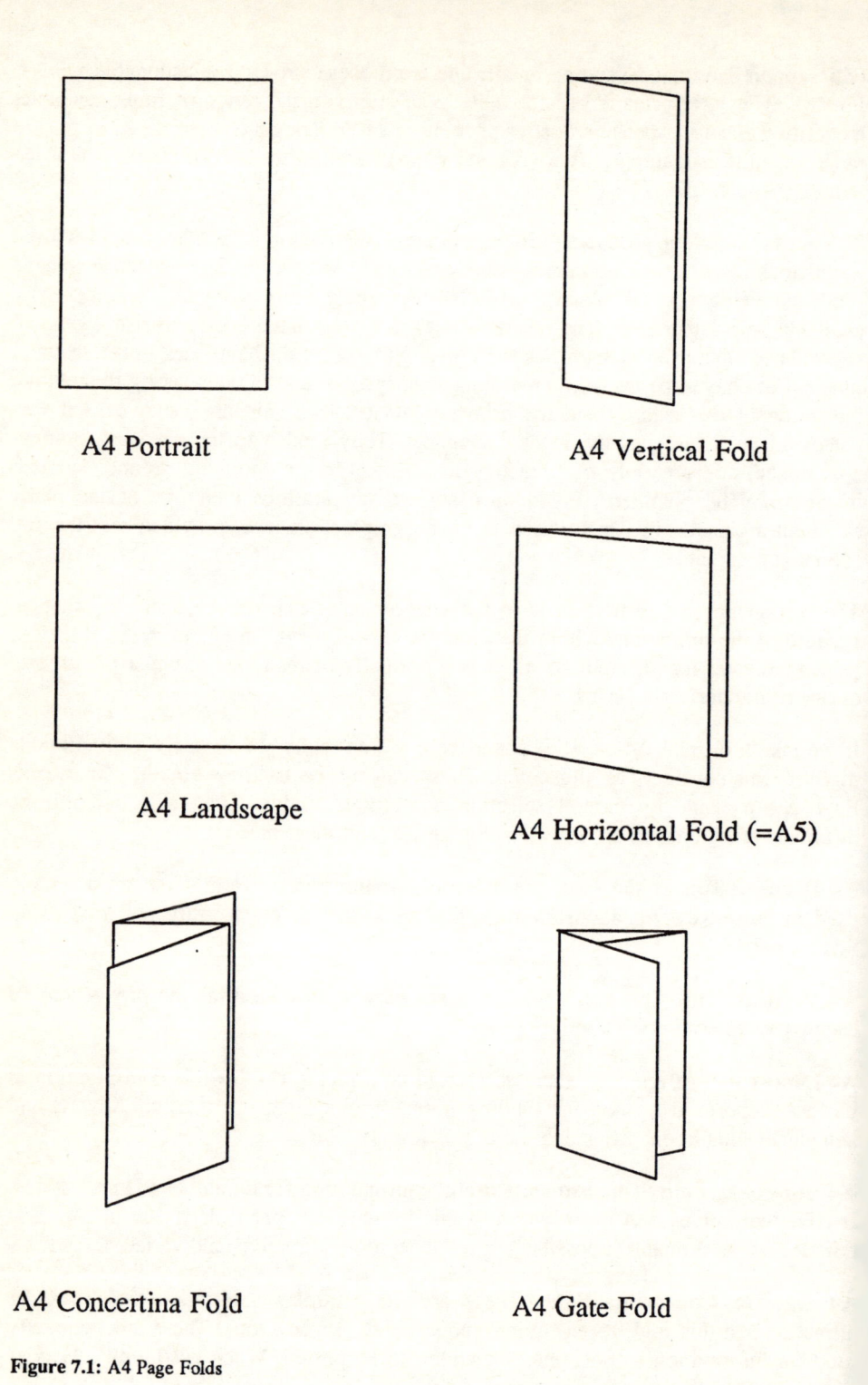

A4 Vertical Fold

A4 Landscape

A4 Horizontal Fold (=A5)

A4 Concertina Fold

A4 Gate Fold

Figure 7.1: A4 Page Folds

grade paper they can stand up, and are, therefore, useful for invitations, menus or displays. With the gate fold, the inside leaf must be slightly narrower than the other sections so that it can fold in easily.

Determining which page configuration to use is an important early step in any document design process. Of equal importance, however, is analysing your target audience to establish what sort of format and presentation is most appropriate.

Business applications, of course, tend to adopt a fairly strict, more formal, approach. Embellishments are normally restricted to the use of logos on the opening page, or cover. Fancy scripts are rarely used, except for headings, and illustrations tend to relate directly to the text content of the report, etc. In such applications the content tends to be of greater significance than the actual format.

Club newsletters, on the other hand, should be designed to produce a more relaxed and welcoming appearance. A strictly formal layout and content tend to discourage readers (although, obviously, the same can be true of a very disorganised presentation).

Documents such as invitations, menus, etc., should be encouraged to demonstrate a little more flair in the design, as generally the appearance is at least of equal importance as the content.

Once you have determined your target audience, and selected the particular page format, then the real design process will start. It becomes important, where a range of documents are to be produced, to determine some form of 'House Style', which will become familiar to the audience. This will discourage totally free format layouts, as these can be confusing if not properly used.

Where only single page documents are to be produced it is possible to have a more relaxed approach to the design, having established some basic ground rules for your work.

The more formal approach becomes necessary where longer documents, such as books and reports, are to be prepared.

You will have to try to determine the relative amounts of text and illustrations, where this is an option, and establish how these may best fit on the particular format chosen. Strangely, one of the more important features of good design appears to be the sensible use of 'white space', in order to break up large blocks of text, and to give a more open layout.

Before considering the final content of a document it is important to establish a general layout to be adopted. This will include factors such as the position and style of any headings, the number of text columns to be used, the relative proportions of any illustrations, and their relationship to the text.

To achieve this it is best to sketch out some form of grid, superimposed on the basic page format, and to assign general areas to particular sections. It is important that some flexibility is maintained to allow the input of differing amounts of text, and to allow different sizes of illustrations.

One of the simplest ways of breaking up large areas of text is to have a number of columns of text on the page. Under most circumstances 2 or 3 columns can be used to good effect. Using a greater number can cause problems with word spacing and justification, and may require the use of smaller text sizes to achieve a sensible text layout. There is no need for multi-column layout on the gate and concertina fold layouts, as the individual page area is already relatively small.

Symmetrical and asymmetrical layouts can be applied, although more care is required with the latter to retain control. See Figure 7.2 for some variations using a basic 3-column layout.

The illustration demonstrates how a basic three column layout can be varied to achieve different combinations of text and graphics. Similar considerations can be given to other basic grid layouts. In general, it is best to adopt both vertical (Columns) and horizontal alignment guides to prevent an erratic appearance. Remember, however, that these are only 'guides' to help in alignment and to achieve some consistency of design. Where appropriate, these can be over-ridden in order to achieve different effects.

The best way to obtain ideas for your own publications is to review other documents that you meet in your day to day activities. In this context it is surprising how much material can be produced with an attractive appearance, using very simple layout guidelines. Very few layouts fall outside the ability of Timeworks Publisher.

Having taken due care of the physical layout of the page, in view of the particular application, we can then look at the use of fonts.

When some of the "professionals" have viewed Timeworks Publisher they have tended to be quite impressed, but to say "What; only two fonts!", and proceed to demonstrate the several megabytes of disk space that they have occupied with their font selection.

In reality, however, especially for the beginner, this limit comes as something of a blessing in disguise. Some of the more blatant examples of poor design have arisen because users of various packages have appeared to try to use all available font types within one document. This generally resulted in a confusing, and unpleasant mess on the page.

In practice there is very little need to mix several fonts on the same page; indeed, in all my own applications, I try to stick with a single basic font, and use the size and weight variations within that to achieve the required effects. Having only two fonts available certainly limits the tendency to go overboard with their use. In addition, I rarely find the need for more than two or three variations of the individual fonts in any single document.

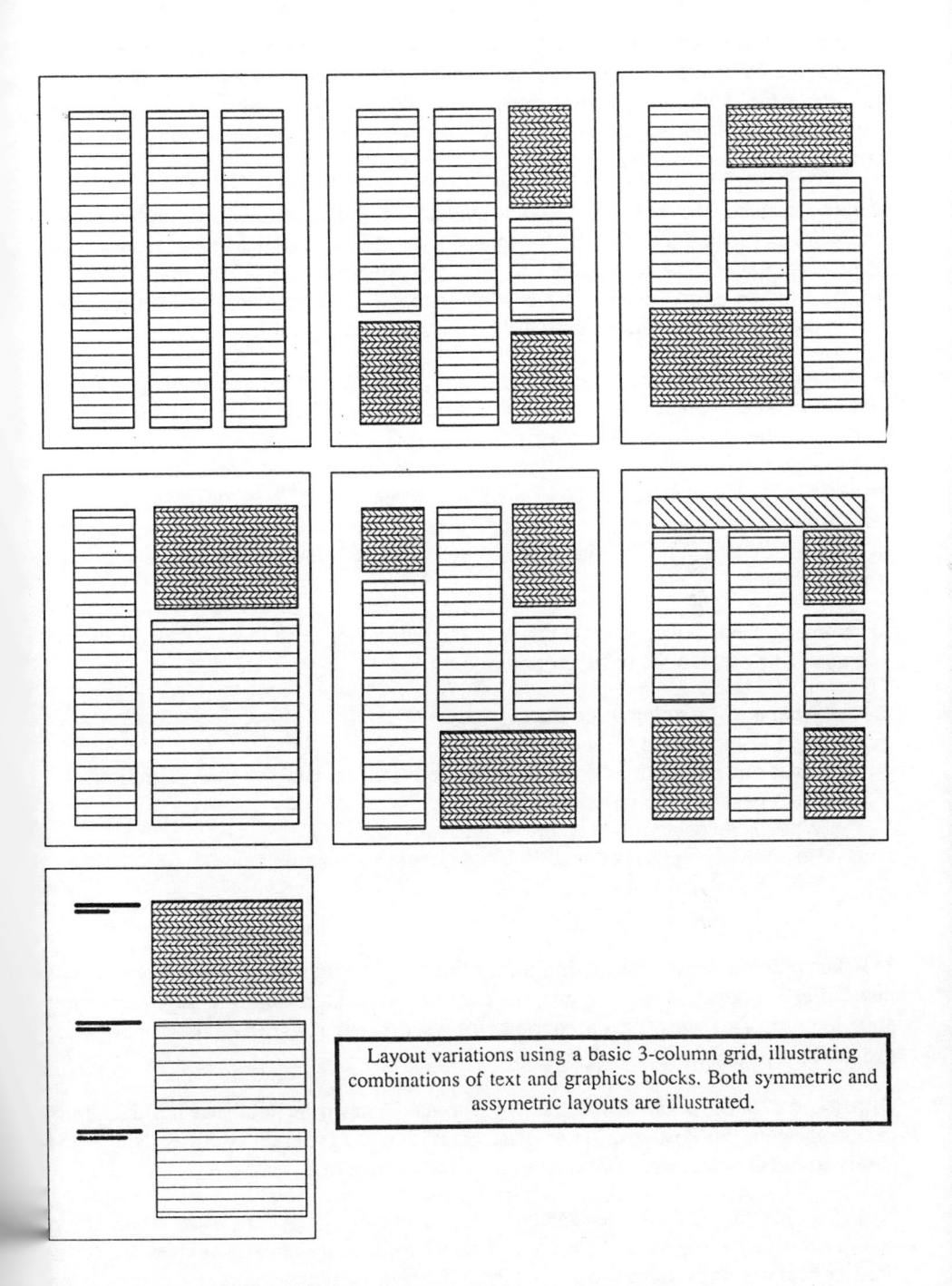

Layout variations using a basic 3-column grid, illustrating combinations of text and graphics blocks. Both symmetric and assymetric layouts are illustrated.

Figure 7.2 Options Using Basic 3-Column Page Layout

Should you find that you want to extend the range of fonts available to you then, if you have a hard disk, this presents very few problems, and we look at this in a later section of the book. A hard disk is necessary because of the space occupied by the individual fonts, and the current font creation programs themselves require substantial memory for their operation.

Having decided the basic form and content of the document, it then becomes necessary to prepare the material for inclusion in it. For anything longer than a single page, text files should be prepared in advance using your favourite word processor. Be prepared to edit this once it has been input to the document, frequently just to make sure that the text will fit comfortably in the space available for it.

If graphics are to be incorporated then they, too, should be prepared in advance. Particular attention may have to be paid to the scaling of the graphics files, as some conflicts can occur due to the particular source of the graphics and the relative printing resolution of different devices. As an example of this the author has experienced some problems when importing screen dumps from different resolution screens, and then achieving a satisfactory image scale for inclusion in the document. In certain cases I had to abandon plans to include some images, as a satisfactory scale was not found.

In summary, then, before you get down to the mechanics of producing any documents you must first prepare the basic ground rules:

> What are you going to produce?
> Who is your target audience?
> What sort of approach does the target audience demand - formal or informal?
> What page format are you going to adopt?
> What is the content and nature of the material?
> How are the elements (Text files and Graphics) to be prepared?
> What basic text styles do you intend to use? and
> How are the documents to be finally produced?

This last point is worth considering a little further. The natural tendency is to assume that the end production will be on your own printer, with all the limitations that this may impose. This may be appropriate for very small runs, but other options are available.

Of particular value, in this respect, is the fact that Timeworks Publisher has the ability to operate with the PostScript laser printers. Within the program controls there is the ability to direct PostScript print files to disk, rather than to a printer.

PostScript has the particular advantage that, as a universal standard, files produced on one machine may frequently be used on another to drive a Postscript printer. You may have colleagues with access to such a set up or, in particular, your local print shop may well have the facilities to use these files on their equipment.

This means that you can produce your documents as if you had a PostScript printer, and have these turned into hard copy elsewhere at a relatively low cost.

Documents produced in this way may be used as masters to prepare the photography for longer print runs. In terms of relative cost, where more than a few hundred copies are required, it may well be better to have these printed than to use the relatively expensive photocopy process. The quality of the finished result will almost inevitably be much better.

Practical Projects

The examples that we are going to look at now are derived from real applications, with some minor adaptions for the purposes of demonstrating particular points of technique, etc. The final newsletter is a totally fictitious product, and used mainly to demonstrate the construction of a more complex page layout. It is also a vehicle to show the widest variety of features possible within the document. (I do not expect it to win any prizes for the "Design of the Year" competition)

Form Design

This first example is one of the actual applications which have been converted for production on the Timeworks Publisher package, with no embellishments added.

The form is used by a major international company to provide rapid notification of instrument service problems to their subsidiary companies (The name indicated on the form is NOT, however, the real company name)

In terms of defining the task and layout, the following points were considered.

> Type of document: Standard Form
> Presentation: A4 single sheet
> Target Audience: Company/subsidiary/distributor/technicians.
> End Production: Photocopy

The nature of the document is such that it can be produced using just the internal functions of the Timeworks Publisher package.

The final document is illustrated, and the procedures to produce the whole is explained in detail, taking each sector of the document in turn.

The document was produced using five basic elements:

> The main page with the 'Issued By:' line built into the master page. The text styles to be used are set as part of this basic Style Sheet;

> The page heading 'Service Alert';

A single frame to include the 'Instrument or Product' line;

A single frame, reproduced four times, with text edited within each frame, to produce the body of the form; and

A single outlined frame with the 'Originated By:' text block.

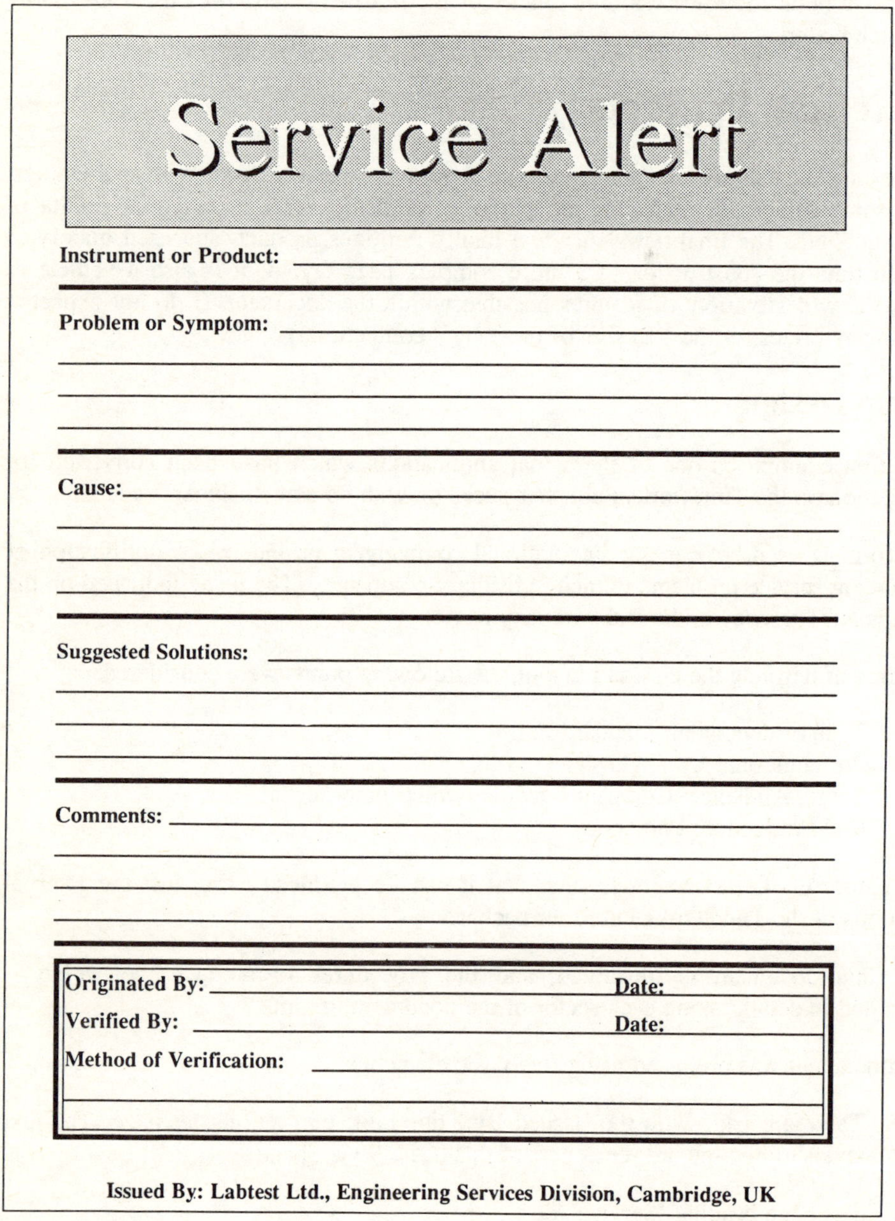

Service Alert

Instrument or Product: _____

Problem or Symptom: _____
_____
_____
_____
_____

Cause: _____
_____
_____
_____
_____

Suggested Solutions: _____
_____
_____
_____
_____

Comments: _____
_____
_____
_____
_____

| Originated By: _____ | Date: _____ |
| Verified By: _____ | Date: _____ |
| Method of Verification: _____ |

Issued By: Labtest Ltd., Engineering Services Division, Cambridge, UK

Figure 7.3 Form Document Example.

Creating the Master Page.

As usual, to create a master page, we load in the DEFAULT.STY, Style Sheet and modify that to give us the required format. To fully define the Style Sheet we will need to specify:

> The basic column layout;
> The fonts required (Paragraph Styles); and
> Any page content required.

As we only require a single major frame there is no need to amend the basic column layout. In another session we have modified the DEFAULT.STY sheet to cater for the printer offset, and unless we change the printer this will remain satisfactory.

Use the Page menu to select the master page.

To facilitate the positioning of the graphics constructions at regular intervals select the {OPTIONS} - [Ruler spacing] for inches and tenths.

Create one single frame to cover the entire column outline, and specify a thin line border all around.

In this particular example the font requirements are minimal, and we require to establish only three paragraph styles.

Body Text: Activate the paragraph tool, and list the default paragraph styles in the browser. Select the body text paragraph, and double click on it to bring up the Paragraph STYLE control menu. We wish to set the following options, leaving all those unspecified at the default values:

> Options: Flushed Left
> Font and Size: Dutch 12 Point
> Dimensions: Space above 0.1 inches

Now exit from the Paragraph Style menu, and select text style BOLD. This completes the new definition of our 'Body Text'

Headline: For our heading we wish to modify the existing HEADLINE paragraph style. Activate the menu and select the following parameters:

> Options: Centred
> Font and Size: Dutch 60 Point (or 36 point)

Quit the style menu, and once again select the text style BOLD, completing the definition.

Centre: For the 'Issued by' text create a style, the same as the body text, but using the 'CENTRE' format option.

The two styles BULLET and SUBHEAD are superfluous, and these may be deleted, using the Paragraph style menu.

The final step in the master page design is to insert the 'Issued By:' text at the bottom of the frame. Create a shallow frame, within the page, and the full width of the page. Select this frame, and select TEXT mode of operation. Place the cursor in the new frame, and enter the line of text:

```
Issued By: Labtest Ltd., Engineering Services Division, Cambridge. UK.
```

As usual, by default this text will adopt the body style definition. Use the paragraph controls to assign the CENTRE style to this text, and re-position the frame to fit along the bottom margin of the page. Reduce the frame height to the minimum required to contain the text.

This finalises the definition of the master page, and the Style Sheet, and the next step is to save the Style Sheet in an appropriate directory for future reference.

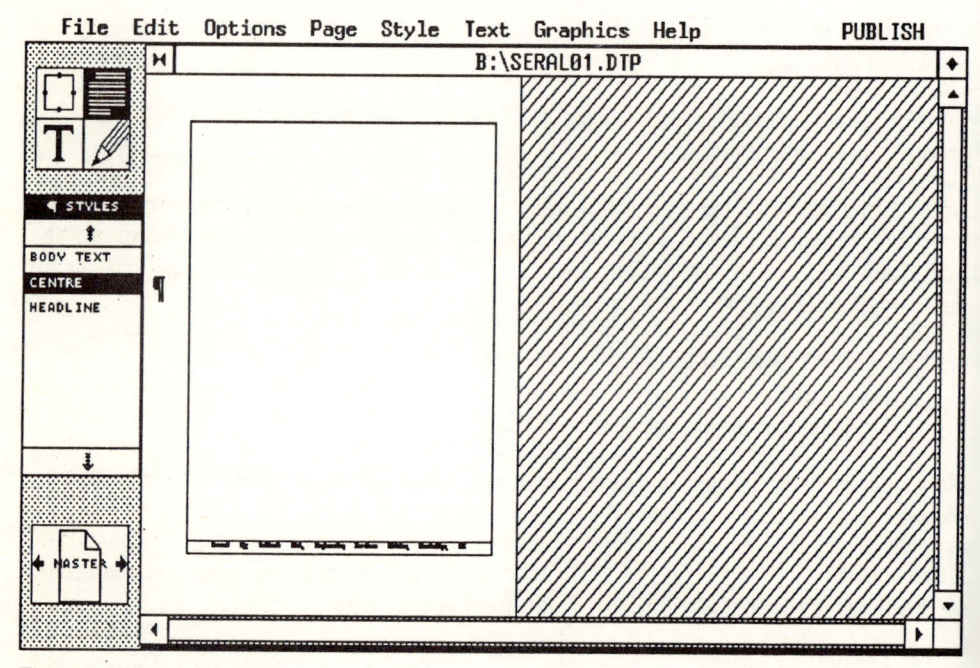

Figure 7.4 Master page layout

Select the {FILE} option, and use [Save style sheet] to save this definition as FORM1.STY in your normal Style Sheet directory. (With a floppy system the DEFAULT.STY file is on your overlays disk in drive B:)

This is important in the real application, as other forms are to be based on the same page layout.

Before producing the form we need to switch from the master page to page 1 of our document.

Headline Section

The headline for this document introduces the technique of shadow printing. This is a frequently used device, quite effective in many applications and, happily, not too difficult to achieve.

We wish this headline to be centred in the page, close to the top, and its position is to be used to determine the alignment of the rest of the form.

Using the default column layout, on the master page, to define the basic page frame produces a frame of width 6.77 inches, and height 9.36 inches. This is determined from the {OPTIONS} - [Size and Position] function, using the default style. The main body of the form is to sit centrally within this frame, and the dimensions of the individual frames will be chosen to suit this. If we choose a basic frame width of 6 inches, this will leave us with a margin within the main frame layout of 0.38 inches on each side (i.e (6.77-6.00)/2).

Create a frame within the page, with dimensions of width 6.00 inches and Height 1.50 inches. This height may be reduced if you are using a smaller size headline text. To have this frame positioned centrally across the page requires a horizontal position of 1.38 inches and, to give the appropriate top margin, a vertical position of 1.20 inches. (Remember that the default column setting gives a basic frame position of 1 inch horizontal and 1 inch vertical, referenced from the top left hand corner of the page).

Select the {OPTIONS} menu and set the [Repel Text] function to OFF, as this is important when we try to position the "shadow" frame.

Select the text tool and enter into the frame the text 'Service Alert', then select the paragraph function and assign the 'HEADLINE' paragraph style to this text. To generate the shadow we require to make a copy of this frame. Switch to frame mode, and using the EDIT menu, copy this frame to the clipboard, and then paste a copy onto the page; for the moment, just below the original frame. Remember that the "Layer" which a frame occupies is related to the time when it is created. This copy frame will occupy a higher layer than the original and will, therefore, appear over the first when we try to position them close together. This is not suitable for the shadow effect, as this second frame is used to generate the shadow, and must lie below the original frame.

The simplest way to get the right level relationship between the two frames is to use the {PAGE} -[Bring to front] option on the original frame, which will place it in front of the shadow frame.

To finalise the definition of the main frame we need to:

Add the border;
Select the frame tint; and
Change the text colour to white.

Activate the main headline frame and select the {OPTIONS} menu - [Frame border..] command and create a frame all around using the second line thickness. Now use the frame tint control to select a medium dark tint, with a clear 'Visibility' setting. (Remember that the shadow must be visible through this frame). To change the text to white, select the text tool, and highlight the text by dragging the cursor across it. From the {STYLE} menu select the 'White' option (or use ALT-W from the keyboard).

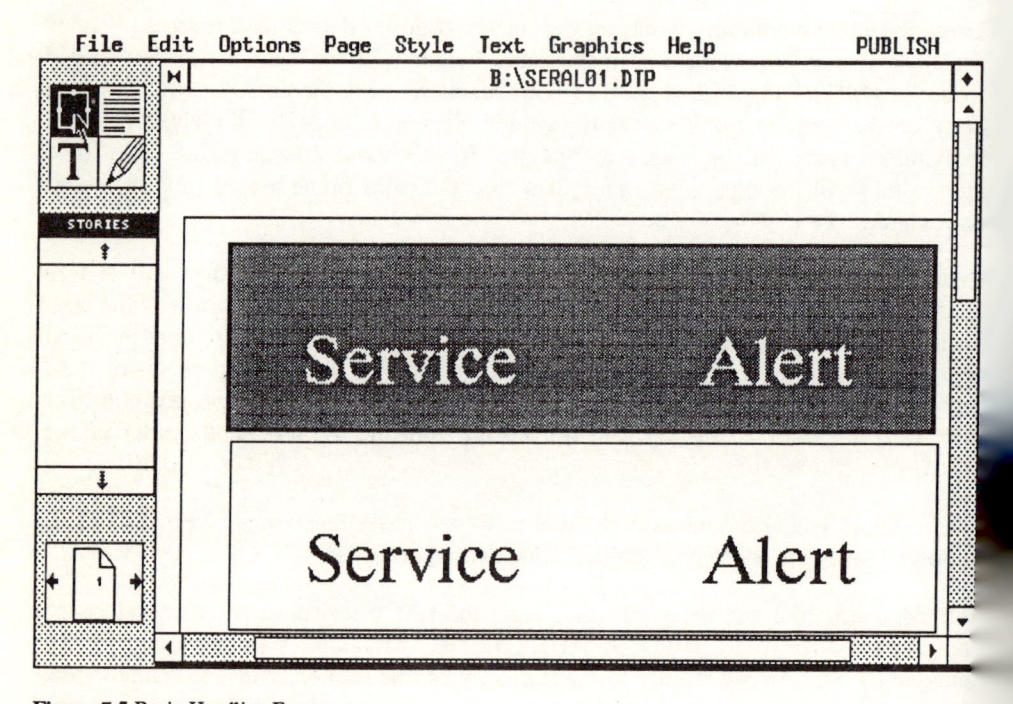

Figure 7.5 Basic Headline Frames

The final step is to position the shadow frame behind the original. The actual shadow effect produced will reflect individual preferences, and some trial and error may be required to achieve the desired result. The shadow is achieved by activating the shadow frame and using the {OPTIONS} - [Size and Position..] control to locate the shadow frame with a small offset from the upper text frame.

Above, we defined the position of the main frame at 1.38 inch horizontal and 1.2 inch vertical.

In the example illustrated a 0.04 inch vertical and horizontal offset has been selected for the shadow, giving a frame position for the shadow frame of:

> Horizontal Position: 1.42 inches
> Vertical position: 1.24 inches.

The shadow effect should now be visible on the screen. If it is not, the two most likely causes are that the VISIBILITY CLEAR option was not selected for the main frame, or that the REPEL TEXT function has been left ON. Selecting too dark a tint for the main frame will also obscure the shadow effect.

If you are not happy with the shadow effect achieved then small adjustments to the frame position can be made using the {OPTIONS} - [Size and Position] function, *before* the frame handles are turned off. Because of the close positioning of the two frames it is sometimes difficult to select the lower frame, and it may become necessary to move the upper frame out of the way. This presents no major problem, however, as re-positioning the frames to the exact location is very straightforward.

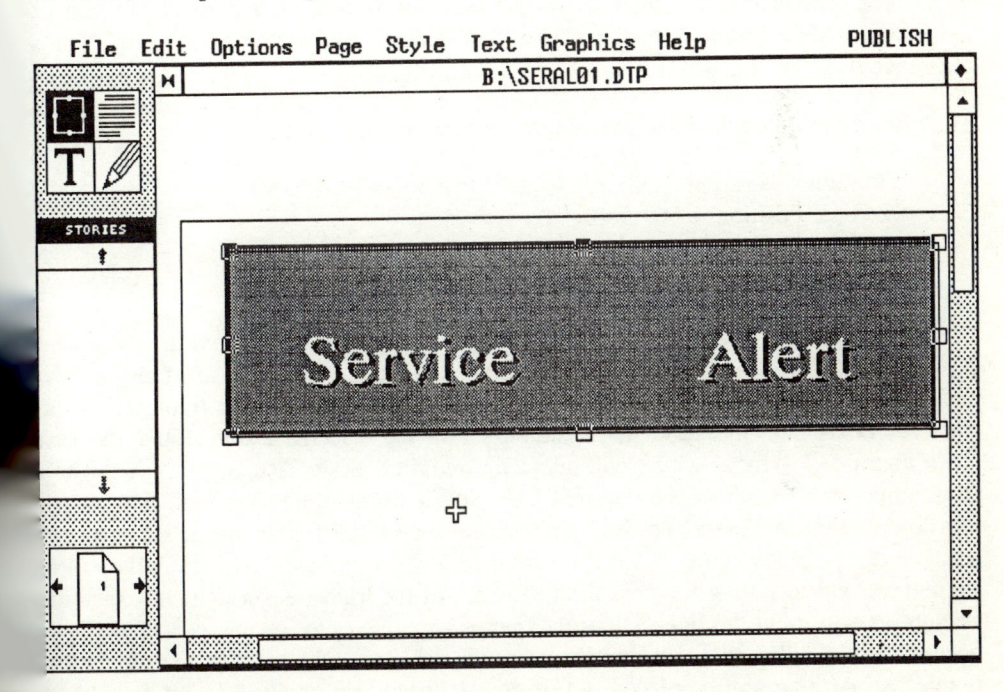

Figure 7.6 Shadow Frame Located

First text entry frame

We now move on to creating the main body of the form, by building up the other frames as required. The first frame is required to hold only one line of information. We have determined some of the basic frame parameters already, by setting the main headline frame as a guide. These are:

Horizontal Position: 1.38
Width: 6.00

The height of the frame can be calculated from the following: Our body text definition specifies a space above text of 0.1 inch, and the 12 point text selection gives a default leading of 14 point (0.2"). To align the line graphics just beneath the text we will select a position, relative to the frame margin, of 0.22 vertical (i.e. leading of 0.2 inches plus clearance (0.02") = 0.22"). Finally, to allow a spacing of 0.2 " above the frame dividing line we arrive at a frame height of 0.42".

Select the vertical position of the frame to give:

Adequate clearance below the headline frame; and
Uniform appearance of the whole page

This latter point cannot be confirmed until the page layout is complete and, initially, to allow a clearance of 0.1 inch below the headline frame, set a vertical position of 2.8 inches. (Main frame vertical position (1.2") plus Main frame height (1.5") plus clearance (0.1") = 2.8").

This now gives us all the basic frame information that we require:

Horizontal Position: 1.38
Vertical Position: 2.80
Frame Width: 6.00
Frame Height: 0.42

Create the frame, initially using the mouse controls to get the approximate size and position, and then using the [Size and Position] controls to finalise the definition. Having created the basic frame we now wish to enter the frame contents. First select the text tool, and place the cursor in the selected frame. Enter the text 'Instrument or Product:' which will adopt the required Body Text Style. Now switch to graphics mode to draw the required line. Select the line drawing tool, and accept the default line thickness. Position the cursor within the frame, and click once to activate the graphics mode. Place the cursor to align with, and just below, the colon in the text, and then drag it across the full width of the frame, ensuring that it remains straight as you draw the line. Allow the cursor to move onto, or just past, the frame border, as this will ensure that the line is drawn right up to the limit. When the button is released the line will be placed in position. If the drawn position is not exactly as required, use the {OPTION} [Size and Position] control to adjust it. In particular, we have specified a vertical position of 0.22" which you should confirm. (Note that a simple line graphic has a height of zero in the Size and Position menu).

Finally, to produce the dividing line, we return to frame mode, and from the {OPTIONS}-[Frame border] control select a frame, of second thickness and specify BELOW on the screen. This gives us the necessary divider, and the reference position for the other frames on the screen.

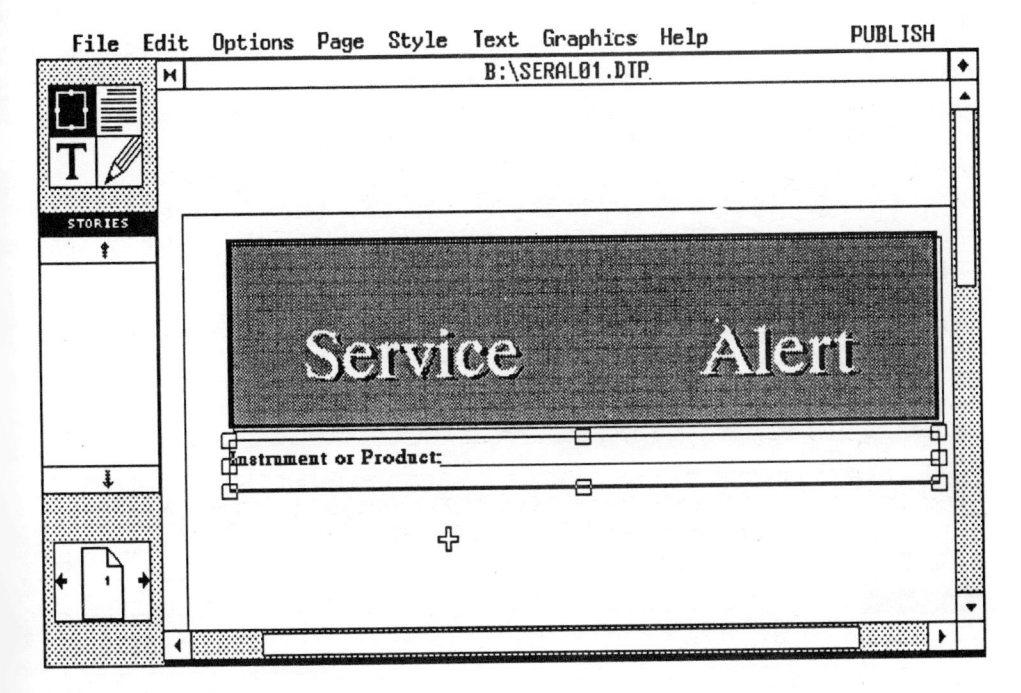

Figure 7.7 Completed First Frame

Main Body Frames

For the main part of the form we will create four identical frames, which will allow for four lines of text in each frame. Again, from the preceding work, some of the basic parameters have been set:

> Frame Horizontal Position: 1.38
> Frame Width: 6.00
> Position of first graphics line: 0.22

In addition to the first graphics line we require three additional lines, for which we will specify a line spacing of 0.25" for each. (This is an estimate based on fairly crude measurements of the space required for the whole frame, and could be amended later if it does not work out as planned). Finally, allow a final 0.2" spacing, as in the previous frame, from the dividing line. We can thus specify the frame height as 0.22 + (3 X 0.25) + 0.2 = 1.17.

As before, allow a 0.1" clearance below the preceding frame, and set the vertical position at 3.32".

Create the frame with the above specifications, by first using the basic mouse controls, and then using the {OPTIONS} - [Size and Position] controls for fine tuning.

Using the text tool place the text 'Problem or Symptom:' into the frame. Switch to the graphics mode to create the lines required. Again activate graphics mode, by clicking once within the frame, and place the first line as before. As graphics objects are positioned in reference to the frame in which they are produced we can confirm that this first line has a vertical position of 0.22. The next line is to be the full width of the frame (i.e. length 6.00) and to be positioned 0.25" below the first line (i.e. at vertical position 0.47). Draw this line, and a further two, retaining the 0.25" line spacing between each (Vertical positions 0.72 and 0.97 respectively).

Finally, create the dividing line by returning to frame mode and assign a frame line, of second thickness, *below* the frame.

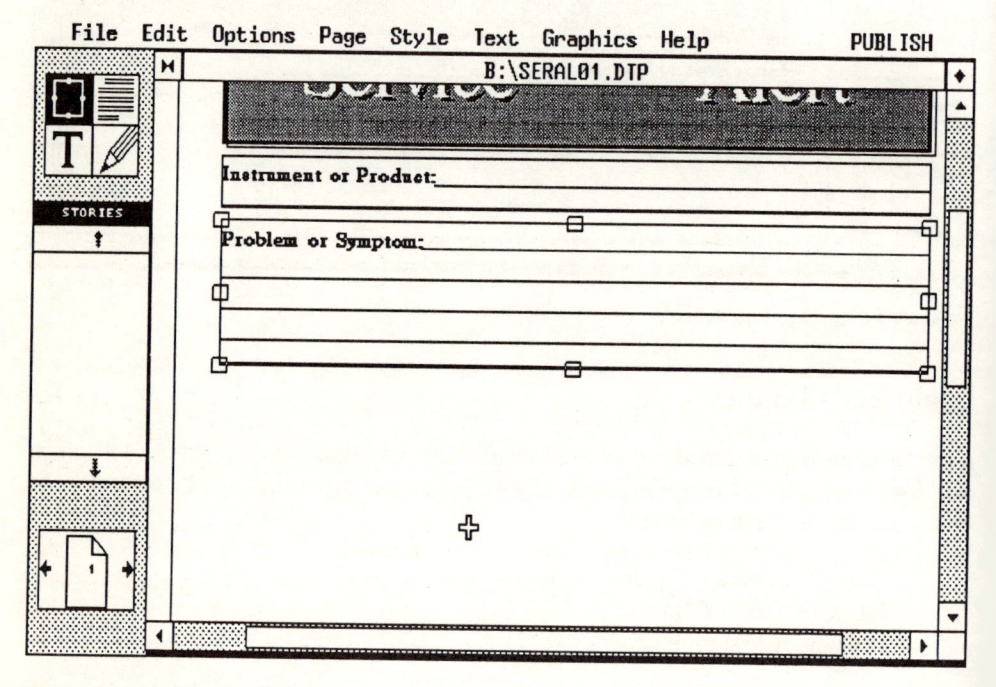

Figure 7.8 Main Text Frame Pattern

To complete the body of the form we need to copy this last frame three further times. Switch to full page view, and use the {EDIT} options to copy this last frame. Now use the paste command three times to produce the three required copies, and place them in roughly the correct position on the page. We will fix these positions as we modify each frame.

The first of our main body frames is now correctly positioned, so we can move to the next copy. We will need to confirm its position on the page, modify the text entry, and edit the first line length to match with the new text. Return to actual, or double, size display to make this easier.

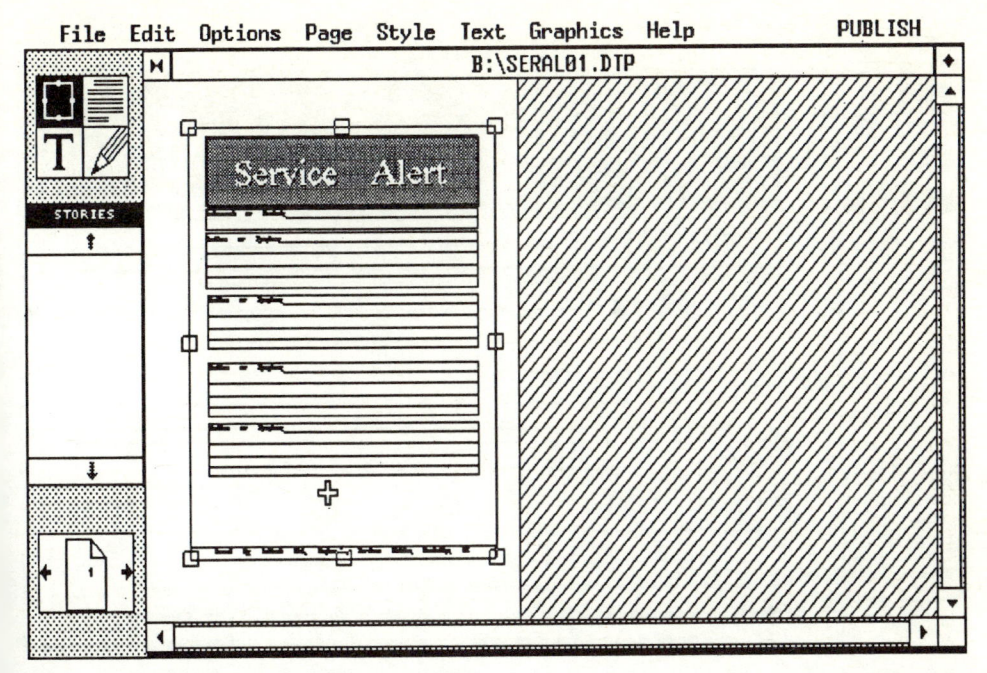

Figure 7.9 Copy Frames in Approximate Positions

Again we calculate the vertical position with respect to the preceding frame, which was given a vertical position of 3.32, and allowing a 0.1 inch clearance between frames. This gives us a required vertical position of 3.32 + 1.17 (Frame height) + 0.1 = 4.59, with a horizontal position of 1.38 as before. Position the frame correctly, and then select the text tool to modify the text.

Place the text cursor in the frame at the colon (:) in the text line, and delete this line of text. The graphics lines may disappear while you do this, but do not worry as we will get these back later. Replace the text with the word 'Cause:'. Switch to graphics mode and click once within the frame, and the lines will be re-displayed as before. We now need to lengthen the line to match up with the existing text, and re-position the start point. By activating the graphics line, and double-clicking on it we can bring up the [Size and position] control menu which shows us that the line has a horizontal position of 1.70 and a length of 4.30 (note that these two must add up to 6.00, which is the total frame width). At this point you will have to approximate the correct position for the line, with reference to the length of the text. As it happens the word 'Cause:' in 12 point has a length of almost 0.5", so we will use this to give the horizontal position. To allow for the change in the start position we will also have to increase the length to 5.50 inches. Use the size and position controls to set these values, and – Hey Presto! – the line is re-sized correctly.

The remainder of this frame needs no editing, so once it is placed we can move onto the next. We have to repeat this exercise with the other two frames. Modify the text content, line positioning and frame position to create the required page layout.

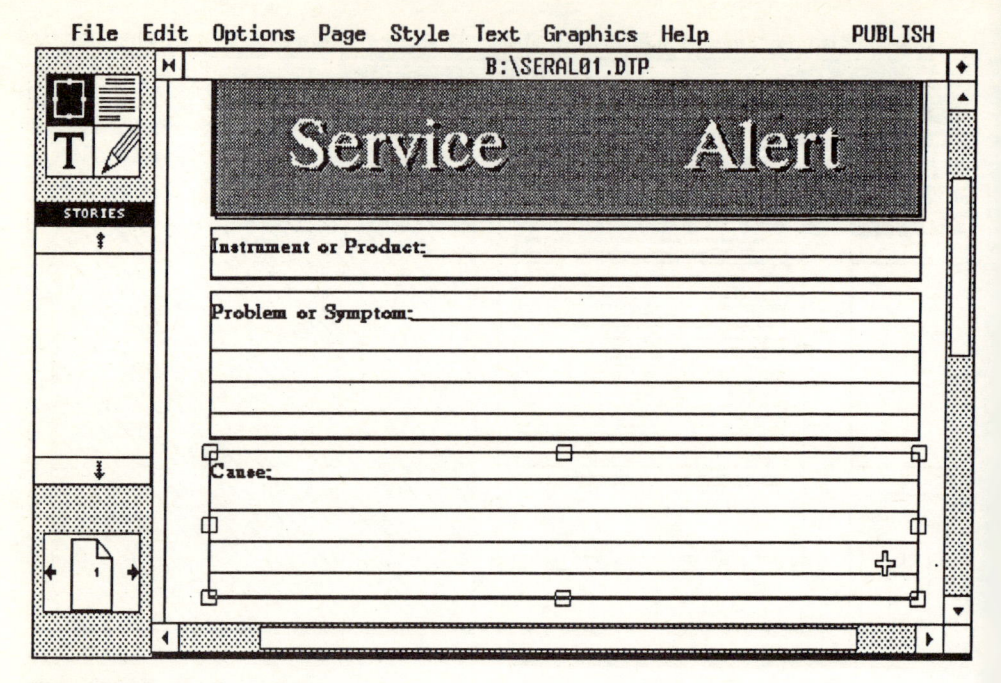

Figure 7.10 Second Frame Edited

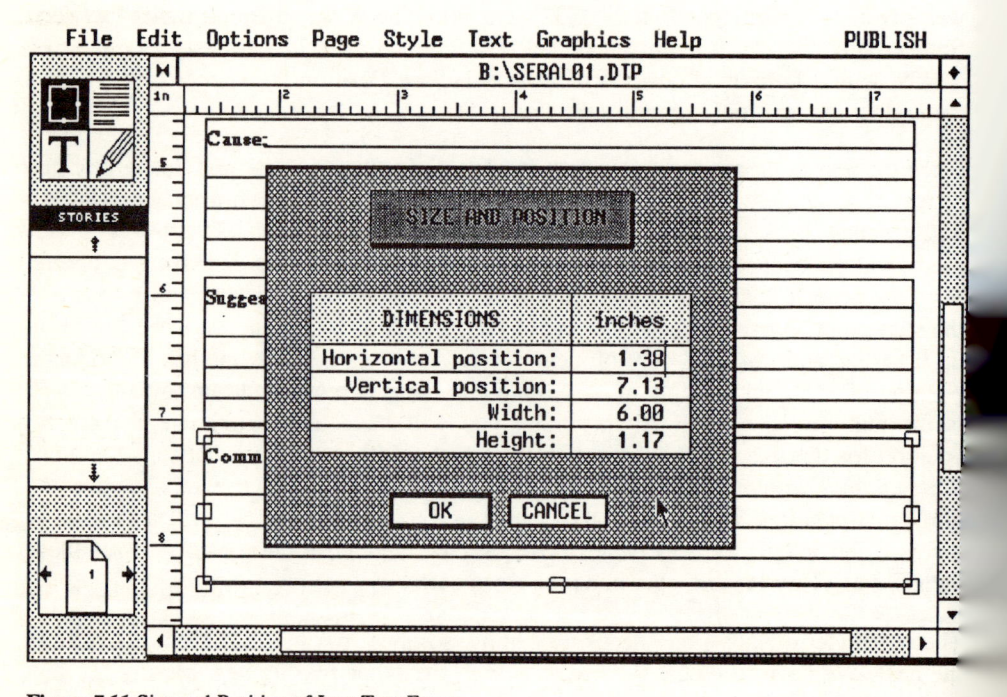

Figure 7.11 Size and Position of Last Text Frame

The first of these has a position of 1.38 horizontal and 5.86 vertical, with the first line at a horizontal position of 1.63, and a line length of 4.37 to accomodate the edited text. The second has a position of 1.38 horizontal and 7.13 vertical, with a first line at a horizontal position of 0.88 and length of 5.12.

The final frame on the page is a little different from the rest, chiefly in that it contains more text. When drawing the lines we have to take into account the actual spacing between the lines of text, which is pre-determined by our settings for BODY TEXT paragraph style.

As an example of the type of calculation that may be involved in this we can estimate the space between each line of text. First remember that, as we use the [RETURN] character between each line, Timeworks Publisher will regard each line as a new paragraph, and apply the 'Space before' dimension to each line. In practice, the line spacing between lines across a paragraph boundary, as discussed in an earlier chapter, is equal to the 'space before' dimension, added to the "leading" of the text selected. Now, our body text point size is 12, with a default leading of 14 point, or approximately 0.20 inches. Add to this the space before figure of 0.1 inch, between each paragraph, suggesting a line spacing for the text of approximately 0.3 inches.

Because the calculations to determine this spacing are a little obscure, in this case we will do this by trial and error, to verify the above calculation. By the process used earlier to determine the position of each frame we can calculate that, for uniform spacing, we require a frame vertical position of 8.40, and use the standard horizontal position of 1.38. As we are uncertain of the overall size that we will require to make the frame, we will estimate about 1.5", as this will fit comfortably in the space remaining.

Create the required frame, and select the text tool, to enter the lines of text. Enter the text 'Originated By:', and then use the space bar to move to a suitable position along the line to enter 'Date:'. Press the [RETURN] key to move to the new line and enter the appropriate text. Use the space bar again to position the 'Date:', lining it up visually with the preceding line. Press [RETURN] once more to move to the third line and enter 'Method of Verification:'

Before switching to graphics mode use the {OPTION}- [Frame Border] command to set the frame border as illustrated. This is necessary as this particular frame border intrudes into the frame space, and has a small effect of the text and graphics positioning. Setting the graphics lines first, and then setting the frame border, will disturb the appearance of the frame.

Select the graphics mode, and activate the frame as before. Position the cursor close to the colon(:) in the first text item, and drag it across to the frame edge, under 'Date:', to give a solid line. Because of the intrusion of the border into the frame space the line position becomes better at a vertical position of 0.26, as compared with the 0.22 of the frame without the border. Note also that we need to calculate the line length required at slightly less than the nominal 6.00 frame width to prevent it running across the frame border. By trial and error it was found that the effective length between the inner frame lines is 5.93, and this should be used to determine the required graphics line length for each text line.

Once the first line is placed, we repeat the sequence for the second line of text. In the example calculation above we suggested that a line spacing of 0.3 inches might be appropriate. Use this to position the next graphics line, at a vertical position of 0.56 relative to the frame top, and perform a test print to try it out. In practice, although a very small variation is allowed, this calculation did produce the most appropriate spacing. To keep the bottom line within the inner frame side margins the settings were:

> Horizontal position: 0.08
> Line length: 5.85

Finally, to determine the frame size we can calculate the spacing required as:

> Position of first line: 0.26
> 3 lines @ 0.3": 0.90
> Bottom line clearance: 0.20

This gives a total frame height requirement of 1.36. However, to make allowance for the frame border we can increase this to 1.40. Modify the frame size using the {OPTIONS}- [Size and Position] controls.

This completes the page layout, and the document becomes ready for duplication and use as required. Earlier we had assumed that we required a clearance between frames

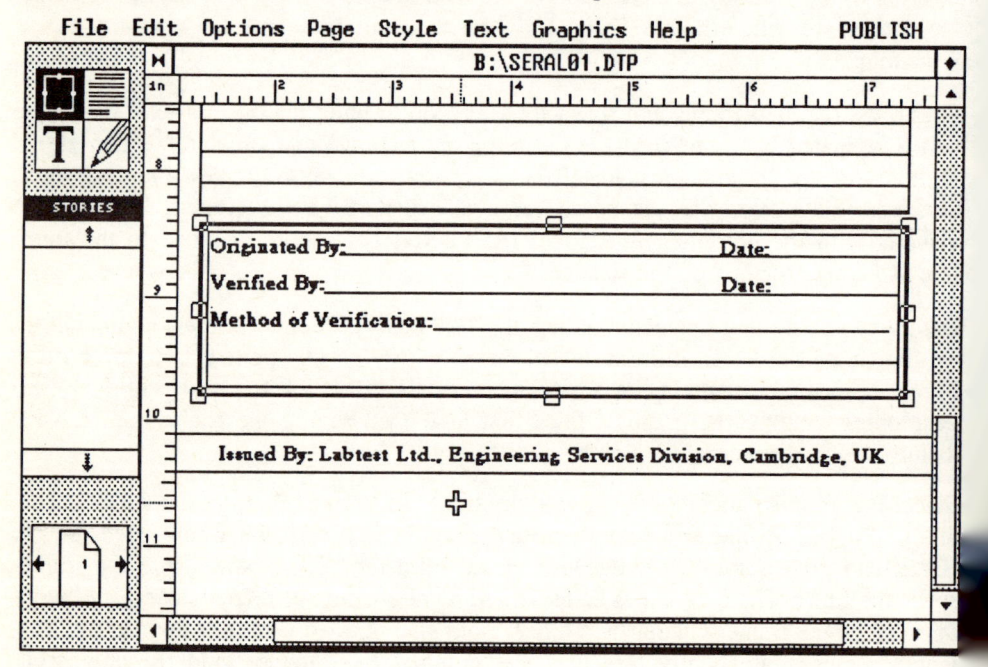

Figure 7.12 Completed Final Frame.

of 0.1", and this turns out to have been a good guess. The finished document does not require this to be modified.

In developing this form we have taken an established design and merely reproduced it using the Timeworks Publisher package, so the basic design work had been done, and many of the measurements required could be deduced from the original.

When designing forms from scratch, however, it is necessary to have a good idea of the general appearance of the forms, and the relevant spacings involved. In this application I have chosen to use the [Inches and Tenths] ruler option as this made it easier to actually measure the original document to obtain the spacings, and to perform measurements on trial prints to check document progress. Where there is a heavy text content in a document, it becomes more useful to use the picas and points ruler options. This was becoming apparent in the final frame, where the positioning of the graphics lines had to relate to the text positioning. This, in turn, is always set in terms of picas and points, irrespective of the ruler settings chosen for the document. Using this measure would have produced some simpler mathematics in estimating the best line spacing, but nevertheless would produce the same end result.

Where you are creating forms which are to be filled in by typewriter or computer it is useful to remember that the most usual line spacing (i.e leading) is 6 lines per inch, equivalent to a 12 point leading, and that the typewriter may be set to give single line spacing (12 point), one and a half line spacing (18 point) or double line spacing (24 point). In this case, it is most helpful to organise the spacing of your form lines to match with one of the above.

It is extremely frustrating trying to fill out a form with a printer where these parameters have not been considered, and the line spacing is not consistent with normal practice. In the example above, this was not an issue as the form is normally completed by hand.

CommunityNewsletter

This second project is again based on a real application. The original document was created on an Apple Macintosh system, by a professional designer, and printed using the Apple Laserwriter PostScript printer (i.e. a very expensive set up). I have chosen to reproduce the document for printing on a 24 pin dot matrix printer, as it is possible that future editions will be produced on an Amstrad-based system, without the luxury of a laser printer.

In re-producing the document the only restriction that arose was in the relatively smaller range of font sizes that are available with the non-laser printer. This arises because of the ability of the PostScript printer to accept font sizes in 1 point increments, where the dot matrix printer is restricted to the range supplied with the package. (Again, even this restriction could be overcome to a substantial degree by a number of font/print enhancement packages which are available and mentioned elsewhere in the book)

WISHING WELL

The Newsletter of the Practice Participation Association
125 Stowmarket Road & West Bramwell Health Centre

Issue No 17   December 1988

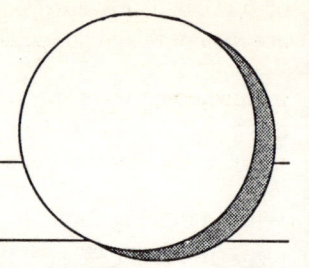

HEALTHY TURNOUT

Community Health Fayre Bramwell Sat 15th Oct

As you will see from the press cuttings, the Fayre was judged to be a great success. Of course its not easy to evaluate a Health Fayre in terms of sucess or failure, but all of us who were involved agreed that despite the hard work, we had fun!

Actual 'feedback' from all the agencies involved may take time but we hope they found it worthwhile, and we were glad of their support in promoting positive health.

Attendance was far above our expectations, and, more importantly, people were participating in the activities, getting health checks, asking questions, and generally having a good time. They certainly enjoyed the good food!

From my own point of view, one of the most rewarding aspects was the way in which everyone worked together to make it a sucess and I hope this is something we can build on. Normal PPA activities virtually came to a standstill during the month when the Fayre was being organised, but we shall be holding our AGM in February (See details) and it would be marvellous to see many new faces there.(We'll be showing the Health Fayre video).Do come along and bring some ideas for future PPA events, suggestions for fundraising activities etc. It may well be that we shall need to look at an entirely different structure for PPA committees, but we do need you and your ideas - it would be a shame not to build on the fun and friendliness we enjoyed over recent months. Thank you to everyone who took part.

Health Checks at Fayre

What a marvellous response! Any initial fears that my colleagues and I may have had that we would be sitting down and twiddling our thumbs on the day of the Community Health Fayre proved to be completely unfounded. Everybody who came to see us had their weight, height and blood pressure measured and they were asked to fill in a short questionnaire about their own particular lifestyle.

We were delighted to discuss and give advice to all those who showed a genuine interest in working to lead a healthier life, perhaps by changing their diet, or losing a little excess fat. I was also encouraged by those who asked for help on how to give up smoking, sometimes the habit of a lifetime. Well, good news - a 'Stop Smoking' group starts in January. Remember, it's never too late to give up!.

The Community Car Scheme Needs You !

My name is Annelie Bartram and I want to tell you about the Community Car Scheme. It was set up to help the elderly, the disabled, and families with young children who have no means of getting to hospital, or the doctor's, the Health Centre, or to other places they would like or need to go.

I know how I would feel if I were housebound because of lack of transport, so I try and do a little of what I hope others would do for me in similar circumstances. It only takes a little of my time and gives people so much pleasure. When I receive a request for transport, I cannot always help, as I have other commitments: so more drivers are needed. At the moment there are 4 of us. So we need more drivers. It only takes a few hours of my time, for which I am paid 17p a mile. Not a fortune, I agree, but then I am not doing it for profit. And one day, who knows, I may need the same help myself! So could you!

We also need someone to help co-ordinate between people needing lifts, and drivers.

Please give a bit of your time to help our Community Project.

Figure 7.13 Wishing Well Document

The finished document is illustrated and, as before, we will go through the processes of creating the document step by step. The pictures have been omitted because in the actual application these were inserted as photographs at the final printing stage, and thus not an integral part of the DTP process. All that was required of the package was to leave space for the addition of these illustrations

The use of the very small point size text in this example means that output onto a 9 pin printer would be of marginal quality, as experience indicates that the minimum size that reproduces well on these is 10 point.

Although only one page is illustrated here, the actual newsletter was four pages long. It is, therefore, advisable to define a master page for the document, as well as some paragraph styles, and this is the first task.

The Master Page

The first step in this process is to determine the basic requirements for the master page, in terms of the column layout, as well as any fixed textual/graphics content.

For the column layout, it is readily apparent that there is a basic three column configuration, and that the page margins are smaller than usually found on an A4 document. Another feature of the document is that individual stories do not run simply down each column before continuing to the next. On the front page, and to a lesser extent on later pages, the stories occupy blocks across the page running to either two or three columns in width. As the layout differs in detail on each page there is little point in preparing any individual frames on the master page.

Only the front page of the newsletter has the title, logo and heading section. However, as we will be using this layout for further issues it is better to include these, in a single frame, on the master page. After the cover page is constructed it will be necessary to remove this section from later pages. This is readily achieved by using the {EDIT}-[Cut] options to remove the frame, and is easier than having to recreate the title block for each newsletter. Another option which may be taken would be to prepare one master page for the front sheet, and a separate one for subsequent pages. However, as we stated earlier, the actual layout detail in later pages is not consistent enough to make it worthwhile in this example.

Start up the program, and start a new document with an A4 portrait paper selection. When presented with the opening page of the default style document, use the {PAGE}-[Go to page] option to open the master page. Select the [Set column guides] option from the {OPTIONS} menu, and set the following parameters:

No of Columns	3
Right Margin	0.33 inches
Left margin	0.33 inches
Top Margin	0.5 inches
Bottom Margin	0.5 inches

Choose the page offset parameters to suit your own particular printer, and to produce the above final margins. It is frequently useful at this point to actually create a frame, with a border, showing the overall column layout, and print out a copy just to ensure that the margins are as expected.

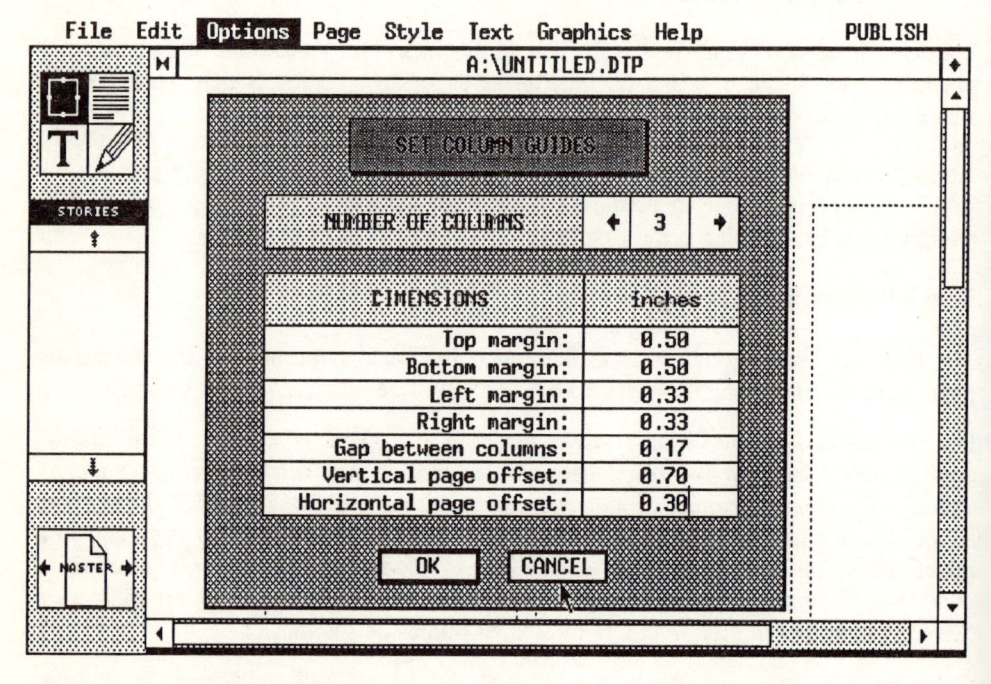

Figure 7.14 Set Column Guides Display

To do this, at this stage, you will first need to save the Style Sheet, which only contains the basic column layout at the moment. After you have done this select page 1 of the document, using the {PAGE} - [Go to page] instruction, and draw a single frame around the column limits, or around each column, and set a frame border of your choice. Select the PRINT option from the file menu, and examine the results to ensure they meet your requirements. When the printout is complete, return to the master page to complete the definitions.

Later in the document we require to construct some graphics which need to bridge all three columns, and a frame will be required to contain these graphics. Rather than create a separate frame for each of these, it is better to create a single overall frame which will contain all the newsletter elements, and additional graphics. This frame should be the full width of the frame guides set above, but should extend to both extremes of the page, top and bottom, for maximum flexibility. Create this frame, and set the FRAME TINT visibility to clear (So that we can still see the column guides)

The next step is to create the title block, which is to be inserted into a single frame.

During this process there was quite a lot of trial and error in order to get the text and graphics positioning as required.

When a document is to contain a lot of text it is frequently more convenient to select the units of measure in Picas and Points. This is achieved using the {OPTIONS} - [Ruler Spacing] function to make the selection. The overall title block frame height cannot be fixed before the final layout has been determined, so this was initially set to 12 picas (2 inches). The width of the frame was set to match the overall width of the column layout which, with the margins set earlier, gives a measure of 45,09 (in picas and points, remember). To get the title as close as possible to the top of the page we will actually position this frame at a vertical position of 0,00. The horizontal position is determined by our margin setting of 2,00 (0.33 inches). The basic frame parameters are then:

Horizontal Position	2,00
Vertical Position	0,00
Width	45,09
Height	12,00 (To be modified)

It is easier to create the frame using the full page view, and then to revert to actual size view for all editing work.

We wish the title to be printed with the following characteristics:

Point Size	46
Typeface	Swiss
Style	Bold
Format	Left Align

The PARAGRAPH STYLE Menu controls should be used to set the above parameters, to a paragraph style which is called 'TITLE', and which, as in the previous example is created by modifying the basic Body Text style. Remember to position the text cursor on a new line, using the [RETURN] key before assigning the new paragraph style.

Once the paragraph style parameters have been set, select the text tool and place the cursor within the frame. Enter the text 'WISHING WELL' into the frame, which will adopt the BODY TEXT style initially. Now select the paragraph tool, highlight the title text, and assign the 'TITLE' style from the browser.

The next step is to enter the small text information for which we shall create a style called HEADTEXT. The basic parameters we require for this are:

Point Size	10
Typeface	Swiss
Style	Bold
Format	Left Align

Each line will be treated as a new paragraph, as we will end each line before the normal wrap around function takes effect. To prevent the line spacing becoming too great we will want to look at the 'space above' parameter. By experiment, using some test prints this was set at 0.02, to give a marginal increase over the normal default line spacing. Set these parameters to this paragraph style and, as before, then select the text cursor, and enter the lines of text into the frame. To create the necessary space between the title and this block, a single blank line was inserted before the text. The date block is separated from the 'Issue No' by using the space bar. Now use the paragraph tool to assign the HEADTEXT style to these three lines of text. Check that the appearance on screen matches the required layout.

I will introduce a reminder at this point about one of the difficulties in using different size text within a frame, which is covered more fully in the next chapter. When you assign a large size to a single line of text it is usually better to ensure that a new line is created, by pressing ENTER, before the large size is applied. To ensure the correct spacing this blank line should be assigned the appropriate style ('Headtext').If you do not, then the next time you use the text tool within that frame it will automatically adopt the spacing of the larger text. For example, this caused some problems with the relative positioning of the title and the 'headtext' above, when I was a little lax in this procedure. A new line was created while the large text cursor was still active, which resulted in all the other text disappearing from the frame. Although not difficult to recover from this, it is best avoided by a little care.

Having entered the text, and assigned the appropriate characteristics, we can then place the graphics elements in the required positions. Select the graphics tool and click once in the frame to activate the graphics function. Choose the single line option from the browser, accepting the default line thickness selection. Increase the page view to double size (Use [ALT] 2), and position the graphics cursor at a suitable position above the text, ensuring that it lines up with the left hand frame edge. Now draw a short horizontal line, above the text, and ensure that the position is satisfactory. Rather than change the page view to extend the line we can use the {OPTIONS} - [Size and Position] function to increase the line length. We wish the line to be the full width of the frame, and we know from earlier that this has been set to 45,09. With the short line active, double click on the line, or select the {OPTIONS} menu, to activate the [Size and Position] control screen. Specify a width of 45,09 for the line, and this will be drawn automatically.

Repeat this general procedure for the lower line, and then switch to full page view to see the overall result. (Use [ALT] 3). See Figure 7.15.

The final step is to produce the circle logo, which is simply built up of two copies of the same circle, with differing fill characteristics. The size chosen is a matter of personal preference but, in the example, a size of 10,00 was adopted. (Remember that this size here refers to the size of the containing graphics frame). Switch to double size page view ([ALT] 2), and locate the screen window over the right hand frame end. Select the circle option from the browser and create a circle with the lower edge

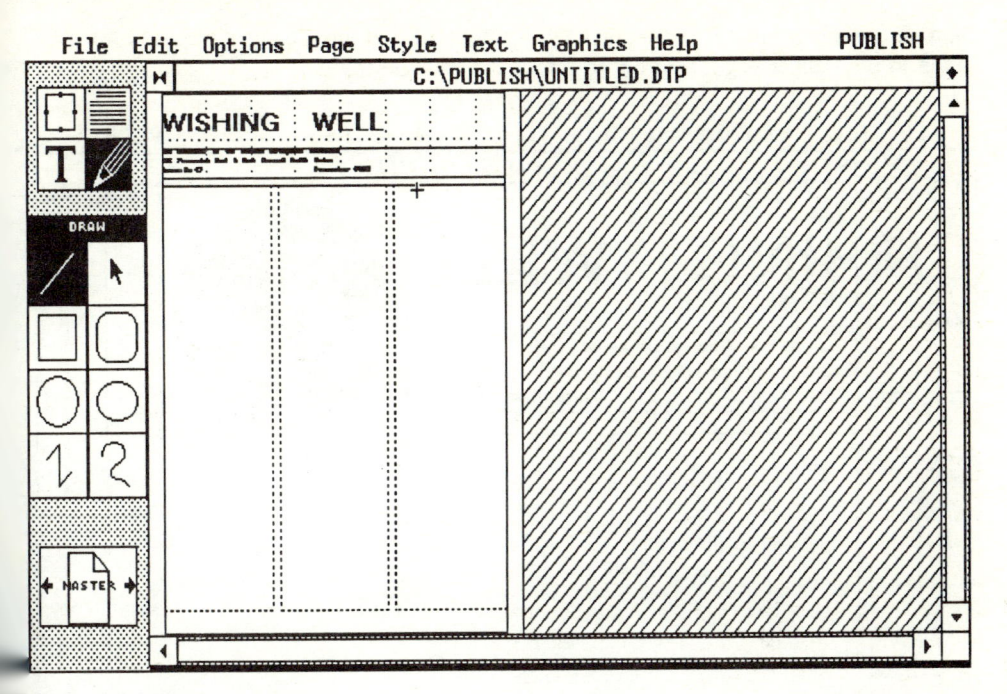

Figure 7.15 Basic Heading Frame

on the frame bottom, extending to the appropriate height. (REMEMBER, when drawing a circle, that we do this by defining the frame within which it is located, and not directly locating the circle itself). When the circle is drawn, and the frame is still selected, use the {GRAPHICS} -[Fill style] menu to select the appropriate shading. Now switch to full size view to check the overall appearance, and to produce the copy circle. See Figure 7.16.

With the original circle frame selected use the {EDIT} -[Copy] function to create a copy, and then use the {EDIT} - [Paste] function to place the second copy in the frame. Unfortunately this appears, on screen, at the left hand edge of the frame, and has to be dragged across to the right hand side for final positioning. (This will happen only where the graphics is created so close to the overall frame border, that there is insufficient space to generate the second copy at that location.) Move the copy approximately into the required position, and then switch to double page view for final adjustments. With the copy frame selected use the {GRAPHICS} - [Fill Style] menu to select a WHITE OPAQUE fill, and then position the new graphic in the appropriate position. Remember for final positioning very fine resolution can be obtained using the {OPTIONS} - [Size and Position] function. In the original the circles are located to intersect at the point where the lower line graphic meets the lower circle. This positioning was easily achieved on screen, and duplicated exactly in the final printout.

It is worthwhile, at this point, saving the Style Sheet, and then doing a test print of the page to ensure that it is satisfactory. Remember that any changes required must be made to the master page, in order to retain the style definition.

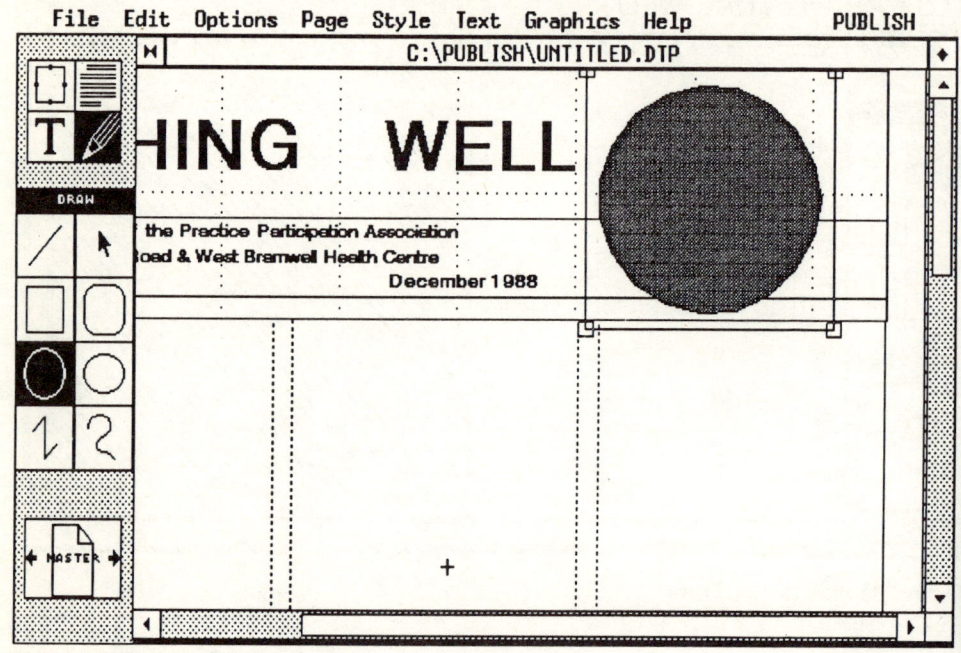

Figure 7.16 First Circle Created

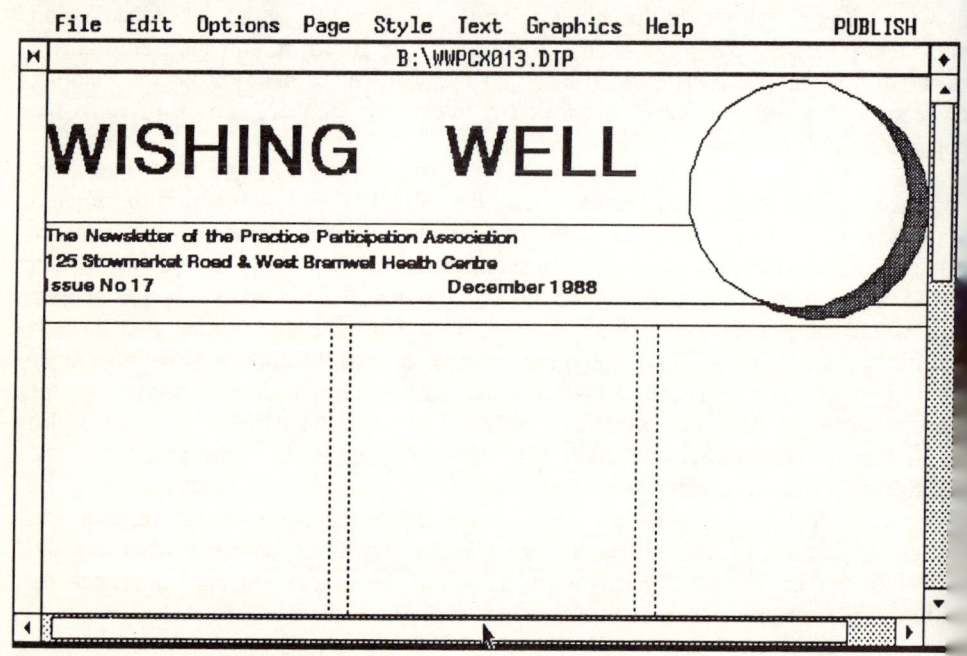

Figure 7.17 Newsletter Title Block

If the title block has been completed to your satisfaction we can now progress to the final style definitions for the body of the newsletter. Again, ensure that the master page is selected before making any changes to the Style Sheet.

The main body of the text within the newsletter was chosen to be 8 point Dutch, with only a small space between paragraphs. The only other apparent feature was that the first line of each paragraph was to be indented by 3,00 (0.5"). We can modify the default BODY TEXT style to achieve this quite easily. Select the paragraph tool, and then double click on BODY TEXT in the browser to bring up the Paragraph Style control sheet. We will not change the style name, but should use the other controls to set the following parameters.

FONT & SIZE	Dutch 8 point
OPTIONS	Format Justified
DIMENSIONS	Space above 0,01; First line left indent 3,00

All other settings can be accepted as for the default style.

The story headings also require a style to be set, and for this the following parameters were required, which we achieve by modifying the default SUBHEAD style to give the following:

FONT & SIZE	Swiss 14 Point
STYLE	Bold
OPTIONS	Format Centred
DIMENSIONS	Space above 0,01

As each of the headings are to be entered into the text individually, it was felt that it would be easier to change the text to white print after it had been entered, and the frame size, etc., determined.

The default Paragraph styles HEADLINE and BULLET are not required, and should be deleted from the Style Sheet.

The other major headlines on the newsletter are entered as direct text and assigned their characteristics later, using the normal text controls.

We have now completed the definition of the master page and the document Style Sheet, which includes:

The Title Frame;
Body Text Paragraph Style;
Title Paragraph Style;
Headtext Paragraph Style; and
Subhead Paragraph Style.

Ensure that this is saved as a Style Sheet before progressing to enter the text onto the page. Once this has been saved, then Goto page 1 to begin entering the body of the newsletter.

The individual stories in the newsletter were produced externally on the Microsoft WORD 4 word processor, and imported as text files. No problems were experienced with this procedure, although no style definitions were applied within the word processor. Each story was produced in a separate file, so that the page illustrated required the import of three story files. The files may be produced and imported before any further frames are created, or may be imported as required, entirely according to individual preference.

The first task in constructing the text layout was to create the initial headline HEALTHY TURNOUT. This caused some problems in that, with the limitations on font size available, and requiring a larger size than the newsletter title, the only choice available was to use 60 point. (With a PostScript printer there would have been a greater range to choose from). The simple problem was that the two word-headline would not fit across the page in 60 point, and some careful manipulation was required.

To make life a little easier for this we will create a new paragraph style for this headline which we will call 'HEADLINE', replacing the default style we deleted earlier. We need to assign this the following characteristics:

 Format Centred
 Font/Size Dutch 60 point

Create a frame to hold this headline, extending the full width of the page, and of height 6,04, or the minimum required to accomodate the text size.

Select the text tool and enter the text 'HEALTHYTURNOUT', in upper case, which will initially adopt the body text style, with the first word inset from the frame edge. Now use the paragraph controls to change the text to adopt the headline style.

We now have the headline constructed as a single word, but of the correct general format.

To make the headline more acceptable in appearance we will use the kerning function to change the letter spacing to give a better result. To achieve the desired balance it was necessary to print out the headline in the existing form, to see where kerning could be used. In the illustration we show the original text, and the modified text for comparison. The points at which it was felt the kerning could be used to improve the appearance were:

 Between H and E reduce the spacing (-3.0 points)
 Between L and T reduce the spacing (-7.0 points)
 Between U and R reduce the spacing (-2.0 points)
 Between N and O reduce the spacing (-1.0 points)
 Between O and U reduce the spacing (-1.0 points)
 Between Y and T increase the spacing (+12.7 points)

This latter value was the maximum kerning allowed by the program, and did achieve a reasonable word separation, without unbalancing the text.

HEALTHYTURNOUT

HEALTHY TURNOUT

Figure 7.18 Headline Modifications

With the headline created to our satisfaction we now wish to place it in the correct position. To prevent it causing any problems with the title block, use the {OPTIONS} - [Repel Text] to set the repel text OFF for this frame. Position this frame so that its border just overlaps the title frame border. Again, as this is a fairly critical part of the document, a test print would be appropriate to ensure that everything is placed satisfactorily.

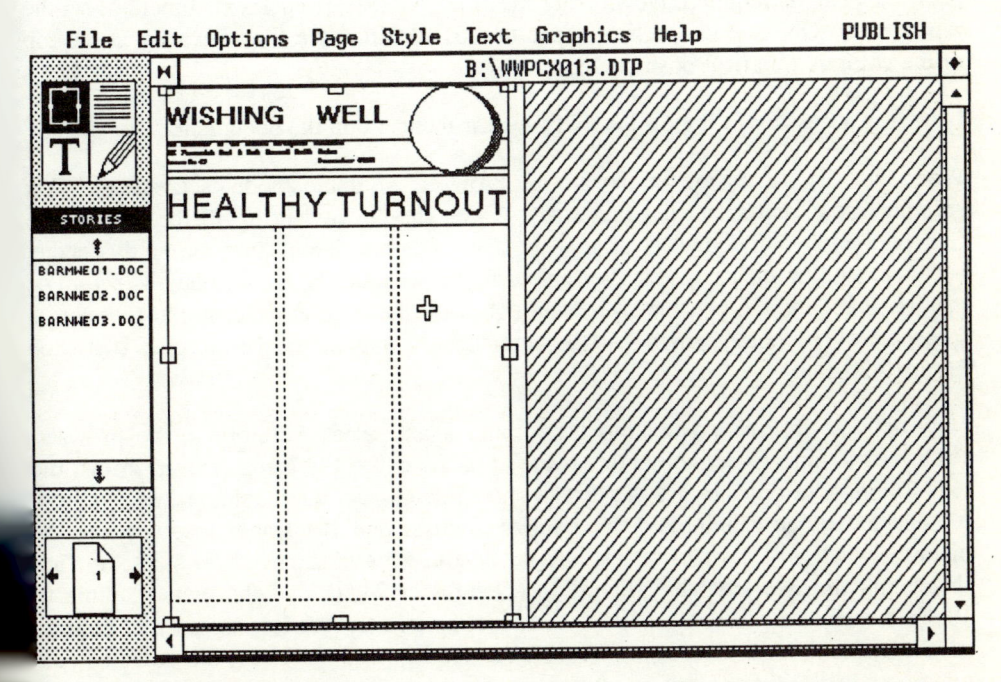

Figure 7.19 Headline Positioned

When this newsletter was planned, the contributors were asked to produce short items for it, but were not given specific targets in numbers of words, etc. As a result of this, all the text frames have to be manipulated individually to fit the text produced, with little editing of the text allowed. This prohibited the setting of a formal layout prior to the text entry, and demands some experimentation as each story is entered. At each stage we will have to make a guess at the size of frame required, and make adjustments as the stories are entered.

As a first guess, for the first story, we will make three equal frames, of height 28,00 (purely arbitrary), in each of the three columns immediately below the headline frame. Across the upper part of the two right hand columns create an additional frame, for the picture space, of height 21,00, and set a border around this. Set the repel text function to ON, but reduce the vertical space to 0,01.

Finally, create a small frame at the top of the left hand column to contain the subheading, again of arbitrary height. When this frame is created select the text tool, and place the cursor in the frame. Enter the subheading text as two separate lines. Select the paragraph tool, and assign the SUBHEAD style to the two lines of text. Re-size the frame to give the minimum height required to contain the headline (3,04). To produce the reverse text effect select the text tool, and highlight all the text in the frame. From the style menu select the WHITE option, or use [ALT]-W, which will cause the text to disappear. Now use the frame tool, and select the subheading frame, and set the frame tint to black in the ({OPTIONS} menu). The headline text should now reappear, as required. Now, using the {OPTIONS] - [Repel text] function, set the repel text to ON, and the vertical space to 0,01. Position the frame exactly at the top of the column. (Vertical position 18,06)

Now it is necessary to Import the text files for inclusion in the document.

When the file names are in the stories browser, in frame mode, activate the first column frame, and select the first story, which should flow in to fill the frame. The first paragraph is assigned a larger text size, and this should be done at this stage, before extending the story into the second frame. Use the TEXT tool and select all of the first paragraph. Open the style menu and use the Font & Size option to select a font size of 10 point, which will be immediately applied to the selected text. See Figure 7.20.

Now activate the second column frame, and again select the story in the browser. With the columns as set above this resulted in the entire file being entered in just the two columns. In order to get the text to spread across the three columns, as required, it is necessary to manipulate the column frames, and the frame reserved for the picture, which will have to be reduced in height. This is achieved, in steps, by first shortening the two left hand frames to a height of 24,00, and the picture frame to 18,00 to maintain a balance. This is to cause the text to overflow the second column so that when the third column frame is activated, and the story file selected, the remaining text will flow into this frame.

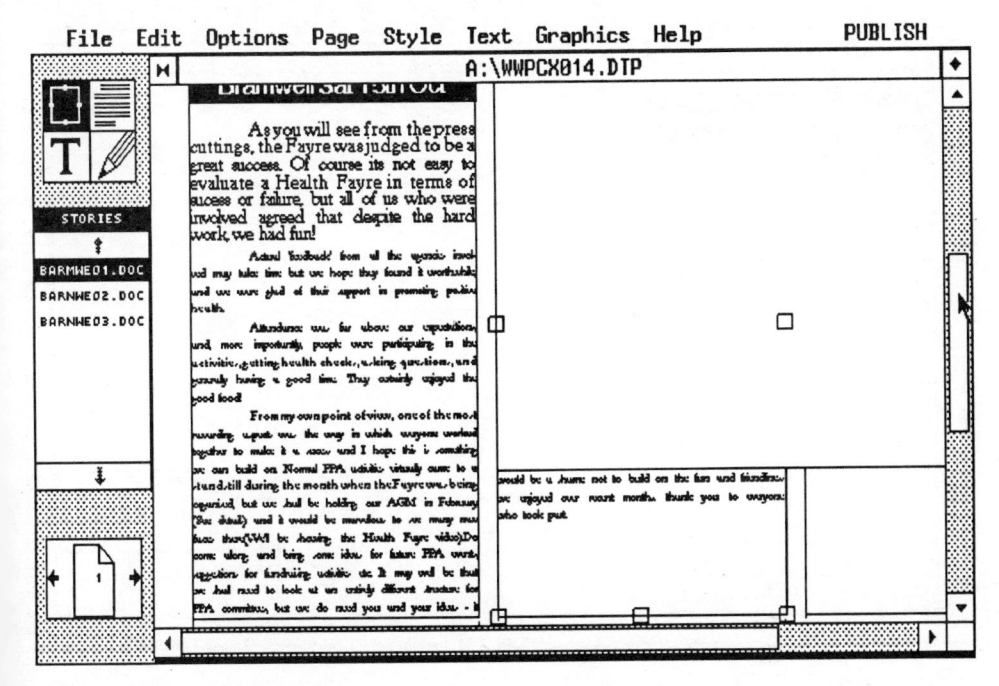

Figure 7.20 First Text Entry Results

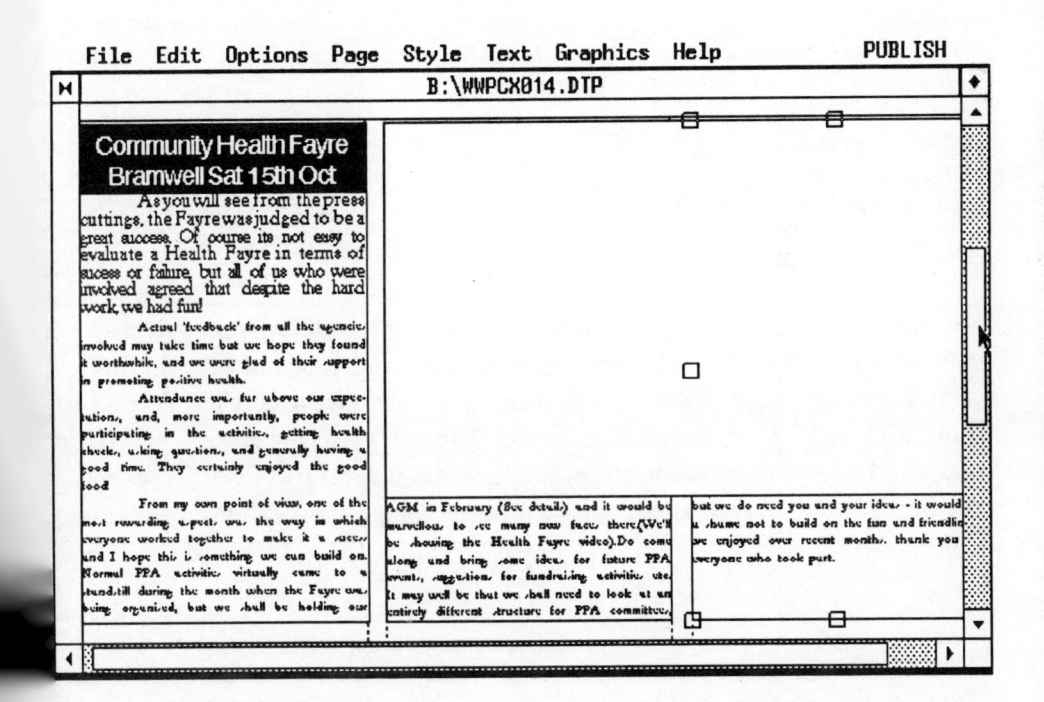

Figure 7.21 Modified Frame Dimensions

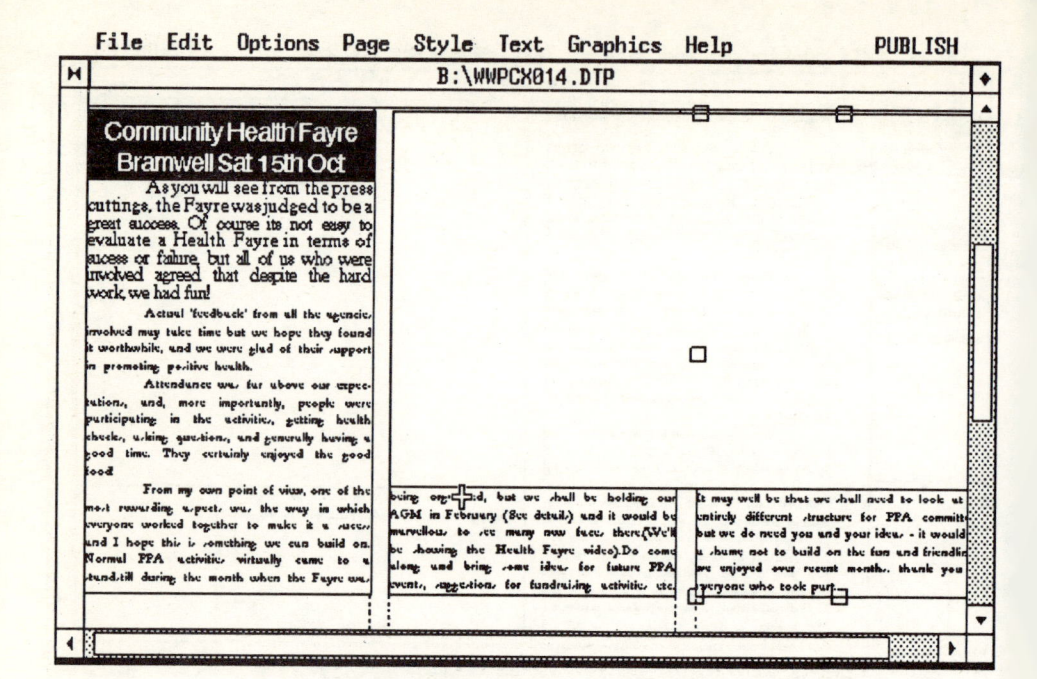

Figure 7.22 Third Adjustment to Frame Size.

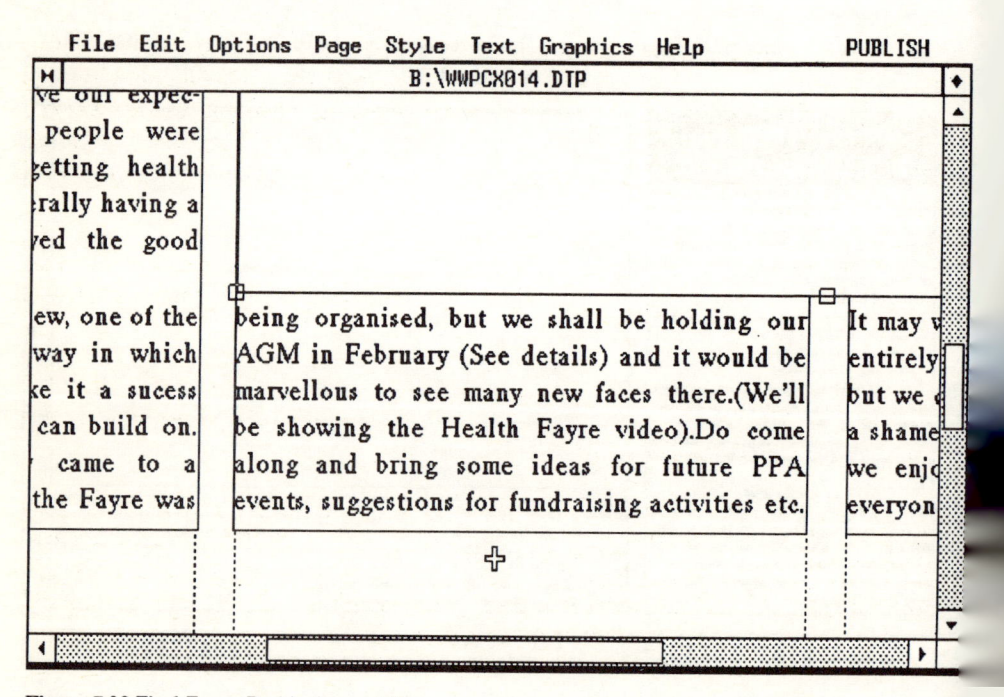

Figure 7.23 Final Frame Positioning and Size

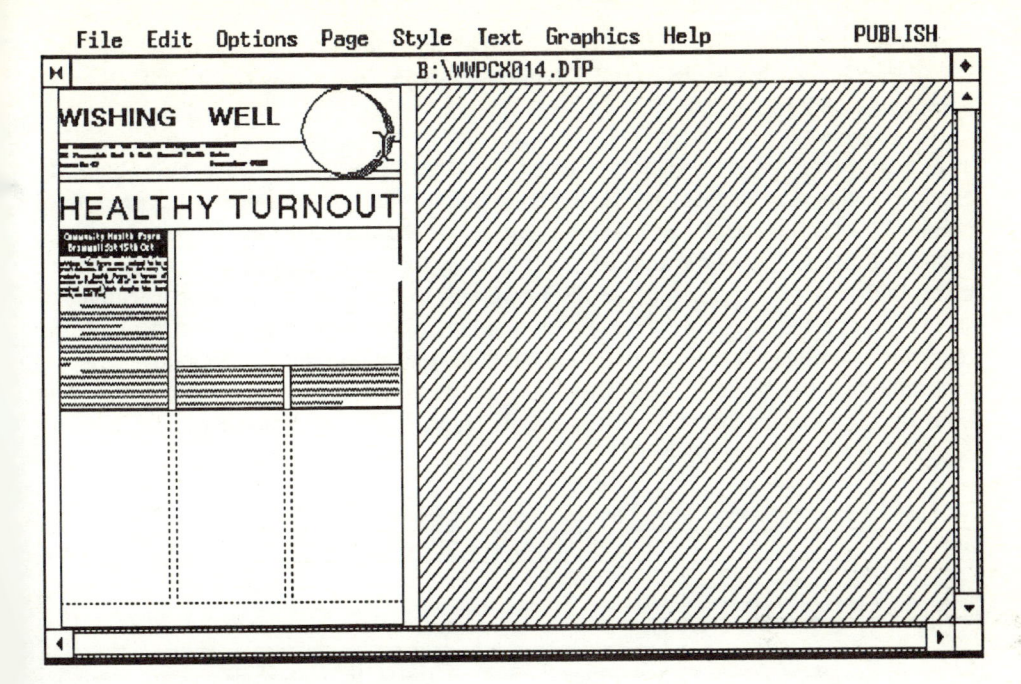

Figure 7.24 Final Frame Layout (First Story)

This produces results which are almost correct, but we need to cause two more lines of text to flow into the third column, to get the final balance. Effectively, this means reducing each of the first two columns by a single line of text. Now the text leading in the BODY TEXT paragraph style is 10 points (the default value for 8 point text), and we should reduce the column size by at least this amount. The frame height of each column is reduced to 23,02 to accommodate this, which is satisfactory in that all the text now fits evenly across the three columns.

However, to be absolutely precise the lines of text in the first column are a little higher than in the other two. This is adjusted by shortening the picture frame by 4 points to 17,08 to bring all the lines of text to the same uniform level.

The next item to complete is the line across the page, dividing the above from the following text. This is a simple graphics line, created on the background frame, and positioned just below the text frames created.

Switch to full page view, and locate the screen window so that the bottom of the text block is visible. Select the graphics tool, and click once in the background frame to select graphics mode. Select the line tool, and choose the second line thickness ({GRAPHICS} menu). Use the 'FULL BOX' to remove the tools column, as this will enable you to view the full width page. Position the cursor on the left hand frame edge, at a suitable point below the columns of text, and draw the line required. Remember that fine adjustments to the position and width of this line can be made, to 1 point accuracy, using the {Options} - [Size and position] function.

If the final position of this line falls within the text frames created for the above, then the frames can be made clear ({OPTIONS} - [Frame Tint]), which will make the line completely visible.

The next block of the page is created in exactly the same way, but obviously excluding the graphics frame. First create three small frames in each column, of height 7,00 (1.25''), and leave a small gap below the dividing line. Create a separate frame for the sub-heading and, as before, enter the text, 'Health Checks at Fayre', using the body text style, and use the paragraph tool to assign the correct 'Subhead' style. Change the text colour to white, and the frame tint to black, to achieve the reversed printing effect. Fix the final size of the frame just sufficiently large to accommodate the heading (2,00), and position it at the top of the first column. The final position can be fixed when the text is entered. Set the frame REPEL TEXT to on, with a vertical spacing of 0,01.

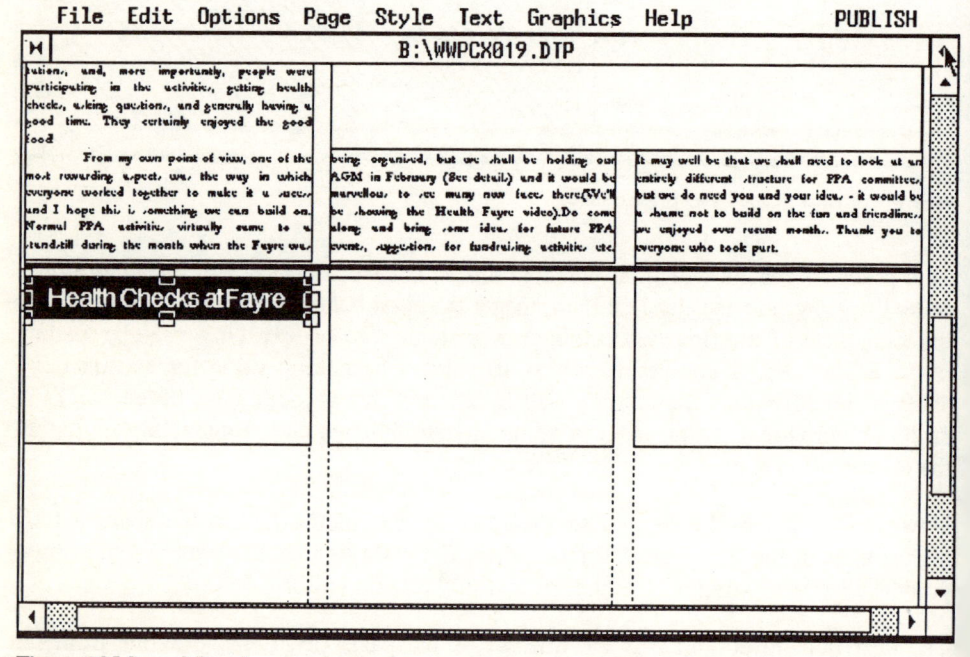

Figure 7.25 Story 2 Step 1

Select the first of the three columns, highlight the appropriate story from the browser, and allow the text to fill the frame. Select each of the frames in turn until the whole story is placed within the frames.

Examine the results to see if any adjustments are necessary. In my example, this frame size was too large, and the optimum was found to be 6,04, to give an even amount of text in each column. To complete the text editing, the last sentence was selected using the text tool, and allocated a new size of 10 point, and a bold style to emphasize its content.

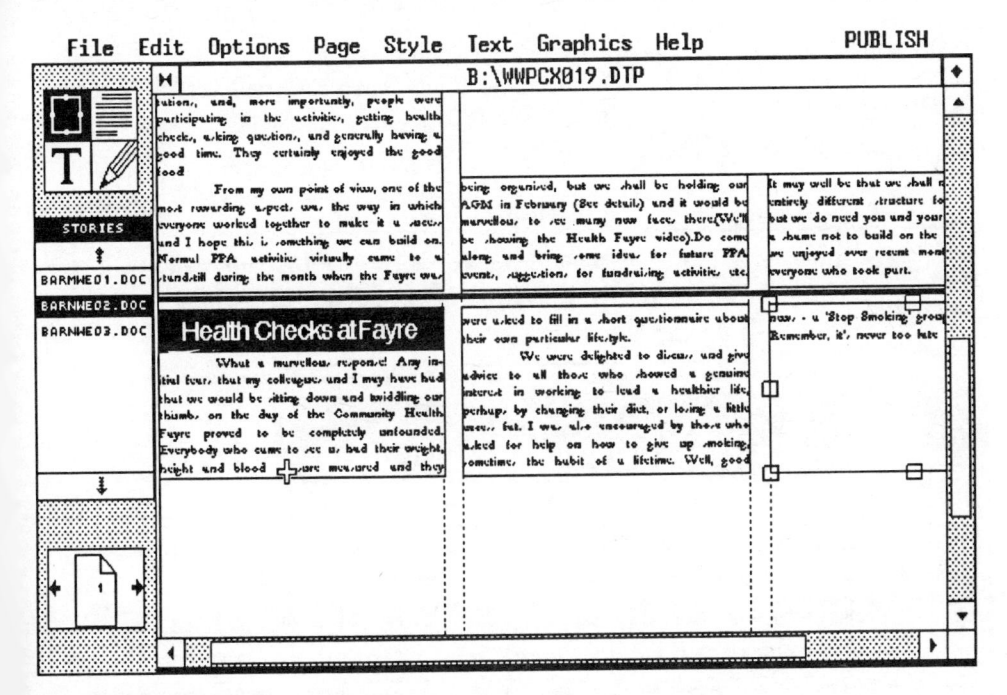

Figure 7.26 Story 2 Step 2

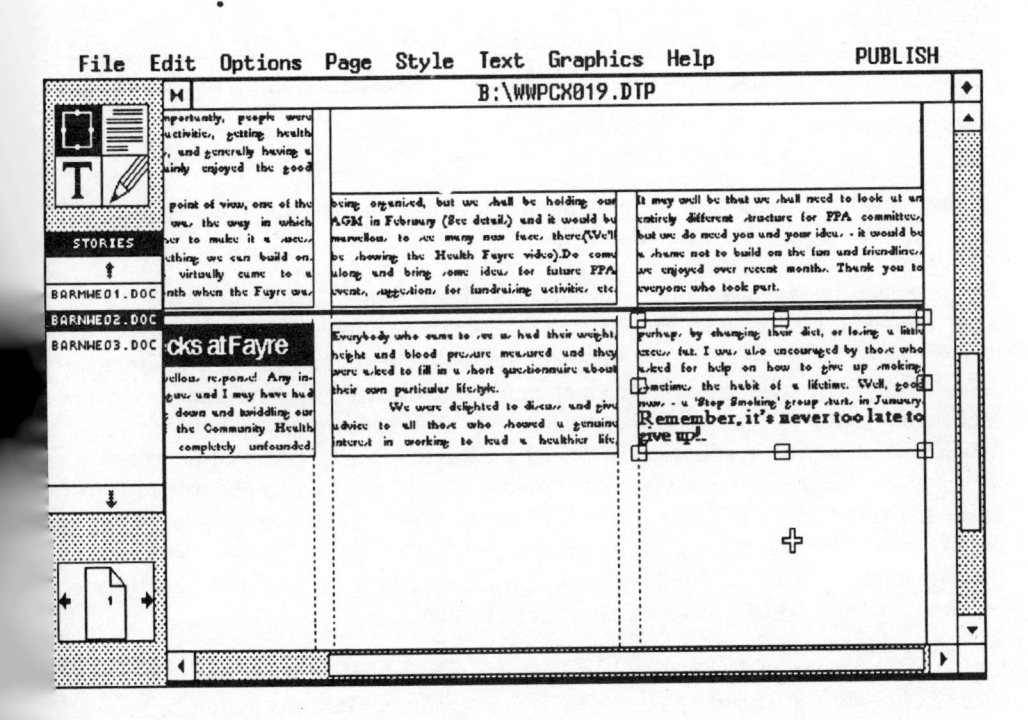

Figure 7.27 Story 2 Step 3

Finally, when viewed on screen, the text was observed to be slightly misaligned between columns one and two. The headline frame was positioned vertically, using the {OPTIONS} - [Size and position] controls to adjust the text position in the first frame to line up with the other columns.

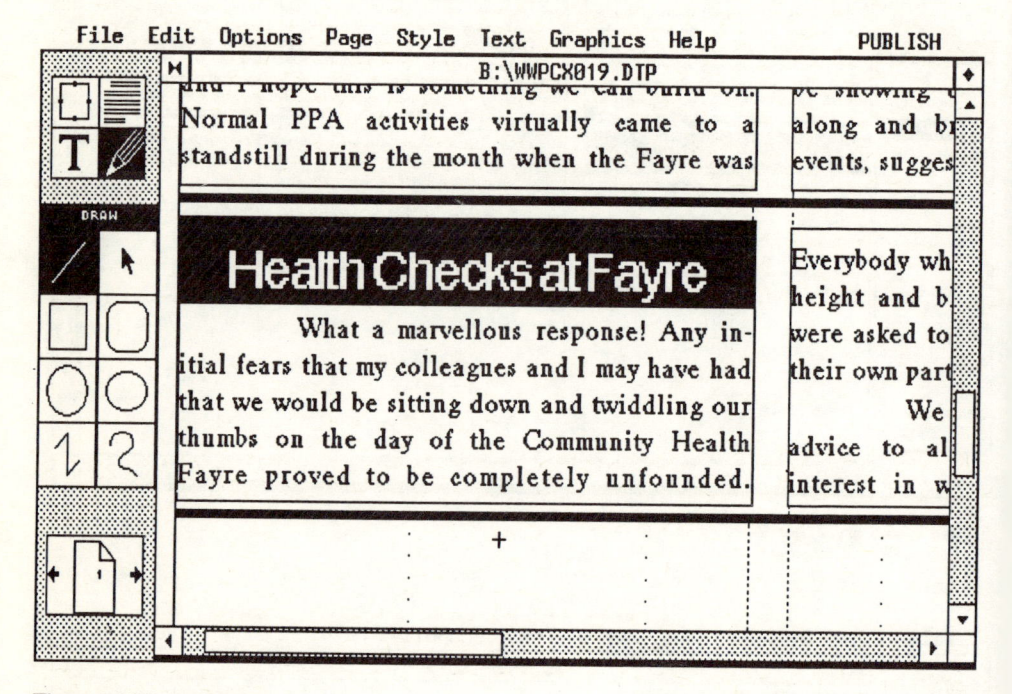

Figure 7.28 Story 2 Step 4

Use the graphics facilities, exactly as before, to create the second dividing line, and move on to the final part of the page.

The first step in this last block is to create a single frame, across the whole of the page to contain the headline, again fixing the final frame height after we have set the text size, etc. Using the text tool, enter the text into the frame, which will adopt the default body text style. Select the paragraph tool, highlight the text and assign the subheading style. To finalise the headline we assign the maximum text size available which will allow the headline to fit across the page. Use the text tool to select the text, and choose the 24 point text size. Finally, adjust the frame height so that it just holds the text size (2,06), and position it on the page. (Note that it is possible to modify text styles while using the paragraph tool, but remember that this will modify the paragraph style for the whole document, which may not be desirable. Use the text tool to assign individual text styles to avoid this situation)

Create three frames, of height 12,00, as before, to hold the third story, but in this case give the left-most a border, as this will contain a picture. The final story can be used to fill up the other two frames.

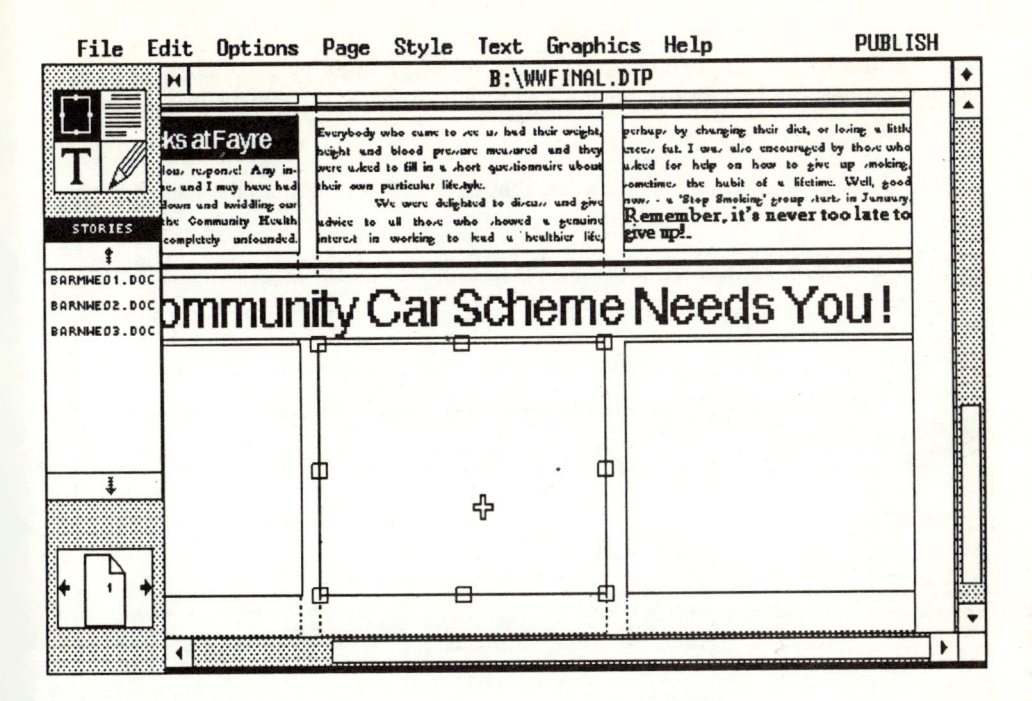

Figure 7.29 Story 3 Step 1

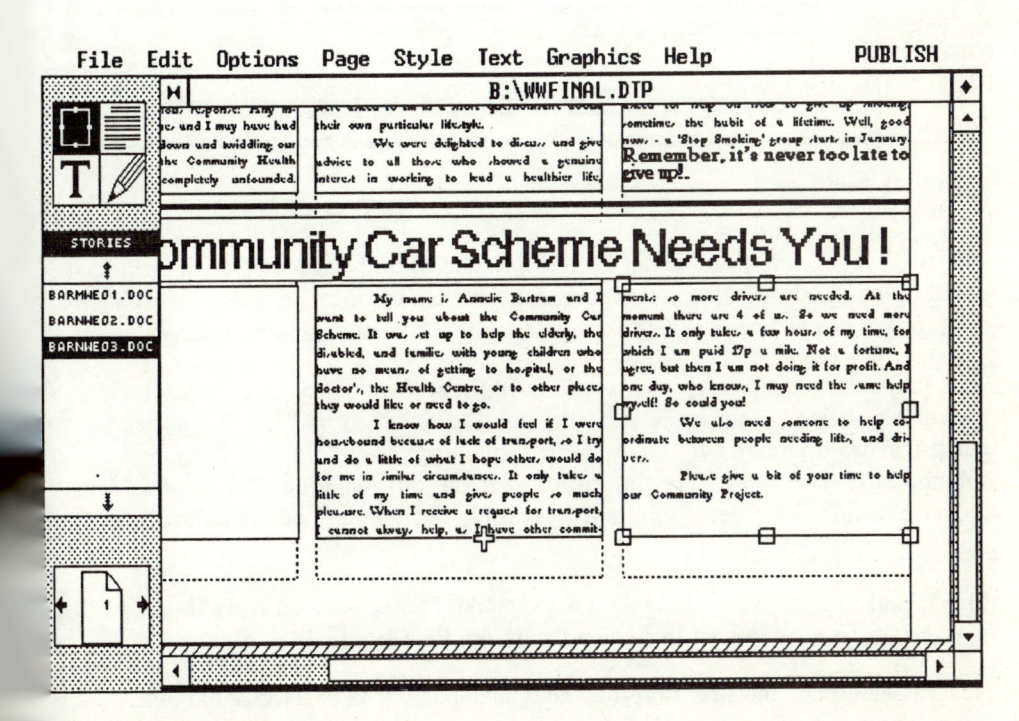

Figure 7.30 Story 3 Step 2

Once again we have made the frame a little too large to contain the sections of the story uniformly, and the height needs to be modified slightly. By a little bit of trial and error, the optimum frame height was found to be 11,06, which was set for all three frames.

Adding the final line graphics, below the frames as before, finalises the page design.

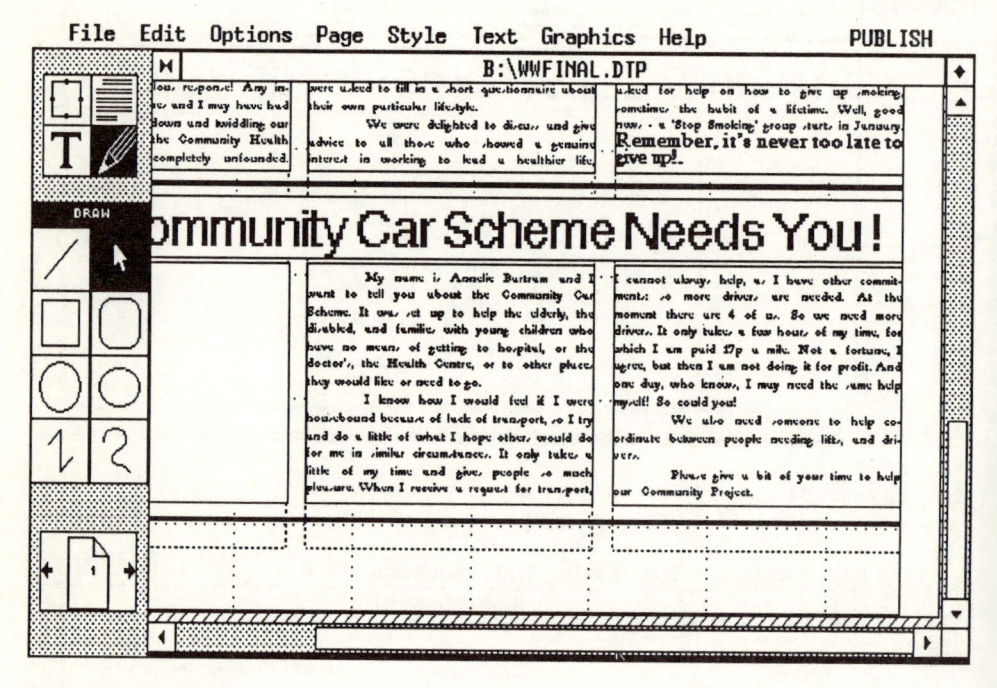

Figure 7.31 Story 3 step 3

The final step in the page layout is to review the overall page on a test printout, and make some final adjustments of frame positions, in order to achieve a balanced appearance. In practice with this example very few adjustments were necessary.

This particular example represents a fairly difficult layout from the point of view of text manipulations. This arose from the basic decision to allocate the stories in the particular way chosen, in order to accommodate, and isolate, short individual submissions. The more straightforward method of assigning text to full length columns would have been substantially easier, but perhaps not appropriate in this case.

This added complexity in design, however, should be considered early in the process as it does have a significant impact on the design time required.

Nevertheless, once the first story had been manipulated satisfactorily the others were fairly simple to produce, requiring just a few steps.

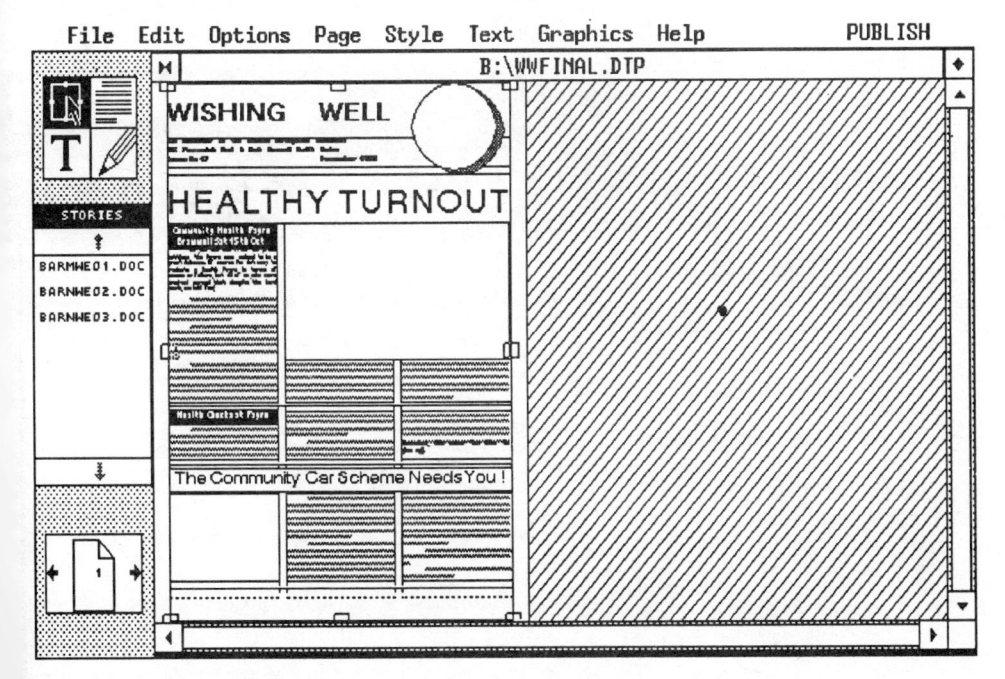

Figure 7.32 Final Page Layout

The selection of the ruler spacing in picas and points was also helpful in allowing manipulations in frame sizes to relate to text dimensions. In particular, this was important where it was necessary to make very small adjustments in frame size and/or position in order to get text to align properly across the columns.

Travel Club Newsletter

This third example is a contrived newsletter, designed specifically just to show how a very complex page design, such as that shown in Figure 7.33, can be put together using some very basic ideas.

We are not going into a detailed explanation of how this page is designed, as it is now time that you started to use your own initiative.

Most of the techniques used in this document have been covered in some detail in earlier sections of the book.

The newsletter is constructed by assembling a number of different frames, from a variety of sources, with the text frames constructed using only the internal functions of the Timeworks Publisher program. The individual frames used to build up the final page are isolated, and identified in Fig 7.34 (a) and (b).

Frames 1,2,3 and 8 are all derived from clip art files which are available commercially, and scaled to suit the page layout using the normal controls.

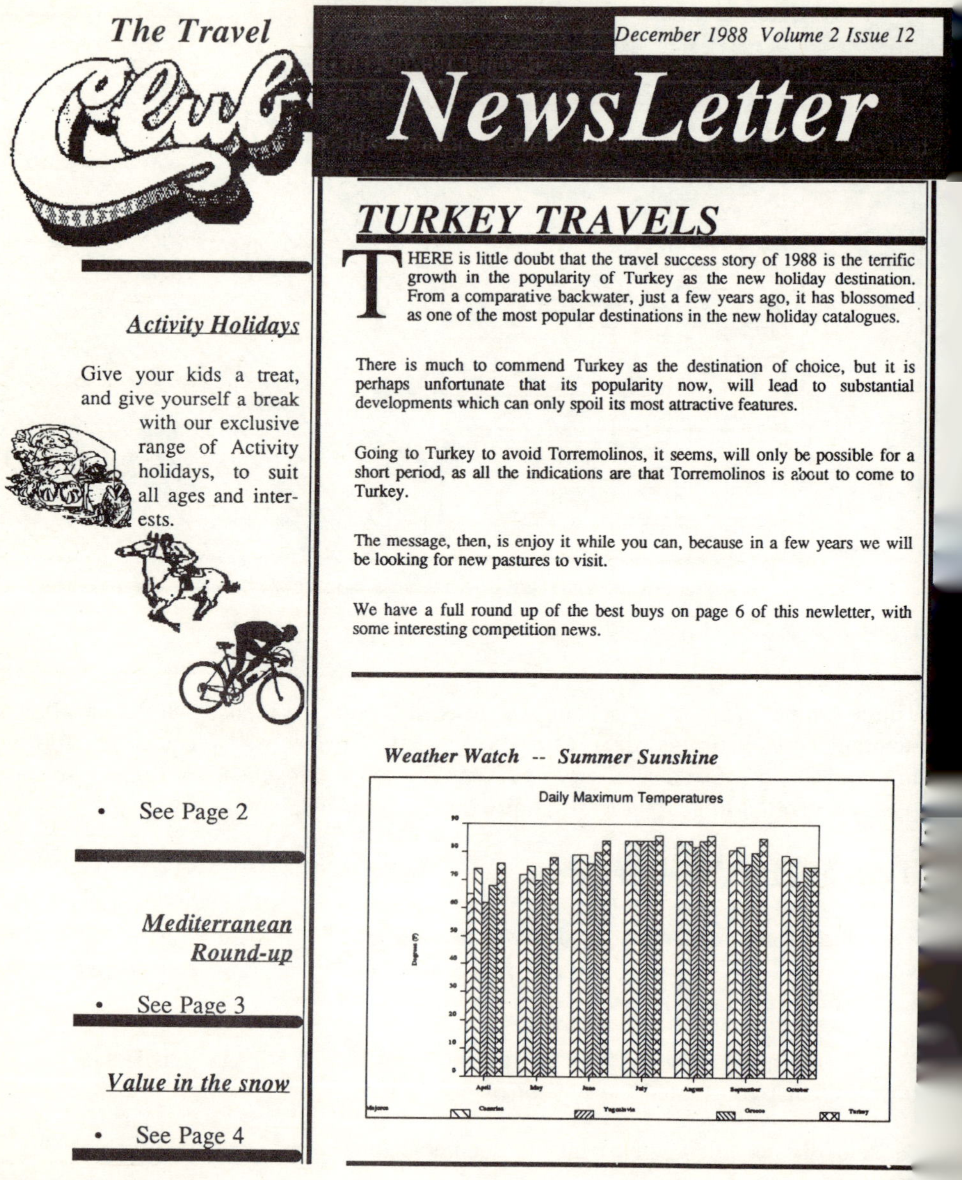

The Travel Club NewsLetter

December 1988 Volume 2 Issue 12

TURKEY TRAVELS

THERE is little doubt that the travel success story of 1988 is the terrific growth in the popularity of Turkey as the new holiday destination. From a comparative backwater, just a few years ago, it has blossomed as one of the most popular destinations in the new holiday catalogues.

There is much to commend Turkey as the destination of choice, but it is perhaps unfortunate that its popularity now, will lead to substantial developments which can only spoil its most attractive features.

Going to Turkey to avoid Torremolinos, it seems, will only be possible for a short period, as all the indications are that Torremolinos is about to come to Turkey.

The message, then, is enjoy it while you can, because in a few years we will be looking for new pastures to visit.

We have a full round up of the best buys on page 6 of this newsletter, with some interesting competition news.

Activity Holidays

Give your kids a treat, and give yourself a break with our exclusive range of Activity holidays, to suit all ages and interests.

- See Page 2

Mediterranean Round-up

- See Page 3

Value in the snow

- See Page 4

Weather Watch -- Summer Sunshine

Daily Maximum Temperatures

Figure 7.33 Club Newsletter

Frames 6, 7, 9, 10 and 12 are text frames, produced using the normal functions of the program, with the text in frame 7 using the techniques described later for producing dropped capitals.

Frame 11 is, again, a normal text frame, using white text on a selected darker fill style.

TURKEY TRAVELS

HERE is little doubt that the travel success story of 1988 is the terrific growth in the popularity of Turkey as the new holiday destination. From a comparative backwater, just a few years ago, it has blossomed as one of the most popular destinations in the new holiday catalogues.

There is much to commend Turkey as the destination of choice, but it is perhaps unfortunate that its popularity now, will lead to substantial developments which can only spoil its most attractive features.

Going to Turkey to avoid Torremolinos, it seems, will only be possible for a short period, as all the indications are that Torremolinos is about to come to Turkey.

The message, then, is enjoy it while you can, because in a few years we will be looking for new pastures to visit.

We have a full round up of the best buys on page 6 of this newletter, with some interesting competition news.

Activity Holidays

Give your kids a treat, and give yourself a break with our exclusive range of Activity holidays, to suit all ages and interests.

- See Page 2

Mediterranean Round-up

- See Page 3

Value in the snow

- See Page 4

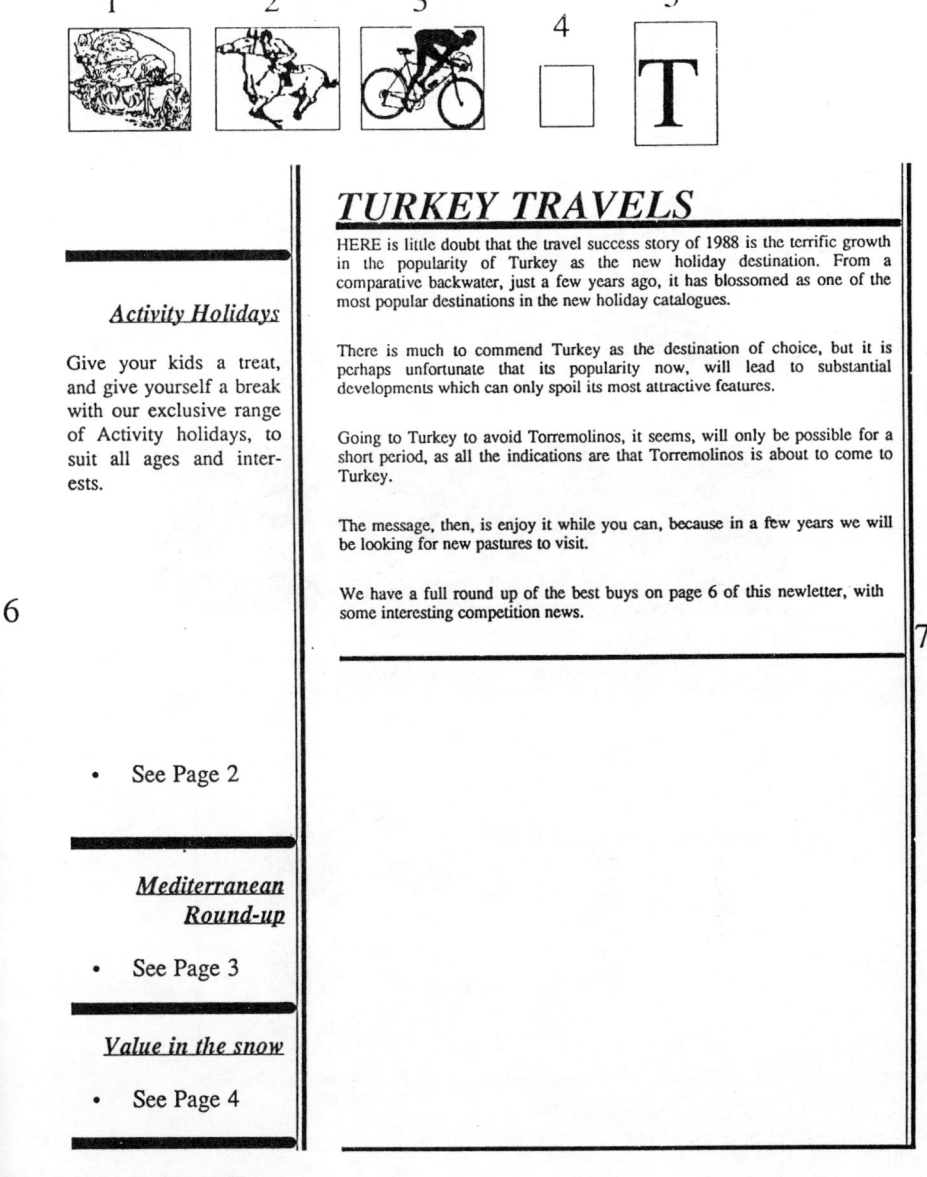

Figure 7.34 (a) Newsletter Elements

The graph in frame 13 was produced on Lotus 123, and imported into the document as a .PIC file, and offered no particular problems. Only one small area of difficulty was apparent with this. If you look closely at the frame you will note that the left and legend block has not appeared (lower left hand corner), although this was apparent on the original file. This appears to be a minor problem with importing these files, as no manipulation would allow this block to appear in the printed document.

8

9
The Travel

December 1988 Volume 2 Issue 12   10

11
NewsLetter

Weather Watch -- Summer Sunshine   12

Daily Maximum Temperatures

13

Figure 7.34 (b) Further Newsletter Elements

As with the line art file, the .PIC files allow no editing functions beyond resizing the frame, but they also do not demand high memory requirements for printing.

Once all the individual frames are created they can then be assembled to produce final document.

Now it is up to you to show what the program can do for you!

8

A Little Bit More About...

Printers and Printing

When this book was first planned it was intended to devote a whole chapter to printing and printers. However this turns out to be such a straightforward process that only a few short comments are appropriate.

Selecting the Printer

This is carried out during the initial installation process, using the INSTALL program supplied. This is called up from the Timeworks Publisher INSTALL.EXE file, on the DTP master disk 1. However, the printer drivers are those supplied with GEM, and are not specific to the Timeworks Publisher program.

Timeworks Publisher is designed to work with six classes of printer:

) 9 pin dot matrix printers, which allow a print resolution of 120 (Horizontal) x 144 (Vertical) dots per inch (dpi).

    Gem Drivers: Epson Hi (FX/MX Series)
                             IBM Proprinter

) 24 pin dot matrix printers, which allow a print resolution of 180 x 180 dpi.

    Gem Drivers: Epson LQ
                             Toshiba P321,341,351

) Laser printers using dot image processing which allow a print resolution of 150 x 150 dpi.

    Gem Drivers: HP LaserJet +

4) Laser printers using dot image processing, which allow a print resolution of 300 x 300 dpi.

    Gem Drivers: HP LaserJet II
                               Epson GQ3500

5) Laser Printers using the Postscript page description language. This allows a graphics resolution of 300 x 300 dpi, and in addition allow the use of a wider range of fonts.

    Gem Drivers: Postscript 12 (Standard Fonts)
                               Postscript 35 (Extended Fonts)
                               Laserwriter/Laserwriter Plus

6) Xerox 4020 Colour Ink Jet Printer, allowing a graphics resolution of 120 x 240 dpi.

    Gem Drivers: Xerox 4020

All of the printers can work with various different sizes of paper, although the laser printers may well have some restrictions on the sizes which can use the auto paper feed functions. This will need to be investigated if you are contemplating the purchase of such a system. In many cases, however, the standard A4 size will be used, and this is easily accommodated by all the printer types.

Using the dot matrix printers is remarkably easy, once you have specified the appropriate printer driver during the set up process. From the list indicated above it is necessary to choose that which corresponds most closely with your own printer. The graphics capabilities of most printers would appear to be quite similar, within the groups specified above. This is not necessarily true of their normal text characteristics. Although most software now provides for a wide range of different printers, you will almost inevitably find that your printer is not listed on some. In this case you need to determine which of those available most closely matches the characteristics of your printer. Frequently it is necessary to experiment with different selections to get the best results for your particular printer.

Lasers printers are selected in the same way, although they may not be quite as straightforward. There are an increasing number of different laser printers now on the market, and it is unclear how closely they follow any standard in terms of their software control. Postscript printers should safely be expected to adhere closely to that standard. However other types of laser printers have their own systems of operating, though many claim to emulate another standard, usually the HP LaserJet II.

How closely this emulation is effective it is difficult to say. Remember, however, that GEM provides drivers only for the HP LaserJet and the Epson GQ printers, and that any laser selected to work with this application must be capable of emulating either of these very closely. Do not buy a laser printer without first trying it out with your major applications, to ensure compatibility.

Paper Alignment

The only small problem experienced with using dot matrix printers has been in the physical alignment of the paper. Most software assumes that the printer can access ALL of the sheet of paper. In practice, however, most tractor or roller feed printer mechanisms make it difficult to align the start of the print with the top edge of the page. This can be overcome with continuous paper, but not when using single sheets. On many printers, the first print line is at least half an inch below the paper top margin, when using single sheets. A similar problem may arise with the print width, or with the fixed left hand margins of the printer.

Fortunately, this is relatively easy to overcome from within Timeworks Publisher. When setting up our master pages, explained in chapter 3, we noted that within the [Set Column guides] option in the {OPTIONS} menu, allowance is made to adjust printer offset. This allows you to enter the information concerning the actual offsets caused by your printer mechanism.

In order to set this up you need first to test the printer. To do this, enter the Timeworks Publisher program, and accept the default style sheet. Create a single frame which covers all the columns, and which aligns with them. Assign a frame border to this frame, using the thin line border all around. Ensure that your printer is online, with your normal paper set in its usual position.

Open the File Menu, and select PRINT, to display the printer control panel. Ensure that the title line displays your current printer type correctly. Ignore all the other

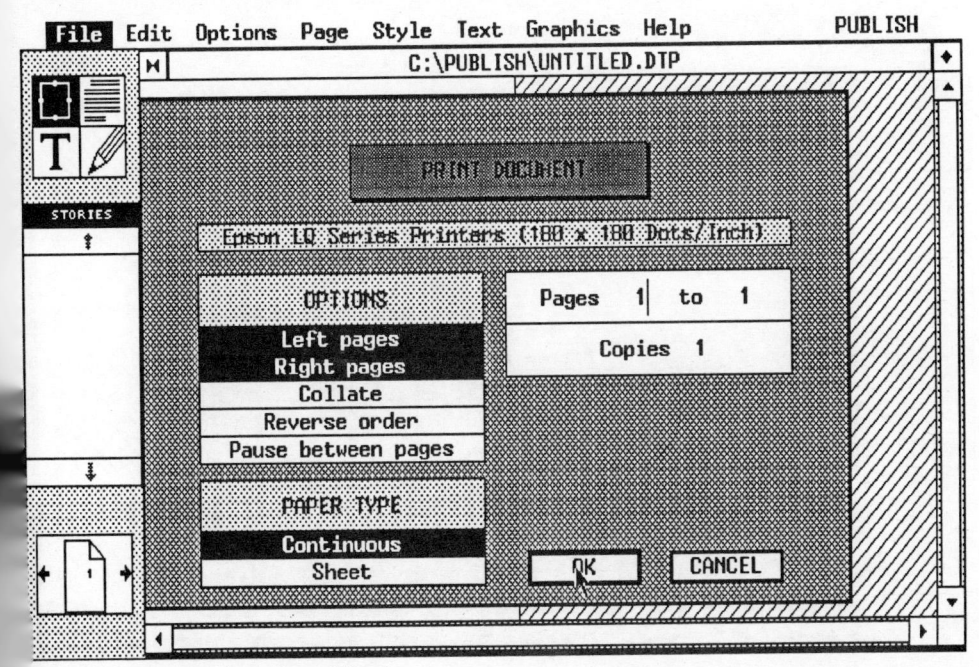

Figure 8.1 Illustrate Printer Control Panel

options except PAPER TYPE, and select either Single Sheet or Continuous as appropriate. Click on [OK], and the printout will start.

When the printout is complete, remove the paper, and measure the top and left hand margin depths, using the edges of the paper as the reference point. With the printer used while preparing this book, for example, this gave the following results:

  Top Margin 1.7"
  Left Margin 1.3"

Now the default column guide setting allows the following:

  Top Margin 1.0"
  Left Margin 1.0"

The difference between these figures represents the page offsets, which in this case gives:

  Vertical Page Offset 0.7" (Top Margins)
  Horizontal Page Offset 0.3" (Left Margins)

If your test has shown similar results these can now be entered into the column guides control screen. Open the {OPTIONS} menu, and select [SET COLUMN GUIDES..], to display the control screen. You can confirm that the defaults are as shown above, and check your own calculations.

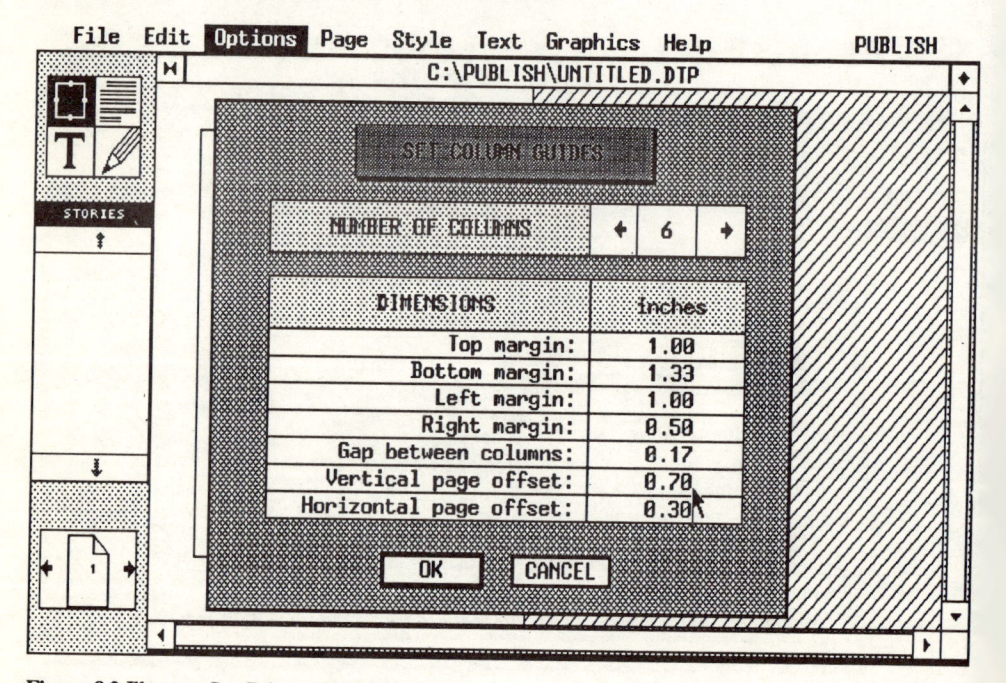

Figure 8.2 Illustrate Set Column Guides Screen

Move the cursor to the Vertical page offset box, and enter the appropriate dimension, and then do likewise for the horizontal page offset.

Now exit from this screen, by clicking on [OK], and print out the page with the new offsets included. Confirm, by again measuring the margins, that the results are now correct.

At any time in the future, when setting up your own Style Sheets, and document formats, these offsets will have to be entered into the Set Column Guides control as above. In the chapter on Style Sheets we discuss how these may be incorporated into the program default Style Sheet, so that they are immediately available when the program is started.

Generally, these offsets will not be such a problem with the laser printers, as their paper feed mechanism normally ensures correct alignment between the paper feed and the printing mechanism. If problems do arise, however, the same process can be conducted.

If you change printers, however, it is probable that you will have to modify your page offsets at the same time.

Changing Your Printer

Timeworks Publisher can only operate with one printer at a time, so if you upgrade your printer, or if you wish to have a second printer option available, then you will have to add the new printer driver to your program disk, or appropriate directory.

The Timeworks Publisher install program allows you to modify the existing set up, by changing the printer type. It is also possible to add a new printer, while leaving the other driver still in place. (Note that with earlier versions of Timeworks Publisher you can *not* use the GEMSETUP program directly for this, as there are some differences in the disk name conventions, which causes the GEM program to fail to recognise the Printer Disk).

If you choose to add a second printer driver, so that you can have greater flexibility, then the decision as to which printer to use, for a particular session, must be made by running the FONTWID program, before entering Timeworks Publisher. If you do not run the FONTWID program then the printer used in the preceding session will remain active.

To replace a current printer, or to add a new printer involves the same process. The INSTALL program is used in exactly the same way that the initial installation was achieved. Place your Timeworks Publisher Master disk in drive A:, make this the current drive, and type INSTALL. (Typing A:INSTALL from the C: drive will not work) As before the process is carried out by making a simple choice as each screen is presented, and inserting the appropriate disks as requested.

Once a new printer is installed it is then necessary to run the FONTWID program to create the necessary files. The FONTWID program can be initiated from the hard disk root directory, or from the appropriate floppy disk by typing FONTWID. It can also be called up from the GEM Desktop in the normal fashion, by double clicking on the program icon.

If you have installed two separate printers, the program will ask which driver to use for the current session, and create the necessary files. To later use the alternative printer it is necessary to exit from Timeworks Publisher and run the FONTWID program again.

It has been mentioned elsewhere in the book that, even if you do not have a Postscript printer directly available, it is possible to produce disk files from Timeworks Publisher which adopt the Postscript format. To do this it is necessary to ADD one of the Postscript printer definitions to your system, and to use this when preparing such documents.

If you have one of the non-Postscript laser printers, or even a standard dot matrix printer, you can get software which will convert Postscript files, with all the increased font sizes and variations thus available, to print out on your standard printer. One such program currently available is the GOSCRIPT emulator, produced by LaserGo, Inc, and available in the UK. For around £200 this gives standard printers the ability to print out Postscript files.

This operates by processing the files saved by Timeworks Publisher to produce the required output. The author only has experience of using this with a dot matrix printer, and found it simple to operate and produce a good quality output. The program uses the maximum print resolution of 360 x 360 available from the printer. However, it took about 50 minutes to produce a single sheet document, that used for the newsletter example in this book. Although this gives access to a wider range of fonts, and all the other benefits of Postcript facilities, in this particular application the overall print quality was not noticeably different from the standard output.

The time taken to print a document, while undoubtedly different for various types of printers, has to be a factor when considering the use of such emulators.

Fonts

The FONTS available within Timeworks Publisher are those determined by the fact that it operates within the GEM environment, and they are therefore restricted by the particular printer drivers available from GEM. All printers will support the two basic fonts supplied, Swiss and Dutch, in a range of sizes. In addition, the more advanced laser printers can support an increased number of fonts.

Using dot matrix printers the earlier version of Timeworks Publisher (1.1) allows a selection of font sizes up to 36 point. The later versions (1.12+) allow an increased number of fonts, up to 60 point, using 24 pin printers or better. (Although this still depends on your disk capacity).

With the HP LaserJet II-compatible printers font sizes only up to 36 point are available, even on the later version of the software. Only the Postscript-compatible printers allow a greater range of font sizes, and the additional font ranges.

The HP LaserJet + driver allows a greater range of fonts than the LaserJet II, and accepts the graphics characters (Bullets), although at a lower print resolution.

There are some limitations in the way that GEM handles the various fonts available to it. The fonts provided on the program disks only cover a limited range of sizes, and are only for the basic fonts, without any enhancements. The GEM program will generate intermediate size fonts, and will generate the BOLD and ITALIC enhancements. The fonts that are available for printing, and for display, are therefore a combination of basic fonts supplied on the program disks and the internal manipulations of GEM, including the operation of the FONTWID program. If you look at the FONTS directory you will be able to identify the various files readily.

Printer Fonts are identified by an extension, which relates to the printer type specified. e.g. *.ELQ = Epson LQ, *.B30 = HP LaserJet +

Display Fonts are identified by an extension, which identifies the display type in use. e.g. *.CGA, *.VGA, etc.

The basic Font is identified by the first two letters of the file name. AA = Swiss Font
AI = Dutch Font

The font size is indicated by the 3 numbers following the font identifier. e.g. 060 = 6 Point, 280 = 28 point

The Bullet fonts are identified by the initial letters TWDB.

Additional fonts can be added to the program, if required. This can be achieved using special font generation software, available from a number of sources. The only system of which the author has direct experience is the BITSTREAM FONTWARE program, which is available with some versions of GEM 3 and, of course, from the publishers themselves.

Before deciding to add fonts indiscriminately, however, you should be aware that each font occupies an appreciable amount of disk space. For example, the *.ELQ files, for 24 pin (LQ) printers vary in size from 3246 bytes for the 7 point font, to 32746 bytes for the 60 point font. Separate files, of similar sizes, also have to be created for the screen fonts. In fact, to have the luxury of being able to switch between two printers, using the FONTWID program, and just using the standard fonts available, my fonts directory occupies a total of 638971 bytes.

Some memory saving has been achieved by limiting the range of on-screen fonts available. Within Timeworks Publisher, only certain of the fonts reproduce accurately on the screen, although proper allowance is made for spacing, etc. In practice, the largest screen font to appear correctly is 36 point.

Using the Bitstream Fontware program is quite straightforward, and will not be detailed here. The version available within GEM 3 is provided with the Swiss and Dutch typefaces already available within the Timeworks Publisher package, as well as the Bitstream CHARTER typeface. Note, however, that in the Bitstream Fontware program the basic Swiss and Dutch typefaces in fact provide, as separate typefaces, the Normal (termed Roman), Italic, Bold and Bold Italic typefaces. That is, using Bitstream you would normally need to generate separate fonts for each typeface variation. With the current version of Timeworks Publisher there is little to be gained from adding extra fonts in the same family. (The Charter typeface is so similar to the Dutch that it is not a worthwhile addition).

The range of different fonts available from Bitstream, is extremely comprehensive, and for special applications may well be worth consideration, where the disk capacity is available.

One other point to make is that although it is possible to use the Bitstream Fontware within Timeworks Publisher, the program only recognises the existence of the basic (Roman) font files, and ignores the other variations. Instead, it continues to produce the Bold and Italic variations internally. This point has now been rectified on the most recent release of Timeworks Publisher (1F12 plus), which will now recognise all separate fonts.

At the time of completion of this manuscript the publishers of Timeworks Publisher have introduced their own new font generation program called Typografica. Unlike Bitstream, this will operate on floppy-based systems, making it much more practical to access a wider range of fonts. In addition, at a total cost of £99 (plus VAT) you get full access to a very wide range of fonts, including Symbols and Dingbats. It is possible to generate exactly the screen and printer fonts that you require for any particular application. The system is easy to use and is specifically designed to work with Timeworks Publisher, but is also compatible with the other major DTP programs.

ITC Avant Garde *Italic* **Bold** ***Bold Italic***
ITC Bookman *Italic* **Bold** ***Bold Italic***
Century Schoolbook *Italic* **Bold** ***Bold Italic***
Palermo *Italic* **Bold** ***Bold Italic***
Sans *Italic* **Bold** ***Bold Italic***
Sans Narrow *Italic* **Bold** ***Bold Italic***
Serif *Italic* **Bold** ***Bold Italic***
Courier *Italic* **Bold** ***Bold Italic***
ITC Zapf Chancery Medium Italic
Symbols φ γ η ∴ ζ ξ θ ω ε ρ τ ψ υ ι ο π [ ] α σ δ
Dingbats ❑ ➤ ✳ ✶ ■ ❘ ✿ ❖ ☯ ■ ○ ✗ ✎ ☞ ✪ ▲ ✾ ✽

Figure 8.3 Typografica Font Range

If you wish to extend the typefaces available, using either dot matrix printers or HP LaserJet-compatibles, then this is a realistic route, provided that you have the disk capacity. To preserve valuable disk space, however, only produce those font files that will actually be required, even if it means keeping separate font families on floppy disk, for use in particular applications. For example, it is highly unlikely that in a properly designed document, you would use more than 6 different font sizes, and two or three typefaces.

Remember, also, that when you produce new font files they must be placed in the appropriate directory (C:\GEMAPPS\FONTS), or your FONTS disk in the floppy system, and must be activated by using the FONTWID program before they can be used within Timeworks Publisher. Creating new font families is also quite a slow process, although Typografica seems substantially faster than Bitstream, and may take well over an hour for an extensive range.

Text and Paragraph Formatting and Effects

In the chapters on Text and Paragraph styles we have looked at the more widely used applications. There are, however, a few special effects which can be achieved with a fuller understanding of the system as a whole.

There are a number of special effects frequently employed in producing documents which make use of mixed text sizes and the use of the so-called hanging indent. Various options of this are demonstrated in the illustration (Figs 8.4 a-d). These examples are achieved in the following ways:

> A Hanging Indent is frequently used to give emphasis to particular sections of text. In its simplest form, however is is not particularly attractive.
>
> Figure 8.4(a)

This is a straightforward application of the paragraph style definition. When defining the styles use the DIMENSIONS control to create a Left Indent which is greater than the First Line Indent. In the example shown, these have been set as follows (using picas and points measurements):First Line Left Indent = 0,00 ;Left Indent = 3,00. These values can easily be adjusted to suit the particular requirement.

Figure 8.4 (a) is another very simple effect. The text is entered as normal text, and the first letter is selected and re-sized as required. The normal program actions will adjust the text spacing as appropriate.

> Another common effect is to use a large size capital, as an eye-catcher. This can be used with or without an indented paragraph.
>
> Figure 8.4(b)

> As we can see with this example which uses the same paragraph setting as example (a) above.
>
> Figure 8.4(c)

This combines the techniques of (a) and (b). Using the dimension controls a hanging paragraph is created with a suitable offset. The text is entered as usual, and the first letter is selected and adjusted to suit. It is difficult, for example, to make just the first letter offset from the paragraph, due to the different widths of the individual letters.

This next example is created by using the dimension controls to produce a uniformly offset paragraph. That is, both the first line left indent, and the normal left indent have the same value. The capital is produced in its own frame, and the repel text function is turned OFF. This frame is then positioned in relation to the text, as required. Here the screen resolution

> A similar effect can be achieved using a paragraph with a full indent , and with a large capital inserted, using a separate frame. This can be a little difficult to implement due to some of the problems with the screen representation of fonts of different sizes.
>
> Figure 8.4(d)

may be a significant problem, and a trial print will be necessary to make the positioning precise. This is one of the cases where using the Pica and Point measurements become most useful, as the best position match is provided by adjusting the capital frame location in discrete 1 point steps to match in with the normal test spacing. Some aspects of the following, relating to text styles and frame sizes, may also be appropriate.

The last example of this group is, relatively, the most difficult to achieve. There are probably a number of different ways to get this effect, and the following is only one approach.

> THE most difficult to achieve is the true 'DROPPED' capital effect, within the text body itself. There are a number of individual ways to approach this problem, and here we present one possible solution. Once more the main difficulty arises because of the limitations on the screen display.
>
> Figure 8.4(e)

Screen representation is once more a limit here, and the usual trial prints will be required to confirm the final output. To achieve the neatest effect particular care has to be taken to match the size of the capital with the size and spacing of the main text. The best, and visually the only really acceptable, arrangement is for the capital size to match up exactly with a uniform number of lines of text. This can be achieved with a good degree of precision with sufficient care. But, as usual, it is a personal decision as to whether the precision required is justified in the particular application. To make this latter step a little easier the table in Figure 8.5 shows the parameters necessary to achieve this match using the standard range of fonts available for dot matrix printers. This involves selecting both the text size of the capital, and the text size *and* leading for the normal text.

TEXT SIZE & LEADING	2 LINE	3 LINE	4 LINE	5 LINE
7/8	20			
7/9	20			60
7/10		36		
8/9				60
8/11	24			
10/11			60	
10/12	28	46		
14/15	36	60		
14/16	36	60		
16/19	46			

Figure 8.5 Point Size Table for Dropped Capitals to match given lines of text.

Using a PostScript printer you have the ability to change the capital height in steps of one point, and although the same type of calculation is necessary it is easier to achieve a perfect match. With the table indicated only a few of the items provide a close enough match for most work, but this gives quite an adequate range of choices. If you wish to perform the calculation yourself, the equation used is:

$$P = 1.5 * [(\text{Point size of text}) * 0.66 + (\text{Leading} * (N-1))]$$

where P is the point size of the dropped capital and N is the number of matching lines. The values 0.66 and 1.5 are derived from the heights of capitals and descenders and may need to be altered for different fonts. As an example, to match a drpped capital with N=3 lines of text set in 10 point on 12 point leading:

$$P = 1.5 * [10 * 0.66 + 12 * (3-1)] = 45.9 \text{ (i.e., approximately 46 points)}$$

Once the selection has been made the normal text can be entered using the set parameters, in the normal way. If the dropped capital is to be the first letter of the paragraph then this should be omitted from the text, as this will be added later, in its own frame.

When the text is entered we wish to adjust the position on the appropriate number of lines to make room for the capital. To do this the most consistent method is to create a 'DUMMY' frame, and position this so that the appropriate section of text is moved. The size of the dummy frame will need to be adjusted for each particular application, depending on the capital size chosen. The height is consistent for all letters, and can be the same as the line and spacing dimension for the appropriate text selection. The width may need to be adjusted slightly to cater for the different width of the various characters, within a fairly narrow range for each text size used.

The dummy frame is created outside the text area, and the size is set using the {OPTIONS} - [Size and Position] control. It can then be positioned on the screen to make appropriate space for the large capital. The repel text function must be ON for this frame, but the horizontal and vertical spacing should be set to 0,00.

Finally, as in the earlier example, the capital letter is created in a separate frame, and dragged into position on the page. The frame parameters for this must include setting the repel text to OFF, and the visibility to CLEAR. The actual size of the frame required to hold the capital does depend on the text size chosen, and the frame should be sized at the minimum required to contain the letter.

To help minimise the size of the frame to hold the capital, as this will simplify the positioning, it is worth creating a paragraph style (DROPCAPXX) which sets the following (and where XX represents the point size of the capital):

> Dimensions: Set all values to 0,00 (except leading)
> Leading: Set leading to *half* the point size of the selected capital text. (Do not ask for an explanation of this, as this figure arises from substantial experimentation with different settings, and probably defies explanation).
> Options: Flushed left
> Font/Size : As required
> Style: As required.

The letter should be entered into the frame using the normal body text style, and then reset using the paragraph style controls. The frame should then be re-sized to the minimum required to display the text.

As a final point of design, it is thought that the appearance is enhanced if the letters of the first word in the text are all entered as capitals, and then reverting to normal for the balance of the text.

To ensure that the above is valid you should attempt the following exercise. After a little practice, this seemingly cumbersome exercise becomes quite straightforward.

With a clear screen, select the {OPTIONS} - [Ruler spacing..] controls to set the ruler to picas and points. Create a single frame of width 21,00 and height 14,00, approximately. Select actual size or double size page view as required. From the table (Fig 8.5), which shows the text combinations where the best matches can be achieved, we choose the combination text size 10/12, with a capital size of 46 point.

Create a Body Text style with Font/Size set to Dutch 10 point, for which the default leading is 12 point. Enter the following short text, exactly as shown:

```
'HIS is a demonstration of one method of achieving a true
'DROPPED CAPITAL' effect in the Timeworks Publisher package.
This involves a few, basically simple, steps, although using a
mixture of frames to get the desired effect. For this demonst-
ration we have selected a text size/leading of 10/12 to match
with three lines for a dropped capital size of 46 point'
```

(Note that the 'T' is deliberately omitted from the first word.)

Create a dummy frame, outside the current frame, with the following parameters:

> Height: 31 point
> Width: 31 point (this may need adjustment later)
> Repel text: ON
> Vertical & Horizontal Spacing: 0,00

Move this into the text frame so that the left hand edges of both frames align. The vertical position should be adjusted so that the upper and lower edges of the dummy frame align with the top three lines of text, and create a space for the large capital.

> HIS is a demonstration of one method of achieving a
> true 'DROPPED CAPITAL' effect in the Timeworks
> package. This involves a few, basically simple, steps,
> though using a mixture of frames to get the desired effect.
> For this demonstration we have selected a text size/leading of
> 10/12 to match with three lines for a dropped capital size of
> 46 point.

Figure 8.6(a) Dummy Frame in Position

Create a paragraph style 'DROPCAP46', which has the following parameters:

> Text Size: 46
> Point Font: Dutch
> Leading: 23 Point (From the dimensions control)
> Format: Flushed left

Create an additional frame, outside of the main text area, initially of size about 6,00 square. Use the text control to enter the letter 'T' into this frame, and apply the paragraph style 'DROPCAP46' to this. Re-size the frame so that it is just large enough to fit the letter, which in this example requires:

> Width: 3,11
> Height: 4,04

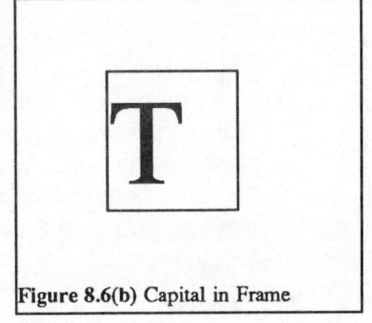

Figure 8.6(b) Capital in Frame

This last step is perhaps the most difficult, as with this size the font is not correctly represented on screen.

Horizontal alignment is achieved by aligning the left frame edge with that of the main text frame. As you can see from the screen dump illustrated below, the vertical alignment required is not well reproduced on screen.

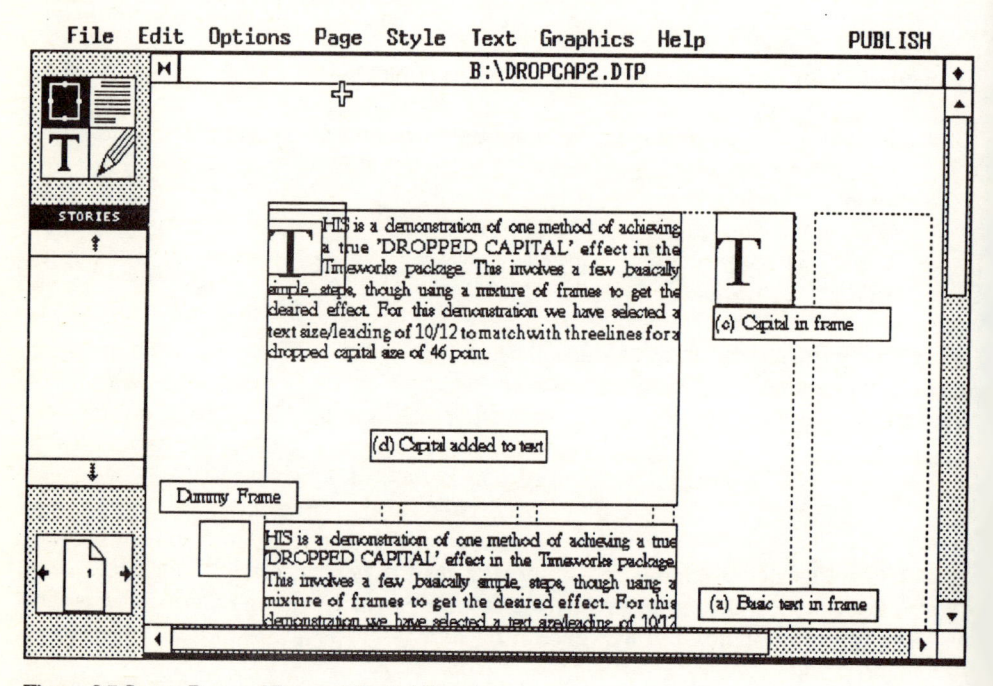

Figure 8.7 Screen Dump of Dropped Capital Exercise

Here it is necessary to first set this frame approximately central with the vertical position of the normal text, and create a trial print. Final positioning can be fairly well estimated from this printout, and adjustments in the vertical position to an accuracy of 1 point can be made using the [Size and position] controls. In the example, this required a horizontal position of 6,00, which corresponds to the normal page margin, and a vertical position of 5,08.

> THIS is a demonstration of one method of achieving a true 'DROPPED CAPITAL' effect in the Timeworks package. This involves a few, basically simple, steps, though using a mixture of frames to get the desired effect. For this demonstration we have selected a text size/leading of 10/12 to match with three lines for a dropped capital size of 46 point.

Figure 8.8 Dropped Capital Printout

After a little practice with the different point sizes it becomes quite straightforward to estimate the correct position for this frame, within very close margins.

To adjust the horizontal spacing between the capital and the rest of the text you can adjust the width of the dummy frame, or set the [Repel Text] vertical spacing to any required value. This latter method should be used, for example, if you want to give the dummy frame a tint, to provide a background for the dropped capital.

Item Lists

The hanging indent facility can also be used to generate the layout for itemised lists, although there are some limitations to using this.

The list illustrated in Figure 8.9, which is an extract from some training material produced using Timeworks Publisher, was achieved using the following settings, in a style called DOUBLEIND (For 'Double indent').

First line left indent:	0.00
Left Indent:	2.50
Format:	Table
First tab:	1: 1.00 inch left
Second tab:	2: 2.50 inch left

The main point here is that the final tab position should correspond exactly with the left indent measurement. Then, as before when we were discussing tables, etc., the text should be entered with just a single tab between each segment. The first line of each section will take up the specified tab settings, and all following lines will align with the left indent setting to produce the table illustrated.

There are two major limitations with this system. Firstly, the first text on the line can only occupy a single line, and true side-by-side paragraph configuration is not possible using this procedure. Secondly, it is not possible to select justified text for the main body of the text. Table format and justified text are mutually exclusive selections, within the options menus. (The vertical lines in the illustration are there just to show the tab positions, and are not a necessary part of the process).

To achieve side-by-side paragraph layout the different sections of text need to be entered into separate side-by-side frames, taking care to keep proper alignment between the various sections.

Hyphenation and Word and Letter Spacing

In addition to the major controls over the appearance of text, such as the selection of justified or non-justified paragraphs, and the choice of fonts, etc., Timeworks Publisher allows more detailed manipulation of the text appearance by three principle controls:

The Lotus Function Keys

Within the Lotus 123 program the function keys, labelled F1 to F10 have been assigned special meanings as follows:

F1	HELP	This is used to call up the Lotus help program, which provides additional information to assist the user. The HELP files must be available on the Hard Disk, or on the appropriate floppy disk.
F2	EDIT	This is used when it is required to modify the entry to a cell. With short entries it may be easier to re-enter the data rather than use the edit function. This key operates on the current active cell only.
F3	NAME	Used in conjunction with the RANGE NAME functions, this displays a list of defined range names for selection.
F4	ABS	This is used to specify ABSOLUTE CELL REFERENCES, and switches between absolute, mixed and relative references.
F5	GOTO	Used to move the cell pointer quickly to a particular cell location.
F6	WINDOW	Used to switch between windows, when split screen is in use.
F7	QUERY	Repeats a /DATA QUERY command
F8	TABLE	Repeats a /DATA TABLE command
F9	CALC	Recalculates the worksheet, in READY mode. Converts cell formula to value in EDIT mode.
F10	GRAPH	Draws the most recently defined graph.

Figure 8.9 Itemised List

> Word spacing
> Letter spacing
> Hyphenation.

The first two items are of most importance where we have selected justified text Hyphenation has a part to play in all text layout patterns.

When we specify justified text in a paragraph, the program has to scan the text to arrive at some optimum selection for the number of words that can be fitted in a single line. As it is very rare for a group of words to have exactly the right combination of letters and spaces to fit in any given line, further options are required.

In the normal mode of operation Timeworks Publisher will vary both the spacing between words and, where necessary, the spacing between individual letters to achieve the best appearance.

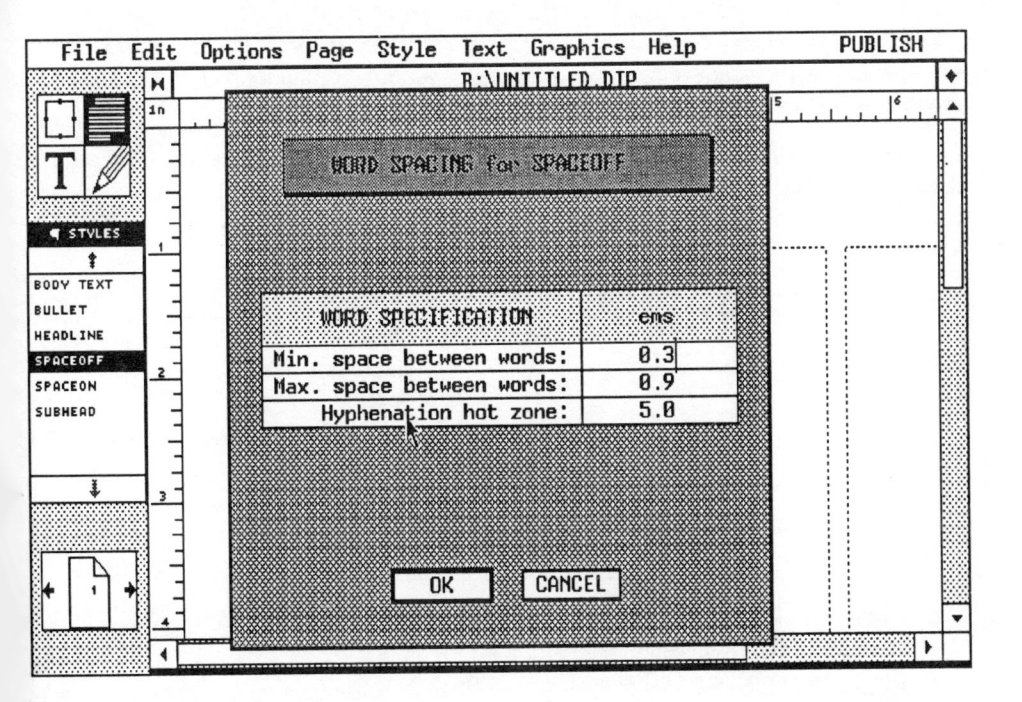

Figure 8.10 Letter Spacing/Hyphenation Controls

The major controls which allow us to set the various parameters relating to this are contained within the paragraph style controls. Specifically, we can select from the following options:

   Letter Spacing ON or OFF
   Hyphenation ON or OFF
   Minimum Spacing between words
   Maximum Spacing between words
   Hyphenation hot zone

If we turn the letter spacing option OFF, then we restrict the ability of the program to spread text along a line to achieve uniform appearance, where a justified style has been requested. The effect of this can be seen in the illustration (Fig 8.10), where (a) has the normal controls in action and in (b) we have disabled the letter spacing option. There are probably few applications where there is any real benefit in disabling this control.

Spacing between words can be adjusted over a range from 0 to 9.9 ems (approximately 0 to 9 character widths), with the default values set at:

   Minimum space between words 0.3 ems
   Maximum space between words 0.9 ems

The main reasons for modifying these values would be to spread, or compress, text to fit within certain space constraints. Changes should be made with care, to avoid creating an odd appearance in the text.

In some cases it is possible to set a group of conditions which create a conflict within the program, and it is evident from some of the examples (Fig 8.11) that the spacing between words does not match the normal maximum value set by the default Style Sheet.

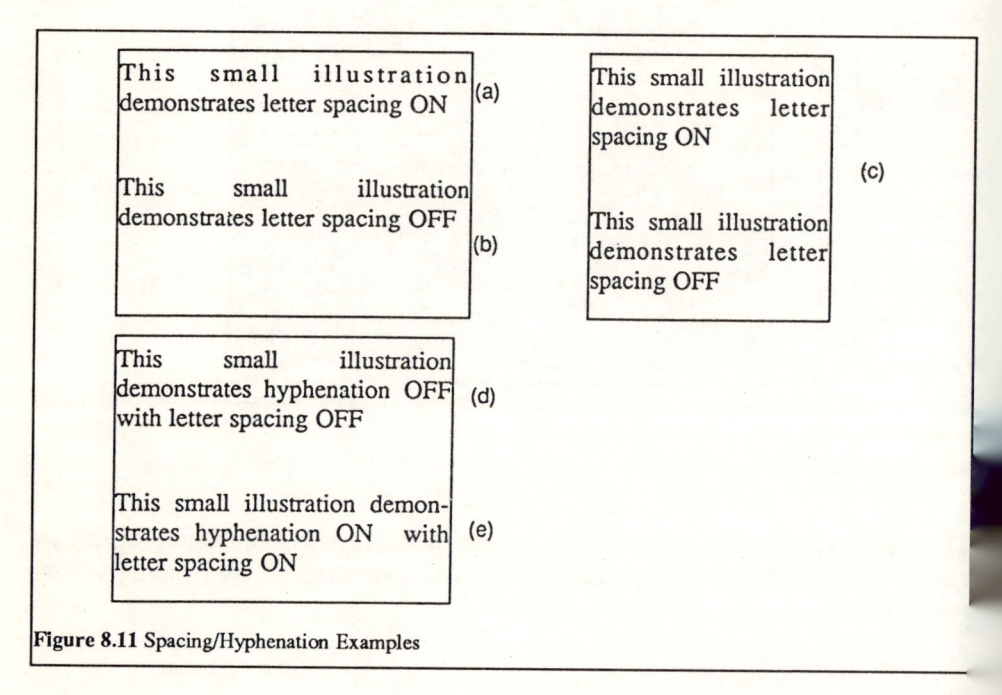

```
┌─────────────────────────────────┐   ┌──────────────────────────┐
│ This   small   illustration     │   │ This small illustration  │
│ demonstrates letter spacing ON  │(a)│ demonstrates    letter   │
│                                 │   │ spacing ON               │
│                                 │   │                          │(c)
│ This    small    illustration   │   │ This small illustration  │
│ demonstrates letter spacing OFF │   │ demonstrates    letter   │
│                                 │(b)│ spacing OFF              │
└─────────────────────────────────┘   └──────────────────────────┘

┌─────────────────────────────────┐
│ This   small    illustration    │
│ demonstrates hyphenation OFF    │(d)
│ with letter spacing OFF         │
│                                 │
│ This small illustration demon-  │
│ strates hyphenation ON  with    │(e)
│ letter spacing ON               │
└─────────────────────────────────┘
```

Figure 8.11 Spacing/Hyphenation Examples

In example (a) Timeworks Publisher has applied the maximum permitted space between individual letters, and spaced the words as evenly as possible along the first line of each example. However, in doing this it has exceeded the normal maximum word spacing allowed on the first line. By reducing the width of the text, as in example (c) the differences become less obvious.

Hyphenation is another aid to enable a more uniform appearance of text. The two most usual forms of hyphenation are:

The 'hard' hyphen, where we type in the hyphen (-) character as part of our text normally because convention dictates the placing of a hyphen to link certain word combinations. This hyphen will appear in all text, and may be used by the program as the point at which to break a word at a line ending;

and

The 'program' hyphen, where the internal Timeworks Publisher controls determine where a word should be split, in order to control line breaks in the text. Hyphens s added may be removed by the program when text is subsequently edited, and the text layout modified.

In examples (d) and (e) the hyphenation and spacing controls have been set as indicated and the frame width adjusted just sufficiently to allow the program hyphenation controls to take effect, and to illustrate the different features. By allowing the controls to split the word "demonstrate", the overall text is given a more pleasing appearance.

On some occasions, however, the program hyphenation controls may not be adequate, or may cause inappropriate splitting of words. Where there is a chance that a word may be split, and where we want to determine where that split should take place then we can use the third of the hyphenation types, the *soft hyphen*. A soft hyphen is entered into the text using the key combination [CTRL (-)]. This hyphen will normally be invisible until the particular word is required to be split. The soft hyphen will force the program to split the word, where necessary, at that point.

Hyphenation, then, is an important element in allowing the program to organise text layout for the best appearance. Where we have specified justified text the program will use all the choices available to ensure the most even spread of text.

Where we have selected non-justified text, however, the situation is a little different. There are two principle differences here, the first of which is that spacing between individual letters is less important, and no special considerations are required. Hyphenation, too, would appear less critical, but this is not always the case.

Even though we have specified a non-justified appearance, there will be cases where either word length or column width will create an exaggerated appearance of the text. In this case, the hyphenation controls will once again come into play. We can control, to a certain amount, how 'ragged' the text should be using the 'HYPHENATION HOT ZONE' controls. This figure, quoted in 'ems', and roughly equal to the number of character spaces, provides the program with information about how ragged the text can be. The larger the 'HOT ZONE' the more ragged the text. The hyphenation controls will act to maintain the required configuration as closely as possible.

The illustration (Fig 8.12) shows the same basic text, where the various controls have been set as below:

a) Hyphenation ON Letter spacing ON Justified Text

b) Hyphenation OFF Letter spacing ON Justified Text

c) Hyphenation OFF Letter spacing OFF Justified Text

d) Hyphenation OFF Ragged Text

e) Hyphenation ON Hot Zone 1.0 ems

f) Hyphenation ON Hot Zone 9.9 ems

Selection of letter spacing controls on or off made no substantial difference in the last three examples, as we would expect.

Using these controls, in conjunction with the normal paragraph style functions enables us to determine the overall appearance and layout of text with a great degree of precision. This is evident in the examples shown. Particular care has to be taken where there is a mixture of narrow column widths with long words, which provides the most demanding combination

(a) The main function of hyphenation within most DTP and word-processor packages, is to assist in achieving a more pleasing appearance to the text. This is most important when narrow columns are used, where it is difficult to achieve such control without this facility. Each program will have its own hyphenation system which determines where hyphens will be placed. Generally they will honour hyphens inserted as part of the text. An optional item, which will be

(b) The main function of hyphenation within most DTP and word-processor packages, is to assist in achieving a more pleasing appearance to the text. This is most important when narrow columns are used, where it is difficult to achieve such control without this facility. Each program will have its own hyphenation system which determines where hyphens will be placed. Generally they will honour hyphens inserted as part of the text. An optional

(c) The main function of hyphenation within most DTP and word-processor packages, is to assist in achieving a more pleasing appearance to the text. This is most important when narrow columns are used, where it is difficult to achieve such control without this facility. Each program will have its own hyphenation system which determines where hyphens will be placed. Generally they will honour hyphens inserted as part of the text. An optional

(d) The main function of hyphenation within most DTP and word-processor packages, is to assist in achieving a more pleasing appearance to the text. This is most important when narrow columns are used, where it is difficult to achieve such control without this facility. Each program will have its own hyphenation system which determines where hyphens will be placed. Generally they will honour hyphens inserted as part of the

(e) The main function of hyphenation within most DTP and word-processor packages, is to assist in achieving a more pleasing appearance to the text. This is most important when narrow columns are used, where it is difficult to achieve such control without this facility. Each program will have its own hyphenation system which determines where hyphens will be placed. Generally they will honour hyphens inserted as part of the text. An optional item, which will be

(f) The main function of hyphenation within most DTP and word-processor packages, is to assist in achieving a more pleasing appearance to the text. This is most important when narrow columns are used, where it is difficult to achieve such control without this facility. Each program will have its own hyphenation system which determines where hyphens will be placed. Generally they will honour hyphens inserted as part of the

Figure 8.12 Hyphenation Control Examples

Scanners

In an earlier chapter we looked at the graphics capabilities of the Timeworks Publisher program, and mentioned the use of scanners as one means of providing graphics input to the documents. Such devices are becoming more common now, with a number of options available, and it is worth having a brief look at their capabilities.

There are two basic types of scanner available; the relatively low cost hand-held units and the more elaborate desk top units. The authors practical experience is limited to the former type, with some appreciation of the latter through reading the available literature.

Figure 8.13 Hand-held Scanner

The illustration shfows a hand held scanner (Logitech Scanman) which has replaced the model AMS Microscan used by the author in the preparation of this book. It has a common format with all such systems. This contains a light emitter which provides a strip of light, the full width of the scanning head (105 mm, or approximately 4 inches). The head contains a photo-detector array, again of full width, which allows a resolution of 200 dots per inch. Some later models are now available with increased resolution, up to 400 dots per inch.

Installing this particular model required the addition of a half card inside the computer, and the installation of the necessary software. This particular device has the facilities to operate under MS-DOS, GEM or Microsoft Windows, which obviously covers most applications. Files, for the images produced during the scan, can be stored either as *.IMG files for GEM or *.PCX files for the PC Paintbrush art packages, as well as the TIFF format. Either of the first two options is suitable for inclusion within the Timeworks Publisher documents.

The product is extremely simple to use. There are a few controls available which allow:

> Selection of image contrast;
> Selection of scan mode for colour or black and white documents; and
> A push-button to initiate the scan.

In addition, the colour mode of operation allows a selection of 'dither' patterns to provide control on the black and white representation of colour shades. Colours are represented, in terms of their density, by varying the dot pattern on the selected areas to give different shading effects. The dither pattern control offers a variety of options for the actual dot patterns that can be selected. Using this, in conjunction with the contrast control, it is possible to get quite a good representation of some colour pictures. The illustration in Figure 8.14 is an example of a colour photograph scanned using this system. As with many things, however, some experimentation will be required with this feature, and it is likely that in most cases the reproduction would not be of adequate quality for professional applications.

Black and white line art pictures, however, scan extremely well, and even complex drawings can be reproduced with a very high quality. The example leaflets illustrated have made use of some line art images available in copyright-free form (Dover Clip Art Series, Dover Publications Inc, New York). These have been scanned and stored as *.IMG files, and subsequently imported into a Timeworks Publisher document. The text has been added in separate frames, using the normal procedures.

The scanner software includes pixel editing facilities, as well as the ability to select specific areas of the picture to save. Files can be rotated before saving, so that the image can be entered onto the page with the desired orientation.

Scanning is performed by pressing and holding the scan button, and dragging the scanner along the required image. A rubber roller wheel provides the position registration, as the image is scanned electronically. There is no real problem with

Figure 8.14 Scanned Colour Photograph

scan speed, and small irregularities will cause no deterioration of image. Some interesting effects can be obtained by twisting the scanner as it is moved, but it is quite difficult to control this with any precision. One problem area with the hand held scanner is in the alignment with straight edges. Straight lines, and some small text characters, may not reproduce satisfactorily. The editing features provide some means to improve this, but care will be required where there are many straight edges in the image.

The screen image produced by the scanner software is a dot by dot representation of the actual image and, therefore, appears very much enlarged from the original. Within the Timeworks Publisher software the image produced can be scaled to suit the individual application. It is possible to enlarge scanned images retaining quite good resolution.

In theory the scanned images can be imported into a suitable art package for finer editing. A problem was experienced when trying to import large images into the GEM Paint software, as there is obviously a maximum file size that this can cope with. Where this size was exceeded the imported picture was corrupted, and satisfactory editing was not possible. Provided that this image size was not exceeded, however, the program was quite effective in producing additional image processing.

The width of the scanner provides an obvious limit to its applications, and there is no satisfactory way of joining separate scanned strips to form a larger image.

The instructions supplied with the scanner were at pains to stress the need to control the scaling of the image, in relation to the relative dot resolution of the scanner and the printing device. They recommend, for example, that the best image is obtained by ensuring a one-to-one dot relationship between the scanned image at 200 dots per inch, and the final printout device resolution. That is, for example, if we scan a 2 inch square image to give a pattern of 400 x 400 dots, and if we use a 24 pin printer with a 180 dot resolution, then the image should be scaled up to (200\180 x 2 = 2.22 inches square. For a laser printer with a 300 dot resolution this would require an image scaled to 200/300 x 2 = 1.33 inches square)

In practice, however, as we showed earlier, the Timeworks Publisher program was able to scale images over quite a wide range without any obvious distortion. Again, unfortunately, this is an area where it is necessary to experiment with each particular case to obtain the best results.

Within these limitations, the scanner was capable of producing excellent quality graphics with the minimum of trouble.

For more exacting applications there are now an increasing number of desktop scanners, which act in a similar fashion to a photocopier or a fax scanner. These can handle full A4 size sheets, and some versions may include character recognition software which will read text from the scanned image. Obviously, as the number of features increase, so does the cost, but for certain professional applications this may well produce some valuable facilities.

One factor always to remember is that scanned images, with a resolution greater that 200 dpi in all cases, will occupy a lot of memory, and may well demand the use of extended memory, especially for full page reproduction. Also, as before, the practical use of such graphics images is largely restricted to hard disk systems.

A final word of warning for those using scanners. The copyright laws will apply just as rigorously to images scanned by electronic means as they do to normal photocopier devices. Do not use images for any commercial, or public, means which may be protected by copyright. As mentioned above, the scanned images produced in this book are included either with permission, or from copyright free material.

Working with large files

In order to work with documents which require more memory than is normally available within the 640K limit for internal memory, Timeworks Publisher supports slaving, either to a hard disk or to a RAM disk, above the 640K limit.

The need for this is normally indicated by a message such as 'Internal error #1' or 'Completely out of memory, save document now'.

The information required to set up the slave file and path is contained within the file PUBLISH.SLV in the PUBLISH directory. This file is empty when supplied, and the necessary information has to be entered by the user.

This can be done using any basic text editor, such as EDLIN or RPED, or even your own word processor in non-document or ASCII mode.

Edit this file to contain the line: C:\PUB_TEMP.SL0

for slaving on the C: drive. Modify the drive designator, but not the filename, if you require to slave onto a RAM disk or an alternative hard disk. (The last character in the file name is the number 0 (Zero) not the letter O).

For users of the cut-down version of Timeworks Publisher, DTP-Lite, the slaving file is called LITE.SLV, and this should be edited to contain the line:

C:\LITE_TMP.SL0

When this is installed all overflow from RAM will be directed to the slaving file and work can progress on longer documents.

9

The GEM System

This chapter is primarily intended for those who are not familiar with the use of the GEM graphics operating system, supplied with the Timeworks Publisher package, and an essential part of its operation. We will look at all aspects of using this system, but particularly at those features which relate directly to the operation of the DTP application.

This also includes a more detailed look at the installation process, as this is likely to present more problems to new GEM users, than to the more experienced. As the installation process is so simple, however, no one need feel concerned. Before we get to that, there are some other things to look at.

The Mouse

Although many of the features of the GEM system can be activated by normal keyboard controls, the full operation of the system requires the use of a MOUSE. Those who are using the AMSTRAD PC systems, or the ATARI or ACORN ARCHIMEDES, are probably already familiar with the operation of these devices, as they are an integral part of the system. It is possible, however, to make full use of any PC system, including the AMSTRAD, without using the mouse at all, as most software still ignores their existence. According to a recent magazine article (January 1989) only about 15% of computer users make regular use of the mouse, or the associated graphics operating system.

If you have any system with which a mouse was supplied as an integral part, then all the preparation for its use is normally a part of the start up procedure. With the AMSTRAD PC system the software to drive the mouse is in a file called

MOUSE.COM, and this is loaded during the normal Startup procedures, controlled from the AUTOEXEC.BAT file on your Startup disk.

If this file has been modified for any particular reason, and excludes the Mouse control file, then this will need to be modified as if installing a new mouse. You may need to refer to your user manual to find out more about this process, and the significance of the AUTOEXEC.BAT file.

If your system does not include a mouse, then before going any further you will need to acquire one. These are available from a number of sources, including your normal computer supplier, and are extremely easy to install. The cost of these lies between £50 and £120, depending on make and type, but they all perform essentially the same job.

There are two basic systems of operation for a mouse, *mechanical* or *optical*. All systems are physically quite similar in that they will fit easily under the hand, and will be equipped with two or three buttons, located to the front of the device, to lie comfortable under your fingers. When in use, movements of the mouse on the desk surface, will cause similar movement of a cursor on the computer screen.

In the mechanical system, a *roller ball* is fitted to the underside of the mouse, which rotates due to friction with the desk surface as the mouse is moved. This rotation is detected by a variety of means, mechanical or optical, and provides the necessary signals to the computer. Although designed for operation on any surface, it is usually beneficial to use a *mouse mat*. These are inexpensive and will have a special surface to prevent any slipping of the roller ball. They provide a defined area in which the mouse is free for operation, and are easy to keep clean. The claimed disadvantage of mechanical systems is that dirt pick up can lead to mis-operation. However, as with most things, a little care can avoid this problem.

The OPTICAL mouse differs in that it does not rely on the mechanical movement of a roller ball. Instead, this requires a special mat, into the surface of which is laid an optical grid. Photo-electronic sensors in the mouse detect movement relative to the grid, and this is translated into the required signal for the computer. The elimination of the mechanical components is claimed to improve reliability.

In some of the available devices there is the opportunity to select sensitivity, or resolution. This is basically the relationship between the amount of physical movement of the mouse, and the corresponding movement of the screen cursor. All devices have adequate resolution, and a higher resolution may have application only in special graphics applications, such as Computer Aided Draughting and Design (CADD).

Whatever type of mouse you select, all will connect to the computer in a similar fashion. The vast majority are designed to connect directly to an RS232 port, and are termed a BUS MOUSE. They are provided with the necessary software, usually in a file called MOUSE.COM, or something similar. The mouse is physically connected to the RS232 port, and the mouse software is loaded into the machine. The operation of the mouse will not become apparent, however, until some suitable software is loaded to make use of it.

If, for any reason, the RS232 port is not available, then some mouse versions are available with their own control card. This will need to be installed into the computer, along with the appropriate software, following the manufacturer's instructions.

Most graphics application software will have provision for selecting different types of mouse during the installation procedure, as we will see with GEM, and this requires only that the necessary software is available in a suitable directory.

Once a mouse is installed it can, of course, be used for any application which has made provision for it. For example Microsoft WORD 4 and the EXCEL spreadsheet, also from Microsoft, make good use of the mouse in their operation.

The mouse system provided with the Amstrad computers is used to simulate the cursor keypad, and any program which makes use of the normal cursor controls can use the mouse. In addition the mouse buttons may be re-programmed using the NVR.EXE program, to provide any necessary special functions.

Mouse Definitions

Once the software is loaded, using the mouse is merely a matter of moving it around the surface to produce a corresponding movement on the computer screen. The buttons are used to activate particular functions, related to the application in use. The functions of the buttons may differ with each application, and this will need to be learned in each case. With GEM, however, and thus with Timeworks Publisher, the mouse is used in its simplest mode, that is, using only one button, the left one, for all functions. The following, repeated from an earlier chapter, are the basic mouse functions that will be used for our current application:

MOVE Move the mouse on the surface to achieve a corresponding movement of the screen cursor.

POINT: Move the screen pointer to a particular location, either within an *icon* or at a *menu item*.

CLICK: Press the left button once, *and* release it.

DOUBLE CLICK: Press the left button twice in quick succession, and release it. Some practice may be required to get the timing right, but nothing disastrous will happen if you do not)

DRAG Press and HOLD the left button while moving the cursor to a new location.

SELECT: *P* oint to an option/menu item and *click*

OPEN: *Point* to a program/application/file icon and *double click*.

ACCEPT: When offered a display with an [OK] box, *point* to this and *click*.

CANCEL: When offered a display with a [CANCEL] box, *point* to this and *click*.

As the mouse software occupies only a relatively small amount of memory it is normal to have this loaded automatically when you start up your computer. Depending on your particular configuration, and the instructions supplied with your mouse, this will be achieved in one of two ways:

Add the line:

```
MOUSE
```

to your AUTOEXEC.BAT file; or

Add the line:

```
DEVICE=MOUSE.SYS
```

to your CONFIG.SYS file.

In either case your mouse driver file must be available in the start up directory, or one indicated by any PATH instructions within your start-up files.

Installing GEM and TimeworksPublisher

With the earliest versions of Timeworks Publisher, installing GEM and the DTP application was part of the same process, and could not be separated. This was extremely straightforward, and unlike many other procedures, behaved exactly as it is described in the manual, with no surprises half way through the installation.

The current version of the program does differ from this, however, but happily is just as straightforward.

The installation process is controlled by the file INSTALL, on the DTP master disk. This uses a menu system to select the various items, and is extremely easy to follow. The install program automatically detects the presence of a hard disk, and will choose to install on that. For this, about 1 Megabyte of space is required.

If you have an earlier version of GEM installed then it is necessary to replace this with the version, 3.0 or 3.01, supplied with Timeworks Publisher. If GEM 3 is already installed the process will only set up the necessary files for the publishing application. Again, all of this is handled extremely easily by the install program.

For the floppy system you will require 5 formatted disks. These will be labelled STARTUP, FONTS, OVERLAY, PRINTER and DATA. Because of the high memory requirement of the DTP program, you are not allowed to have a RAM disk allocation in the computer memory. If your normal startup procedure involves automatically setting up a RAM disk, then you will have to modify this. An error message will be generated if GEM does not think it has enough memory in which to operate.

To minimise the use of disks the Timeworks Publisher program only installs those parts of the GEM system required for its own operation, and no longer installs the full GEM system on the program working disks.

When the necessary disks are prepared, the install process can be initiated by placing the DTP master disk in drive A: and making this the current drive. Type INSTALL [RETURN], and follow the on-screen prompts. You will be asked to identify the various parts of your system in terms of:

   Type of mouse to be used;
   Type of printer to be used; and
   Type of display to be used (CGA, VGA, etc.)

You will also be asked to swap disks as required. Just follow the instructions, and make the appropriate choices, and the whole process will continue smoothly.

Transfer of all the necessary files is handled easily, and provided that you follow the on-screen instructions then all will proceed smoothly. There are four points in the process where you need to make a selection corresponding to your hardware setup, as follows:

Select Display

The following options are offered, and you must choose that which corresponds most closely to your equipment:

```
A Amstrad PC1512 & Colour or Monochrome Display
  (640x200).
B Amstrad PC1640 - CD Colour Display (640x200)
C Olivetti EGC Card 16-Colour Display (640x400)
D Olivetti Monochrome (640x400)
E Hercules card/Monochrome PC Display (720x348)
F IBM EGA/Colour Display (640x200) - Mono mode
G IBM EGA/Monochrome Display (640x350)
H IBM Enhanced card & 16 Colour Display (640x350)
I IBM 16 Colour VGA for PS/2 (640x480) or compatible
J IBM VGA Monochrome for the PS/2 (640x480) or compatible
K MDS THE GENIUS monitor/THE GENIUS Monitor card
  (728x1008)
L Wyse/Amdek Monochrome Graphics Display (1280x800)
M Amstrad PC1640 & ECD Display (640x350)
```

Select Mouse

The following options are offered, and you must choose that which corresponds most closely to your equipment:

```
A No mouse
B Bus Mouse (Requires file MOUSE.COM)
C IBM Personal System/2 Mouse
D Microsoft Serial Mouse (RS232)
E Mouse Systems PC Mouse/SummaMouse/Logimouse
F Summasketch 961 Cursor-Type Tablet
G Summasketch 961 Stylus-Type Tablet
H Summasketch 1201 Cursor-Type Tablet
I Summasketch 1201 Stylus-Type Tablet
J Summagraphics MM1812 Cursor-Type Tablet
K Summagraphics MM1812 Stylus-Type Tablet
L Olivetti Mouse (Requires file MOUSE.COM)
M Amstrad PC Mouse (requires file MOUSE.COM)
```

Options B, L and M require that their driver files, all labelled MOUSE.COM, but all unique to the particular system, need to be loaded into the computer memory BEFORE the program can make use of them. This would normally be incorporated in the AUTOEXEC.BAT or CONFIG.SYS files, which would be activated on machine startup.

Select Printer

The following options are offered, and you must choose that which corresponds most closely to your equipment:

```
A Epson GQ-3500 Laser Printer (300x300)
B Epson LQ Series printers (180x180)
C Hewlett Packard LaserJet II Printer (300x300)
D Hewlett Packard LaserJet+ (150x150)
E IBM/Epson High Resolution Printer (120x144)
F IBM Proprinter (120x144)
G LaserWriter/Postscript printers
H LaserWriter Plus/Postscript printers
I Toshiba P321, P341, or P351 printer (180x180)
```

Selection B should be adequate for most 24 pin printers, and selection E for most pin printers.

Select Communication Port

You are offered five choices here, but in practice most machines will only hav options A and D available. Other printer ports are usually made available as extensions to the basic machine:

```
A Parallel port #1 (LPT1)
B Parallel port #2 (LPT2)
C Parallel port #3 (LPT3)
D Communications port #1 (COM1)
E Communications port #2 (COM2)
```

Items D and E are normally referred to as the SERIAL or RS232 ports, and would be used with serial printers, such as the LaserJet family.

Once you have specified these elements, your choice is displayed, and you are invited to save this setup (Select A) or Change this setup (Select B).

Choice A will allow the install process to continue and you will be requested to make several disk changes as the program gathers its various files together, and this will take several minutes.

Once the install process is complete, all the necessary files are installed on your hard disk, or all the working disks are prepared for the floppy system. The final stage of the install process is to run the FONTWID program. This creates a width table for the various fonts available, so that the program can allocate the correct spacing to each character, and is a necessary step only on first installation or when subsequently changing the printer.

To install the GEM system on floppy disks you will need to run a separate process. This operates in very much the same way as the above, but is initiated using the GEMSETUP program on the GEM system master disk. You have to make the same basic choices, and follow the process as before.

This will create the necessary Startup and Desktop disks to allow full operation of the GEM system.

After this you are ready to run either the GEM system on its own, or the full DTP system, to become familiar with it. We will continue to look at the GEM system in isolation in this chapter, but to make use of the DTP program, even at this stage, go to Chapter 2.

Graphics Environment Manager (GEM)

The term GEM is an abbreviation for Graphics Environment Manager. It is designed to provide a simpler, more intuitive, interface between the computer and the user. It is one of the systems described by the acronym WIMP (Window, Icon, Menu (or Mouse), Pointer), as this represents the main functional parts of the user interface.

Anyone using a computer will already have some experience of a form of interface. The most generally used is the dreaded MS-DOS system, which basically presents you with a blank screen, on which you type the necessary instructions. (That is, once you have found out what they are). It is, to the beginner, an unhelpful system, though is capable of all the processes required to operate the computer, after a brief learning period. For the programmer, however, it is a different beast and makes full provision for all machine applications.

The major optional graphics interface is Microsoft WINDOWS, and anyone who has used this system will have no problems in using GEM. There are many arguments over which is the superior system, but it is up to Digital Research and Microsoft to convince you which may be better. Timeworks Publisher will not operate under the Microsoft Windows system.

The primary purposes of all operating systems, no matter how they appear, is to provide control over the organisation of information on the computer. This is primarily concerned with the organisation of the permanent information that we wish to store on disk, rather than any internal organisation of machine RAM or ROM memory. In fact, the term Disk Operating System (DOS) is entirely appropriate, as that is what we wish to control.

Files and Directories

As it is not possible for the author to know how familiar you may be with the organisation of disk storage, it is necessary to spend a little time discussing various aspects of this before getting down to details about GEM.

If you are happy with the structure and functions of files and directories, skip this next section, and move directly to that on loading and using GEM.

Information for use by the computer comes in two basic forms. The first are the *control programs*, which are basically a list of instructions which will be followed by the computer to achieve a particular function. Timeworks Publisher, and even GEM itself, are examples of this type and, of course, the computer would be quite useless without them. The second type falls under the category of *infirmation* or *data*. These will contain additional information required by the PROGRAM to achieve its function, or information produced during the application. For example, letters produced by a word processor, or drawings produced by a graphics program will be treated as *data*. They may be in quite different forms, but will have the same importance.

The term used to describe a list of program instructions, or the data, as stored on the computer disk is a *file*. Files are given a name, and are stored on the disk with that particular name assigned. The name is used to identify the file for future use by the computer and the user.

In organising files it is sometimes desirable to group them together in some logical way. For example, a usual grouping of files would be a *program* file, and its associated *data* files. Such a grouping would normally be isolated from other files, and is normally termed a *directory*.

Directories and Files, then, form the basic units of storage on the computer disk. How they are organised is more a matter of good practice than any formal structure. Proper organisation of files is important on any system, but more particularly on hard disk systems where the number of separate files possible could lead to much confusion.

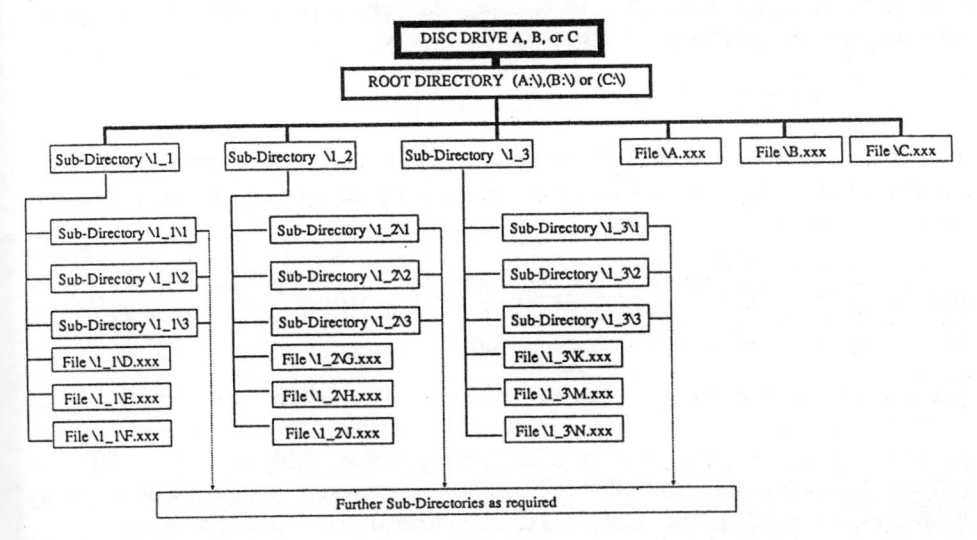

```
                    ┌─────────────────────────────┐
                    │    DISC DRIVE A, B, or C    │
                    │ ROOT DIRECTORY (A:\),(B:\) or (C:\) │
                    └─────────────────────────────┘
    ┌──────────┬──────────┬──────────┬──────────┬──────────┬──────────┐
Sub-Dir \1_1  Sub-Dir \1_2  Sub-Dir \1_3  File \A.xxx  File \B.xxx  File \C.xxx
    │              │              │
 Sub-Dir \1_1\1  Sub-Dir \1_2\1  Sub-Dir \1_3\1
 Sub-Dir \1_1\2  Sub-Dir \1_2\2  Sub-Dir \1_3\2
 Sub-Dir \1_1\3  Sub-Dir \1_2\3  Sub-Dir \1_3\3
 File \1_1\D.xxx  File \1_2\G.xxx  File \1_3\K.xxx
 File \1_1\E.xxx  File \1_2\H.xxx  File \1_3\M.xxx
 File \1_1\F.xxx  File \1_2\J.xxx  File \1_3\N.xxx

             Further Sub-Directories as required
```

Figure 9.1 Directory Structure

The illustration (prepared with Timeworks Publisher) shows an idealised directory and file structure, which can be implemented on any system. Normally a disk will have a main directory, termed the *root directory*. This would have much the same function as a listing of chapters in a book, to direct you to a particular section. The root directory will normally contain a number of *sub-directories*, as well as some program and data files. The sub-directories will be used to store some logical groupings of files; for example, the Timeworks Publisher program and its associated files are stored in a sub-directory named PUBLISH.

To help in organisation, sub-directories can in turn have further sub-directories. The illustration is a stylised picture of this structure. It shows a root directory, which contains a number of subdirectories and files. The terminology shown, i.e. A:\, is the conventional way of indicating the root directory on a disk. Each of the first level sub directories (\1_1, \1_2 and \1_3) can have further subdirectories as required, (\1_1\1, 1_1\2, etc.) as well as individual files. When working with files and directories it is necessary to keep in mind this sort of structure, in order to ensure sensible arrangement of information, etc.

In practice FILES and DIRECTORIES (including SUB-DIRECTORIES) will be assigned names. These names should have some logical connection with their function. A directory name will normally consist of up to eight characters (Some characters, like \ and . etc., cannot be used as they have special meanings). This name would be used to identify the directory on any listing.

Individual files will also be named. The convention with files is to have a two part name. The first part, the *filename*, can be up to eight characters long, with the same basic restrictions as directory names. The second part, termed the *extension*, will be up to three characters long, and will be separated from the file name with a point (.). Thus, the normal format for a file name is:

```
FILENAME.EXT
```

Any characters more than eight in the name, or more than three in the extension will be ignored. It is possible, but not good practice, to omit the extension from a file name.

In creating file and directory names, then, some logical process should be adopted to link the name with the function. Again, as an example, the use of the name PUBLISH for the Timeworks Publisher directory is quite clear.

The filename extension is also used to identify the function of the file. Some extensions are reserved for particular use. For example, the extensions .COM and .EXE are used to signify program files. The extension .APP is used by GEM to indicate GEM application files. Other examples of extensions which should generally be avoided are .BAT, .BAK, .RSC, and .SYS, which all have special meanings.

For fairly obvious reasons each file in a directory should have a different name, and each sub-directory must have a name different from its immediate *parent* directory, (that is, the directory in which it may be contained). Files in different directories may have the same name, but this should only be used for strong reasons, or if the files are identical.

Just to provide some final definitions in this area, and to avoid any confusion in terminology, you should note the following:

The *root* directory is considered to be the *top* of the structure, and each sub-directory level steps *down* from the root (like an inverted tree).

The *path* defines the directory steps to get to a particular file. For example, in the directory illustration the file E.xxx is accessed by the following steps (assuming that it is stored on disk A:):

Go to disk A (written as A:)

Select the root directory (written as A:\)

From the root directory go to sub-directory 1_1 (written as A:\1_1)

In the subdirectory go to file E.xxx (written as A:\1_1\E.xxx).

The Path, then, is written as:

```
A:\1_1\E.xxx
```

and is a full definition of the route to the particular file.

The *path* can be as long as necessary, but try not to get too cumbersome.

Loading and Using GEM

GEM is the system that we are going to describe for the further manipulation of our files and directories. The above section was to give a brief but, I hope, clear, idea of the way files should be structured. This is valid for any operating system, graphics or otherwise.

To load GEM on your system:

HARD DISK: Type GEM when in the root directory (the install process has created a batch file (GEM.BAT) to provide this facility);

FLOPPY DISK: Place your Startup disk in Drive A:, make this the active drive, and type GEM (as for the hard disk). You will be asked to place your DESKTOP disk in the drive when the GEM initialisation is complete.

After a short time you will be presented with the GEM opening screen. The actual screen display will depend on:

- The hardware configuration of your computer; and
- The version of Timeworks Publisher/GEM that you are using.

The screen presentation is controlled by the GEM application program called DESKTOP, which provides the user interface for the GEM system. GEM itself is

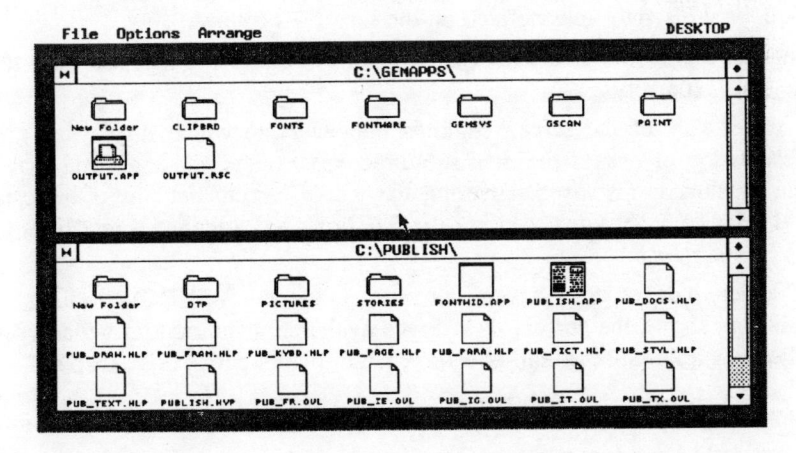

Figure 9.2 GEM Opening Display

much more extensive than this and, like MS-DOS, is used to build applications which have a particular format of screen presentation. However, as we are users rather than programmers, we need not concern ourselves with this.

Whatever display you get, the general principles of the following will apply.

The illustrations used in this section are screen dumps from an AMSTRAD 1640 ECD, with a hard disk (C:), and two floppy disks (A: and B:), and using the more recent version 1B12 of Timeworks Publisher, with DESKTOP version 3.01. There are minor differences in the directory structure between this and some earlier versions which may result in the GEM opening screen showing different directory displays. (Note, also, that the two different versions also use slightly different versions of the GEM 3 Desktop)

The various parts of the screen display will have different functions, and we will look at these in turn.

First, however, we had better make sure that the *mouse* is working correctly.

Somewhere towards the centre of the display a small diagonal arrow will be shown, which represents the mouse cursor. Moving the mouse should result in a corresponding movement of the cursor. If this does not respond then check:

That the mouse is plugged in to the correct port; and

That the mouse software has been loaded in correctly.

If there is any problem with this you will need to exit GEM (Press [CTRL] Q), and check your installation. Remember to load in the mouse software *before* running GEM.

With the mouse operating properly we can now have a look at the GEM display. There are three discrete areas defined on the screen, as follows:

- Along the *top* of the screen is a MENU BAR, which we will use later to select some of the controls;
- The upper half of the screen contains one *window*, which displays a graphical representation of *one* of the disk sub-directories. (Here you may find that only a single window is displayed, covering the whole screen, but this is quite normal. The display may be adjusted using the *full box*, as explained a few lines below); and
- The lower half of the screen contains a second WINDOW which, in the illustration, shows the current disk drives available. (The bottom window on your display may show another sub-directory, rather than the disk drive display).

Whatever the particular contents, each window has the same basic structure:

- The top *left -hand* corner contains a *double arrow* , or *butterfly icon* and is termed the *close box;*

- The top BAR contains the *name* and *path* of the directory currently displayed in the window;
- The top *right-hand* corner contains a *diamond icon*, and is often termed the FULL BOX;
- The *right-hand* bar contains the *scroll* controls for moving around the window display, where all the contents cannot be displayed simultaneously; and
- The WINDOW contains the graphical representation of the contents of the particular directory.

The main window section contains *icons*, which represent the contents of the directory. That is, all the individual *files* and *folders* contained within the selected directory will be displayed.

There are four basic icons used by GEM, which will be apparent on the display as you work with GEM.

The first is intended to represent a cardboard folder, of the type used in a manual filing system. This is used by GEM to show a *directory* as we defined earlier. GEM uses the term FOLDER for the same function. Each folder shown on the display, apart from the one labelled NEW FOLDER, may contain other files and folders.

The second *icon* used is a rectangle with a solid bar at the top, and which may contain an illustration. This is a *program* icon, and represents a program file. The illustration within the icon is used to identify its particular function. Such icons can be assigned when an application is installed to operate under GEM.

The other type of file that we discussed, the *information* or *data* file, is represented by the third icon type. This is illustrated as a sheet of paper with one corner folded down. As with the program icon, this may have an illustration within it to indicate its content.

The final icon is a representation of a disk, indicated as floppy or hard, which appears when no directory is active, and when it is possible to select the different disk drives available on the system. Note also that each icon has its folder or filename identified beneath it, and that the format follows that which we discussed earlier (i.e FILENAME.EXT).

Each of the two windows available on the screen will display the contents of a single directory. These may be the same directory if required, different directories on the same disk, or directories on different disks. This makes this a more useful display than the normal DOS directory displays, which only allow us to see one directory at a time.

As we know from the discussion on directories, each directory is only a part of all the information stored on the disk. To see all the information that we may require, it is necessary to be able to move between directories. As might be expected, this is a feature of GEM, and is easy to achieve.

If we wish to move UP the directory structure, towards the ROOT directory we will use the *close box*. The current directory in our illustration is shown to be:

    C:\GEMAPPS

To move UP the tree we will *close* the GEMAPPS Folder, which will automatically take us into the ROOT directory or folder. To do this, move the pointer to the *close box* and click. The display will change quickly to display the next directory. Do this on your own display to see the effect, even if it does not show the same as the illustration.

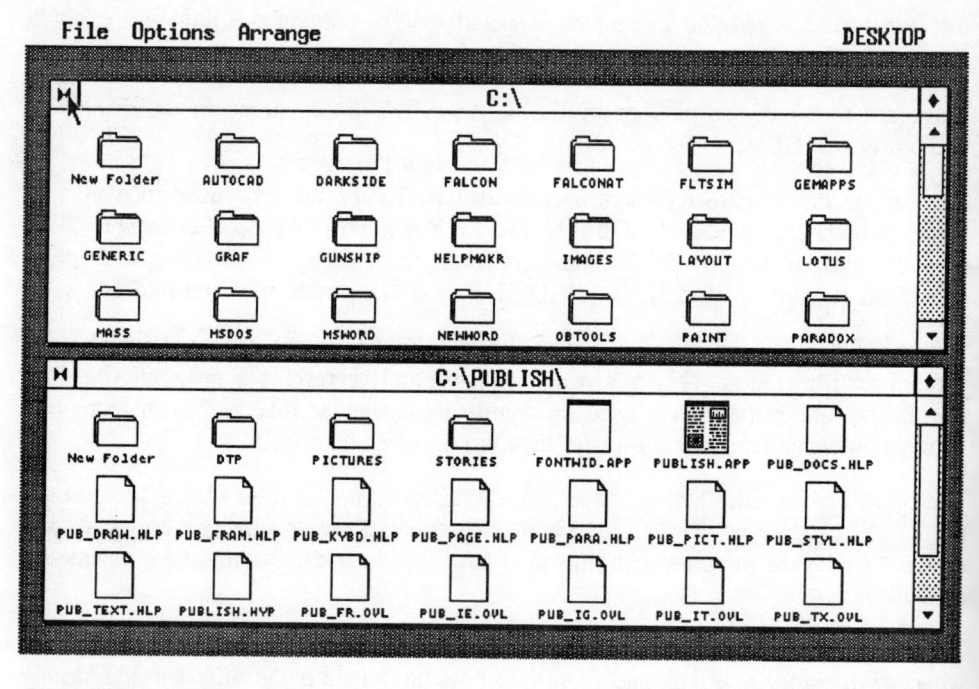

Figure 9.3 New Directory Display

On the new display you will be able to identify the FOLDER which represented the previous display. In our illustration we can see the GEMAPPS folder.

Each time you click on the *close box* you will move further UP the directory structure until the ROOT directory is displayed (C:\). (Above, we did this in one step) If you close this directory you will be shown the disk drive display, which illustrates the drives available on the system. Move up your directory structure until you get to this final display. Any more action on the close box is ignored.

To move back DOWN the directory structure, we need to be a little more selective but this is just as straightforward. With the disk drive display in the upper window move the pointer to one of the *drive icons* and *double click*. The *icon* will first be highlighted in inverse video, but the display will rapidly change to show the root directory of the selected disk. If this does not respond it is because the timing of the double click was not quite correct. Repeat this as necessary to get the result.

If you inadvertently select a drive which does not contain a disk, then an error screen is displayed, as shown in the illustration. If this arises, then check that there is a disk in place before proceeding.

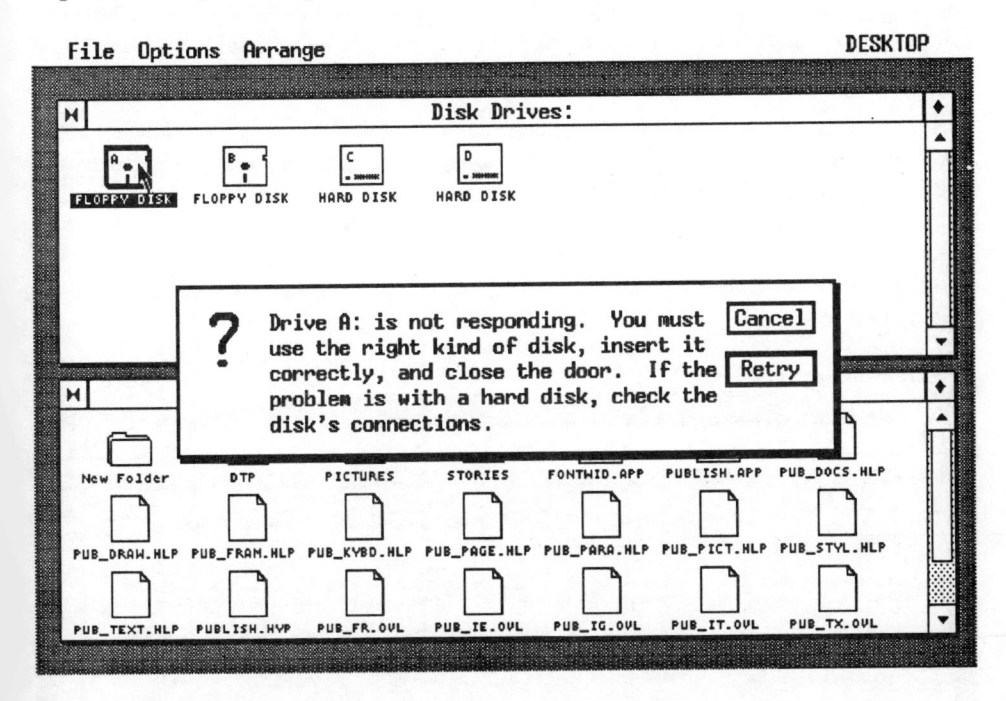

Figure 9.4 DISK READING ERROR DISPLAY

Now, to move into any lower FOLDER we merely point to its icon and double click with the mouse. Using these simple controls we can readily move through the directory structure and, of course, look at any of the disks in the system.

Move around you system using these controls. Do not, for now, double click on any program icon (as this will activate the program), or on any data icon (as this will produce an error message).

As you move through the directory structure you may move into one which has more files than can be displayed within the window. This situation can be identified by watching the SCROLL BAR, on the right hand side of the window, as in the illustration. If the window contains *all* of the files in the directory, this scroll bar will show as solid white, along the full length between the arrow heads. However, if all files are not displayed this bar becomes shortened, by an amount which indicates how much information is *not* in the current display.

To examine the part of the directory which is not currently displayed, move the pointer to the arrowhead by the shaded part of the SCROLL BAR. Clicking on this will move the display by one row at a time, to show additional files. You can achieve a similar result by *pointing* at the scroll bar, and *dragging* it in the direction of the shaded area. This latter process is better for large movements through the display.

As well as for use with directories, this feature of using the scroll bar to move around the display screen is a common feature of many GEM applications, including Timeworks Publisher. It provides an excellent way of moving around displays which may occupy a size greater than the physical screen.

Different parts of the same directory, then, can be viewed by means of the SCROLL BAR controls. If we wish to see more of a particular directory we can increase the size of the window. To do this, point to the *full box,* (the Diamond icon in the top right hand corner of the window) and click the mouse button. The window will expand to fill the whole screen, and more of the files and folders will be revealed. It is still possible for a directory to exceed the full screen, but the scroll controls can be used as before.

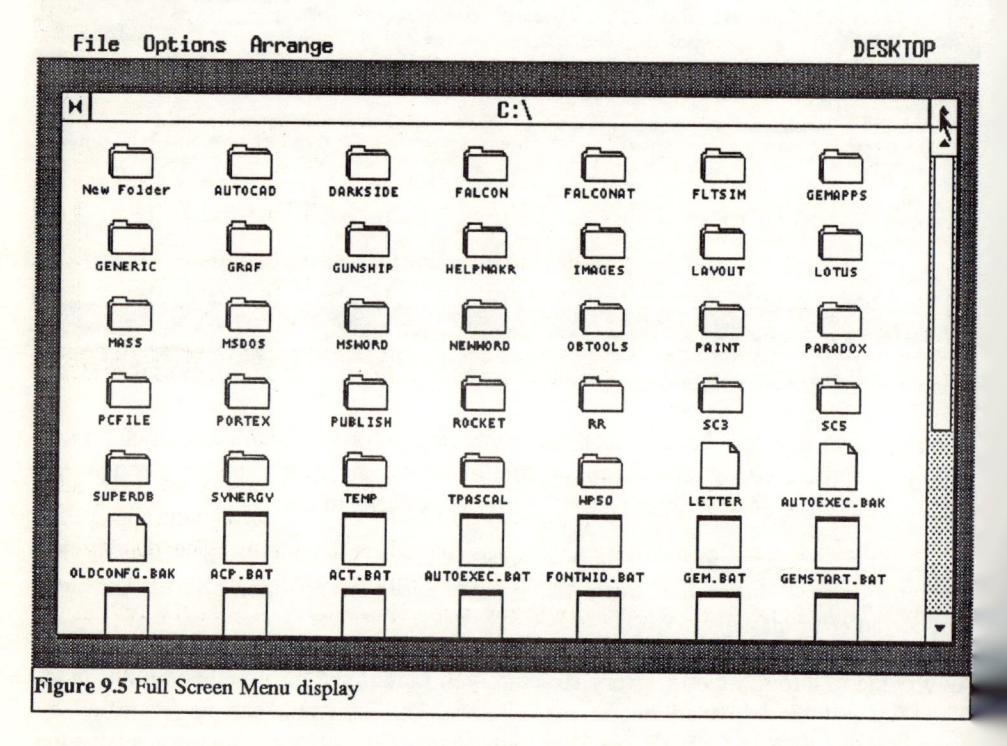

Figure 9.5 Full Screen Menu display

The window can be restored to its former size by clicking once again on the full box.

The above controls, then, enable us to move about the directory structure, and to view all or part of a particular directory. You should become familiar with these controls before moving onto the next section.

As we move around the directories in this way we are effectively following our PATH structure, and we should be able to identify the path to any required file. This is quite important to recognise, as we will frequently be asked to specify *paths* within our applications, so that the program can find the files it needs to operate.

The normal display of GEM directories is as we have seen above, but we are given some flexibility with this. With a directory displayed on the screen. move the pointer to the ARRANGE item on the MENU BAR. This will cause a menu to drop down which will allow us to change the directory display in particular ways.

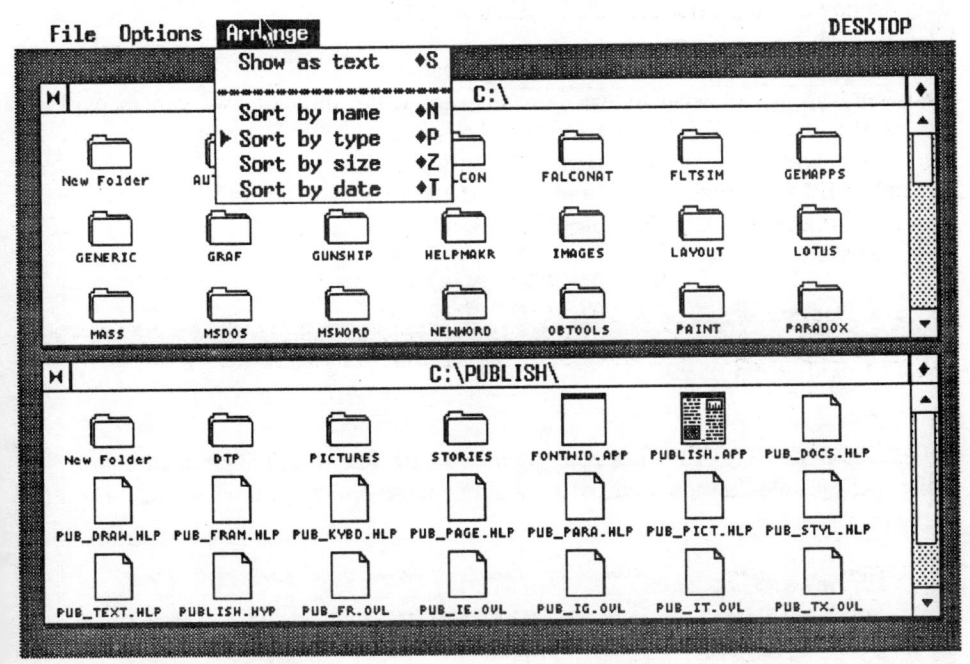

Figure 9.6 Arrange Menu Options

The first option, SHOW AS TEXT, allows us to show the directory as text, rather than as icons, in a similar fashion to the normal MS-DOS [DIR] command. Select this option by moving the pointer until it is highlighted, and clicking. The display will change immediately to adopt the new form. To see more of the files you will need to use the FULL BOX to increase the window size. The SHOW AS TEXT option has the benefits of providing a little more information about each file, as with MS-DOS, but does require more space on the display. However, you are, of course, quite free to adopt the system that suits you.

If we want to return to the icon display we open the arrange menu, and note that the first option is now listed as 'SHOW AS ICONS', and we can select this if required.

The other options that are available on the ARRANGE menu are related to the order in which the files are listed. The default selection is indicated by the arrow head

```
 File  Options  Arrange                                    DESKTOP
┌─────────────────────────────────────────────────────────────────┐
│ ►│                        C:\                              │ ♦ │
├──┴──────────────────────────────────────────────────────────┬──┤
│   ♦ New Folder           00-00-80   12:00 am                │▲ │
│   ♦ AUTOCAD              03-30-89   10:05 pm                │  │
│   ♦ DARKSIDE             02-25-89   02:29 am                │▓ │
│   ♦ FALCON               12-29-88   11:13 am                │▓ │
│   ♦ FALCONAT             01-05-80   04:16 am                │▓ │
│   ♦ FLTSIM               10-22-88   05:44 pm                │  │
│   ♦ GEMAPPS              04-25-89   07:46 pm                │  │
│   ♦ GENERIC              10-27-88   10:30 am                │▼ │
├──┬──────────────────────────────────────────────────────────┼──┤
│ ►│                    C:\PUBLISH\                           │ ♦│
├──┴──────────────────────────────────────────────────────────┬──┤
│   ♦ New Folder           00-00-80   12:00 am                │▲ │
│   ♦ DTP                  04-25-89   07:52 pm                │  │
│   ♦ PICTURES             04-25-89   07:52 pm                │▓ │
│   ♦ STORIES              04-25-89   07:52 pm                │▓ │
│     FONTWID   APP  42362 05-01-89   01:08 pm                │  │
│     PUBLISH   APP 159824 05-01-89   01:07 pm                │  │
│     PUB_DOCS  HLP   1448 05-01-89   01:07 pm                │  │
│     PUB_DRAW  HLP   3331 05-01-89   01:07 pm                │▼ │
└─────────────────────────────────────────────────────────────────┘
```

Figure 9.7 Text Directory Display

against the SORT BY TYPE option. Again you are free to specify which option you prefer. As indicated on the menu display, all of these options can be selected from the keyboard as follows:

```
Show as text (icon)      [ALT] S
Sort by Name             [ALT] N
Sort by Type             [ALT] P
Sort by Size             [ALT] Z
Sort by Date             [ALT] T
```

Please note that the keyboard controls, as shown above, will *not* operate when the menu is visible on the screen.

Once we are familiar with the controls to move freely about the various directory displays, we can begin to make use of the practical functions of GEM.

The primary activities that we will become involved with are :
- Creating new directories (Folders);
- Copying Files; and
- Deleting Files.

We do not normally create individual files as a function of GEM, as this is usually done from within a specific application.

Creating New Folders

We will create new folders as we add programs to our system, to operate within GEM, or as a means to organise files created by our various applications. To create a new folder we must first decide which directory this is to be in. This can be in the root directory, as would be usual for a major application program, or within any other sub-directory.

Remember, as we create new folders, that we must try to adhere to some sensible overall organisation. Bear in mind the general directory structure as we do this.

To create a new folder, then, we first move into the appropriate directory, using the controls learned previously. Point to the NEW FOLDER icon, of which there is one in each directory, and double click. The screen will change, and you will be asked to enter a suitable name for the new folder. There is provision in the name box for an extension to the folder name, and this can be used or ignored. In most cases a single name, of up to eight characters will suffice. Extensions used as part of a folder name will have no particular significance to the computer.

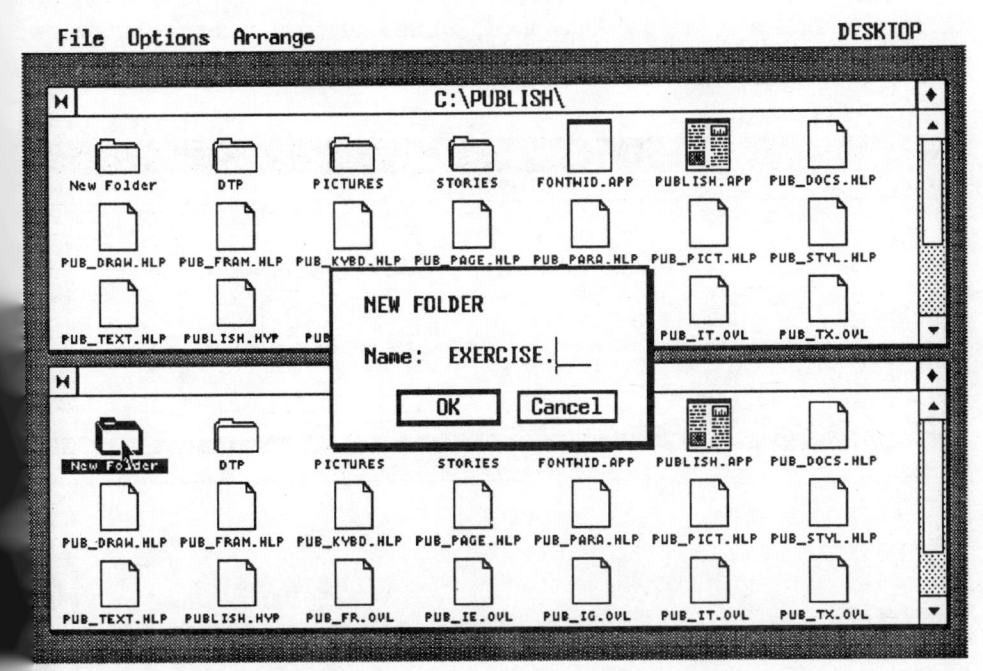

Figure 9.8 New Folder Screen

Once the name has been entered and accepted, the screen display will be restored, and the new folder will be shown. To place files within the new folder we will have to move into the folder, so we can open this by double clicking on the new icon. This folder will be empty, except for a NEW FOLDER icon, which we can use to create further sub-directories.

Some confusion has been expressed by beginners relating to the interaction between GEM and MS-DOS, particularly in relation to the making of directories or folders in either system, with the misconception that the two items are not related.

As GEM operates "on the back" of MS-DOS, in practice, every action that we perform under GEM will be mirrored by the MS-DOS system. Folders that we create with GEM will be recognised as directories by MS-DOS, and vice-versa. Any files we delete within GEM will also disappear from the MS-DOS system. The two systems are used to achieve the same ends, but merely represent themselves on screen in a different fashion.

In order to perform some actual *copy* and *delete* exercises we should create a new folder. If you have a hard disk move into the PUBLISH directory, and create a new folder called EXERCISE. Alter the directory display so that the top window shows the PUBLISH directory, and the bottom window shows the new, empty, EXERCISE directory. With a floppy system you will need to have a formatted disk in the B: drive, on which to create the new directory, and your DESKTOP work disk in the A: drive. Arrange the window display to show the A: drive in the top window, and the B: drive in the lower window. Enter the PUBLISH directory in the upper window, and the new directory in the lower.

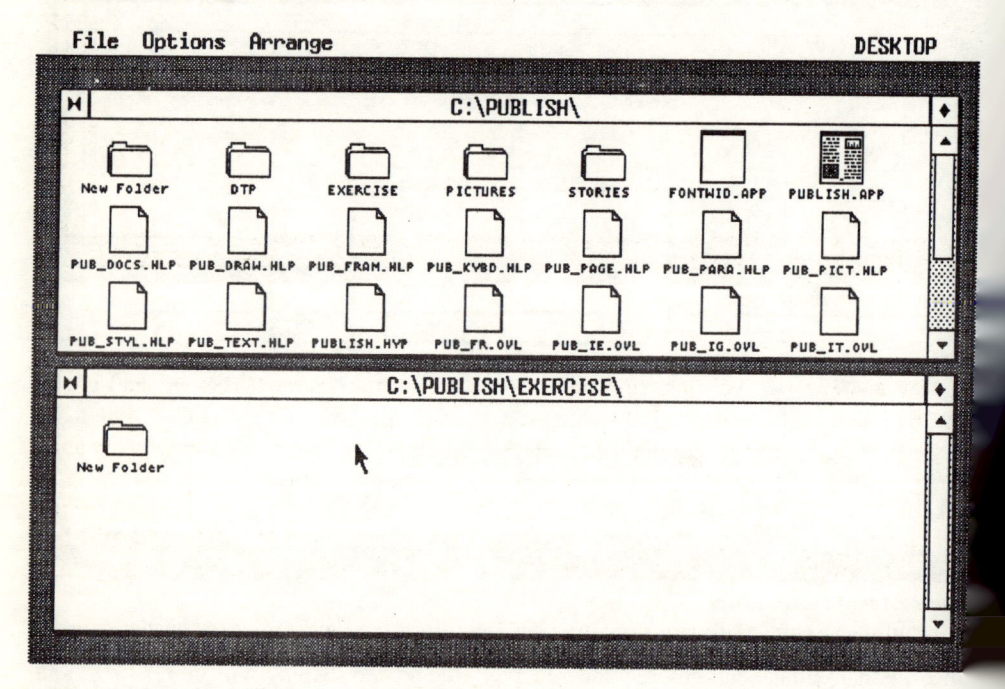

Figure 9.9 Exercise Directory Display (Hard disk)

Copying and Deleting Files.

When we copy files we will normally copy from one disk to another, or we can copy files between directories. As we have set up above, the first step in the copy process is to display the directory in which are listed the files we wish to copy (The *source* directory), and the directory to which we wish to copy the files (The *destination* directory).

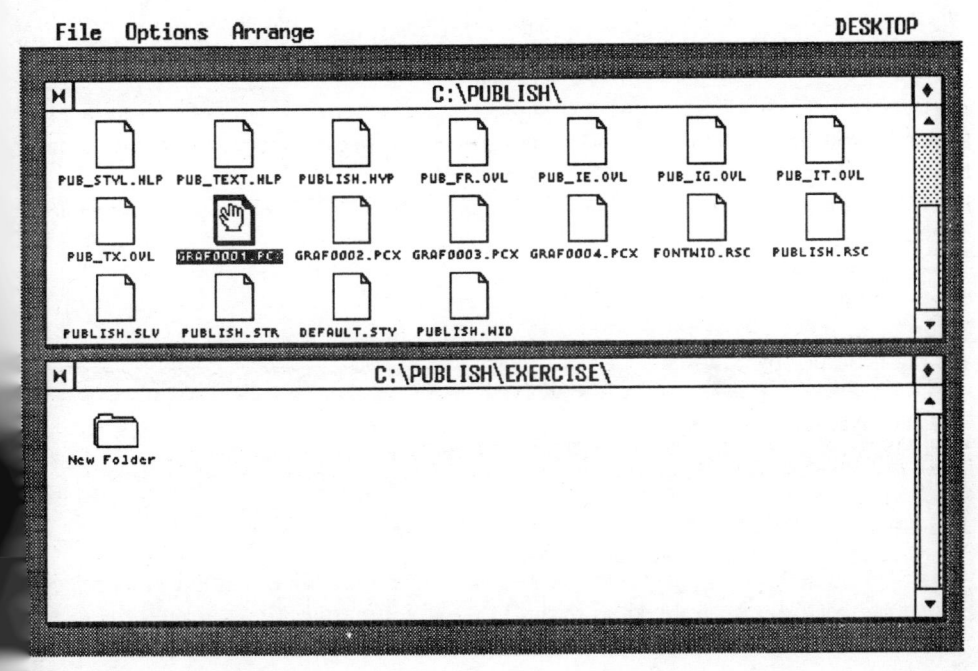

Figure 9.10 Files Highlighted

To copy a single file we must first point to its icon in the source directory, and click once. This causes the file to be highlighted in inverse video, which shows that it is selected. With the screen pointer within the highlighted icon we should now *press* and *hold* the left mouse button. The pointer will change to show a hand.

If the pointer is outside the icon the hand will not appear, and the highlight will be removed from the icon.

Still holding the button down, now drag the hand into the new directory on the screen display. The file icon will *not* move with the hand, and the hand can be moved to anywhere within the destination window. When the mouse button is released the screen display will change, and you will be asked to confirm the copy instruction. If everything is in order ACCEPT this, and the file will appear in the new directory. Note that the original file remains within the original directory.

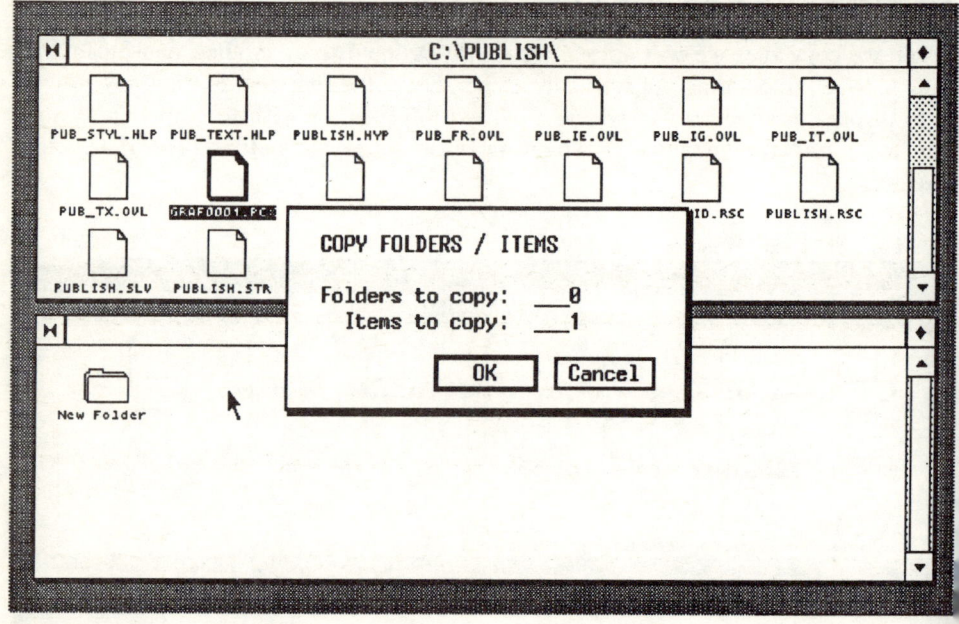

Figure 9.11 Copy Confirm Display

Using this procedure copy two more files into your new directory.

It is also possible to copy several files at the same time. One method is to select a group on the display, arranged so that it is possible to draw a box around them, and treat this as a single block.

Choose a group of three or four files from the *source* directory to copy. Place the pointer at a position on the screen which will represent the *top left-hand* corner of a box to be drawn to surround the chosen files. Press and hold the mouse button, and drag the mouse to form an outline around the files. When the button is released the selected group will be highlighted. Place the pointer within any one of the highlighted files, and press and hold the button to obtain the hand icon. Now *drag* the hand to the new directory, and release the button. Once again we will be asked to confirm the copy process, which we should do, and all the files will be transferred.

Where the files we require are not in a convenient block it is possible to select a number of individual files by holding the [SHIFT] key whilst clicking on the mouse button in the relevant file icon. (Known as [SHIFT]-[CLICK]).

If we attempt to copy a file into a directory, which already has a file of the same name, then GEM will warn us that this is about to happen, and we are given the option to overwrite the current file, or by editing the file name in the window create a new name for the file.

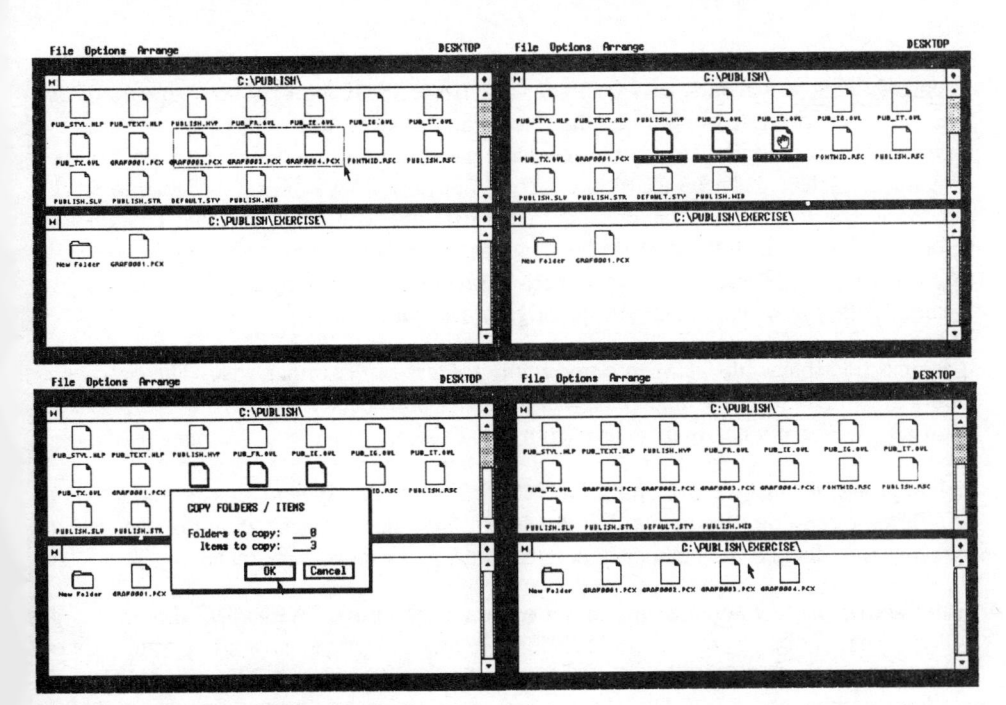

Figure 9.12 Block Copy Display Sequence

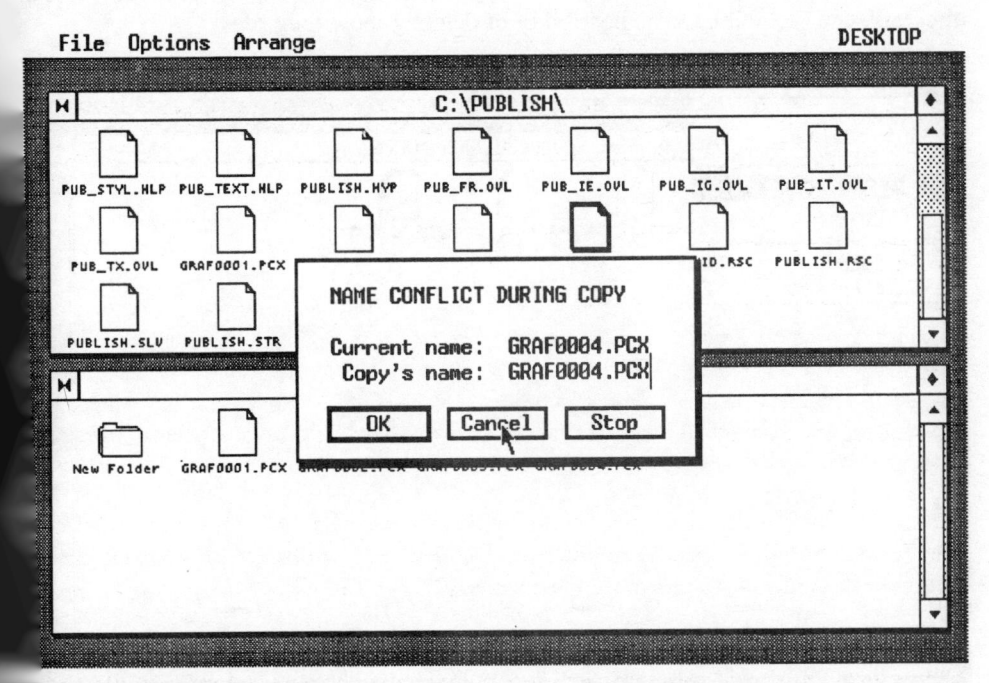

Figure 9.13 Name Conflict Screen

Occasions may arise where we will want to make a copy of a file in the same directory. This would normally occur if we wish to make a safety back-up file of one that we wish to work on. To do this, we would always store the copy under a new name. GEM allows you to do this in much the same way as when copying between directories. Select the original file as before, but now drag it to a new location within the same window. After the request to confirm the copy, the NAME CONFLICT screen, similar to that illustrated above will appear. Now, however, you are required to enter the new name for the file before proceeding. The new copy will then be created, with a new name, leaving the original file intact.

It is also possible with GEM to copy whole folders with similar ease. The process is identical to that for individual files, and need not be repeated here. This is a powerful feature of GEM, not easily available from MS-DOS.

Deleting files is just as straightforward, but as with any system this is a **DANGER ZONE** of operation. You must be absolutely sure that you are deleting the correct files, as once deleted they can only be recovered by extraordinary means.

In the above we have created a number of new files in our EXERCISE directory. We will now use those to practice the DELETE function. Rember now to operate *only* on those files in the EXERCISE directory. To be as safe as possible, change the top window to show the DISK DRIVE display *icons* make our bottom window a FULL window, using the *full box*. Now our display should show only our EXERCISE directory, and we will have no possibility of deleting the wrong files.

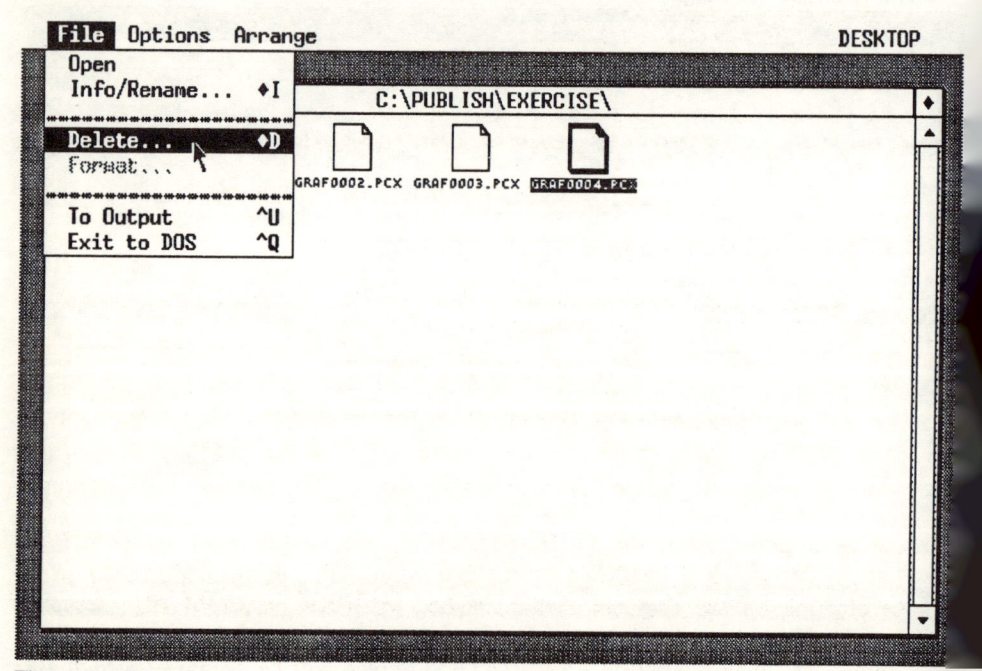

Figure 9.14 File Menu

To delete a file we will make use of the FILE MENU, along the top bar. To see the functions available on this menu, first select any one of the display files. With any file highlighted, move the pointer to the FILE item on the menu bar, and the menu will appear as shown on the previous page.

We will return to the other options later, but for now we can see the DELETE option listed. To delete the selected file we move the pointer to highlight this option and click once. As with the copy process, we are asked to confirm that we wish to delete the file, and if we accept this then the process is completed.

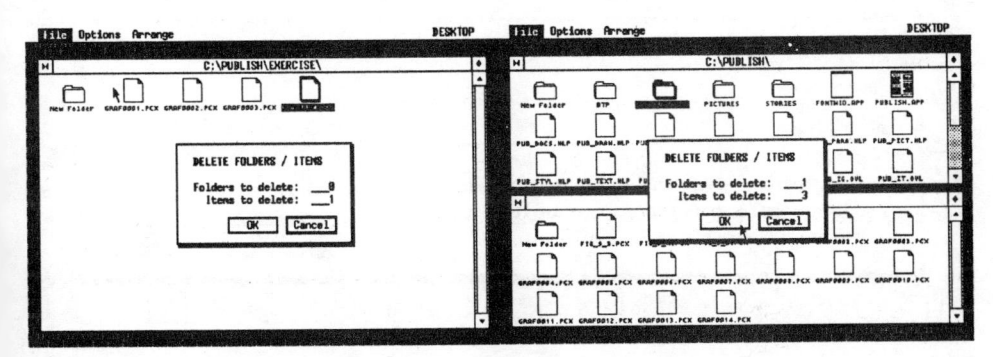

Figure 9.15 Confirm Delete Display   (a)File   (b) Folder

Note from the menu that the delete function can be activated by pressing [ALT] D, on the keyboard, when a file is selected (But not while the menu is displayed).

As with the copy function, we can delete multiple files, and even folders, in the same way. Remember, however, to do this with extreme caution. Practice this for a little while, only using the EXERCISE directory, and by creating further directories within this.

Other File Functions

When we used the FILE menu in the above exercises we noted that a number of other options were available and we will have a look at these now.

OPEN: This can be used as an alternative to double-clicking on an icon, in order to activate a file or directory. It is particularly useful if you have problems with the timing of the double-click action. To use this file feature simply highlight the desired icon with a single click, and then point to the file menu and select the OPEN option.

To use a program, from the GEM DESKTOP, we simply have to OPEN the application file, which is identified by the extension .APP, using this process, or by double clicking on the program icon identified by .EXE or .COM file names. If additional information may be required to start the application, for example, file or path parameters, then the OPEN APPLICATION screen will be displayed, which asks for any relevant details. These may be entered here, or the program may be started without any parameters.(A .EXE or .COM file is renamed as an .APP file when is configured to operate under GEM, as described below)

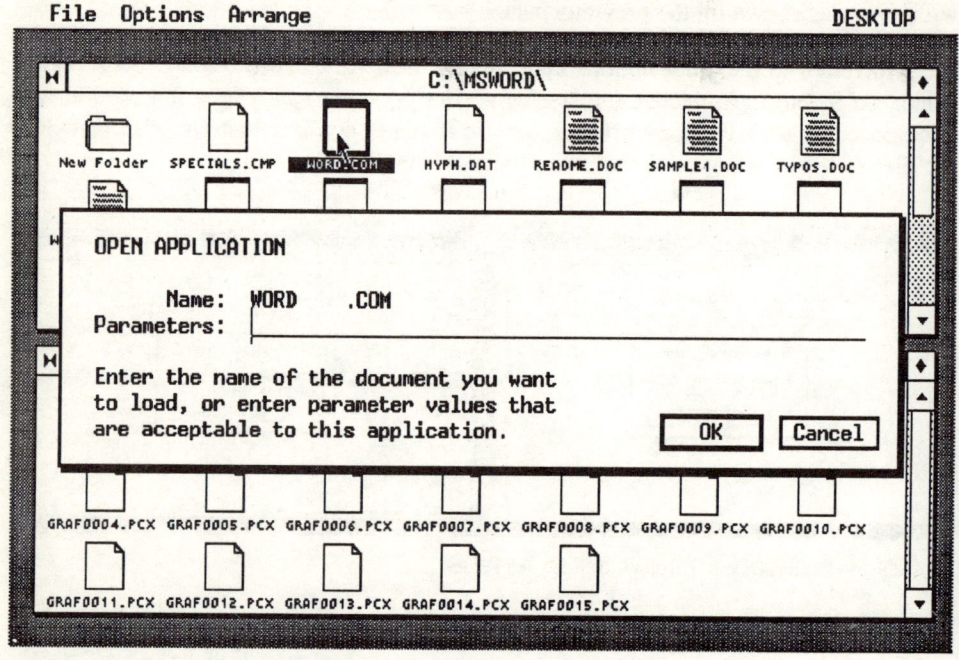

Figure 9.16 Open Application Screen

INFO/RENAME: As suggested by the name, this function allows us to obtain some additional information concerning the selected file or folder. This allows us to change the name of a file, and to set the file attributes to READ/WRITE or READ ONLY. The file is re-named simply by editing the file name on the display screen. If we have selected a folder for this option we are given information only, and there is no provision to change any of the parameters.

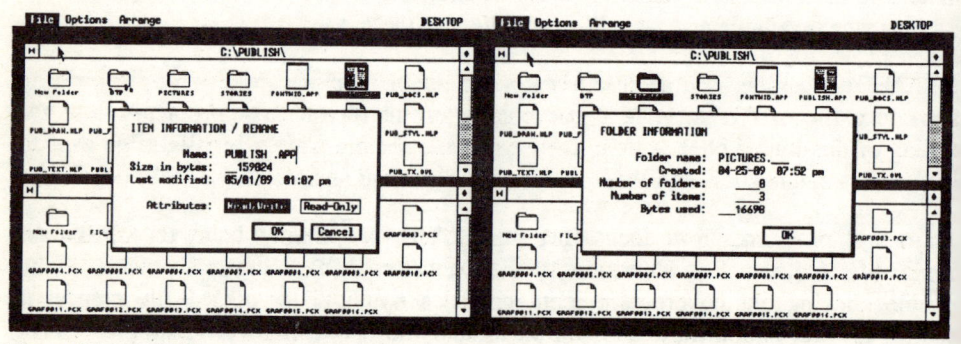

Figure 9.17 (a) ITEM and (b) FOLDER INFO Screens

As with other menu items, this option may be selected by highlighting the appropriate file or folder and using the [ALT]-I key combination.

FORMAT: This has the same basic function as the MS-DOS format command used to prepare disks for use. However, it is *not* identical, and does not, for example give you the option to label the disk, and it does not display error messages or status information. In most cases it is better to use the standard MS-DOS command rather than the GEM version.

TO OUTPUT: This calls up the program OUTPUT.APP which is the GEM printing utility. This enables you to create a list of files for printing. These can be graphics, or text files, provided that they are formatted in an appropriate form. However, this is an item I will leave you to explore on your own, as it is not used for any DTP application. It is quite a straightforward function, with which you should have little difficulty. The version available from GEM 3 is one of the major improvements over earlier versions of GEM. (The key combination to activate this is [CTRL] U)

EXIT TO DOS: This requires no profound explanation. Selecting this option, or using the key combination [CTRL] Q, will quit GEM and return you to DOS.system.

The final functions available from the GEM DESKTOP application are contained within the OPTIONS menu, and we will look at these briefly.

CONFIGURE APPLICATION ([ALT] A): This allows you to set certain parameters for your standard application programs. Before using this function the application should be installed on the computer, in the appropriate directory, following the normal instructions supplied with the program disks. Normally this just means copying the program files into a suitable directory. This directory may have to be created by you first, although many programs have an INSTALL procedure which automates this. Once installed, the relevant files will appear in the GEM directory display. To configure the application select the main program icon, highlight it, and choose the CONFIGURE APPLICATION. This brings up the appropriate display screen, as illustrated.

You are requested to supply certain information to complete the configuration:

Document Type: This requires the input of any special file extensions which may be applied to data files for the program. It can be left blank if there are no fixed formats in use. Many applications, however, will use regular extensions, and this information should be included. Up to eight separate items can be listed. Extension types, e.g. .DOC, .WK1, etc., which are identified for a particular program, will result in documents produced by that program being represented on screen with an icon relating it to the particular application. Where a document type has been configured to work with a specific application, then double-clicking on the document icon will automatically load the application, and the document itself, as a single sequence.

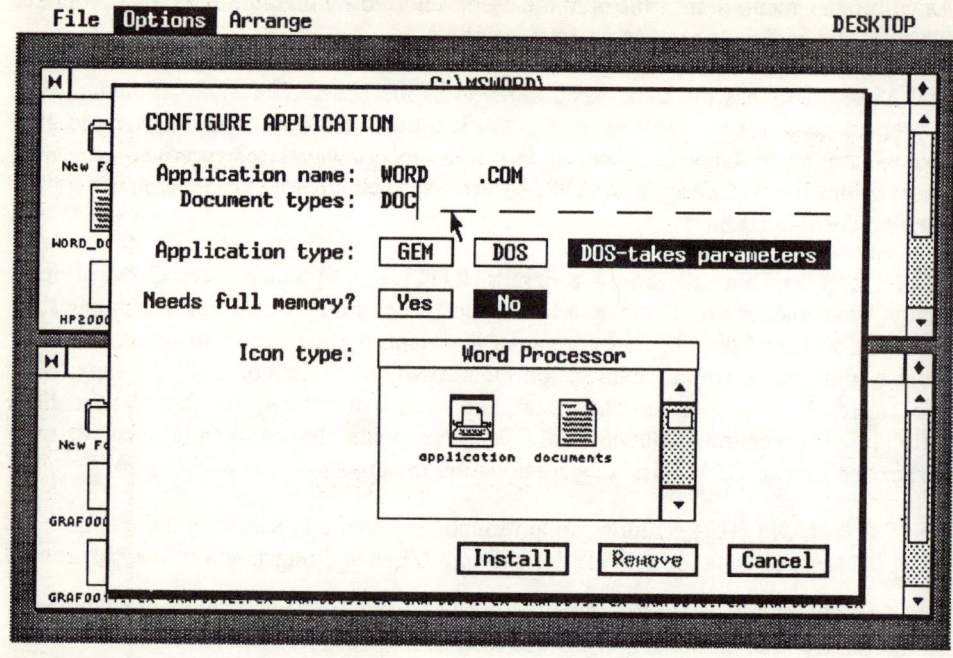

Figure 9.18 Configure ApplicationsScreen

Application Type: This tells the system which operating system is required for the program. If any of the GEM facilities are used, then GEM should be selected. Straightforward applications can be assigned as DOS type. If it is possible, or necessary, to add information to the DOS command line, for example, file names, paths, etc., when calling the program from DOS, then the DOS-takes parameters option should be selected. When an application is subsequently opened, this will result in the OPEN APPLICATION screen being displayed as demonstrated earlier.

Needs full memory: If the program needs all the computer memory, that is, it cannot run with the GEM system installed in memory, then this should be indicated here. If this option is selected before the application is run, the GEM system is removed from memory, and will need to be loaded from disk when the application is complete. You will be prompted to insert the appropriate disk when required.

Icon Type: This sub-screen contains a display of icon illustrations which can be used to identify particular applications. The required icon can be selected by scrolling through the available types. When selected the program icon is assigned to the main program file, and the document icon to any of the identified file types.

Once all the choices have been made the program is installed. It is also a simple process, if required, to remove an application.

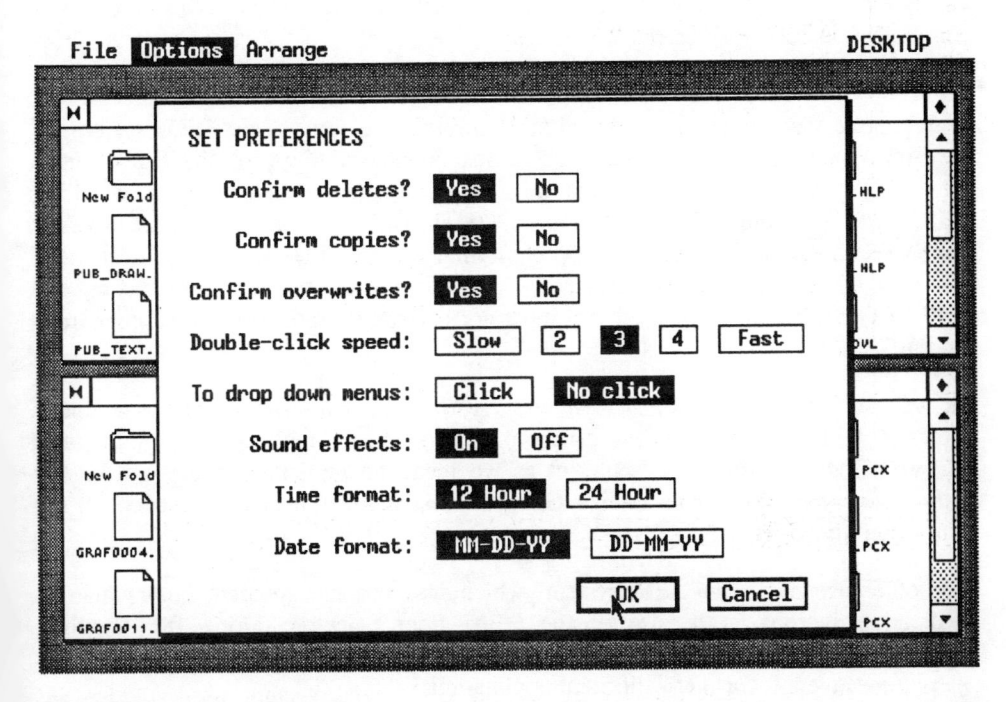

```
File  Options  Arrange                                    DESKTOP

    SET PREFERENCES

    Confirm deletes?    [Yes]  [No]
    Confirm copies?     [Yes]  [No]
    Confirm overwrites? [Yes]  [No]
    Double-click speed: [Slow] [2] [3] [4] [Fast]
    To drop down menus: [Click]  [No click]
    Sound effects:      [On]  [Off]
    Time format:        [12 Hour]  [24 Hour]
    Date format:        [MM-DD-YY] [DD-MM-YY]
                              [OK]  [Cancel]
```

Figure 9.19 Set Preference Screen

SET PREFERENCES: This option allows you to adjust some of the default parameters used in the operation of the GEM DESKTOP system. It is used by making the appropriate choices from the SET PREFERENCE screen display.

The first three options relate to file manipulation features, and allow you to eliminate the need to confirm copy and delete instructions. The safest choice is to leave this option set, as any small inconvenience that this may introduce is easily compensated by the reduction in the risk of erasing required files, by providing a second chance to abort the command.

The double click speed option is a matter of individual taste, and if you are having problems with this function you can experiment with different settings. The rest of the choices are quite easily understood, and need no explanation.

Once any changes have been made it is necessary to save these to disk using the SAVE DESKTOP command ([ALT] V). This will immediately overwrite any previous DESKTOP preferences, and will reflect in all subsequent use of the DESKTOP. The current screen layout, in terms of directories displayed, will also be preserved with the DESKTOP.

ENTER DOS COMMANDS: Selecting this option will cause the GEM screen to be replaced by the normal MS-DOS screen, complete with C:> or A:> prompt. Any DOS command can be entered and will function in the normal way, provided that any of the external files are accessible in the appropriate directory. When this function is complete you can re-enter the GEM system by typing [EXIT] at the normal DOS prompt. This will restore the normal GEM screen and functions, as before.

In the above sections we have looked at all the main features of the GEM system, as they reflect in normal day-to-day use of the computer. Many of the filing duties previously performed using DOS can be used, with some advantage, from the GEM DESKTOP. Remember that many of the DOS external functions, such as FORMAT, DISKCOPY, etc., are treated by GEM as normal program files and can be used from the GEM DESKTOP like any application. You can exit to DOS at any time using the [CTRL] Q command, if required, but most normal applications will run happily from the DESKTOP.

As we use Timeworks Publisher we will become familiar with some of the more extensive GEM functions as they can be incorporated into application programs, and you will find a familiarity of concept as we meet the particular features. Like the author, you may even grow to like GEM, having ignored it in favour of DOS for quite some time.

One other aspect of the GEM system, which will become apparent only when an application is run, is the use of the GEM Item Selector, during file handling operations. This is one of the GEM program functions which gives a common operating sequence, for many different applications.

This screen, illustrated here, is activated whenever a function is selected which requires a file to be loaded from, or saved to disk. It is to provide the means for identifying the Path, Directory and filename of the particular files concerned.

The GEM Item Selector has three areas of interest:

Directory: This specifies the current full directory and path description, as well as any particular file specification that may be expected (i.e. file extensions used as standard for the function in operation) This line may be edited by moving the mouse cursor onto the line, and clicking once to activate a text cursor. The line may then be deleted or changed as required. When a directory specification has been changed, click on the [OK] panel to notify the program to look in the new directory. To delete any line of text on this display, place the text cursor on the line and press the [ESC] key. this can be used for any editing of filenames etc within GEM.

Listing Window: The window below the directory line will show the contents of the current directory. If sub-directories are listed, identified by the diamond symbol, then clicking on one of these with the mouse will change the directory line, to select that particular directory.

```
            IMPORT TEXT FROM: GEM 1st Word Plus (.DOC)
┌──┬──────────────────────────────────────────────────────────────┬─┐
│ ►│                    C:\PUBLISH\UNTITLED.DTP                   │▲│
├──┴──────────────────────────────────────────────────────────────┼─┤
│  ┌──────────────────────────────────────────────────────────┐   │ │
│  │  ITEM SELECTOR                                           │   │ │
│  │  Directory:  C:\PUBLISH\*.DOC_____      │   │ │
│  │  ┌──┬─────────────┬─┐     Selection:  |____.__          │   │ │
│  │  │ ►│    *.DOC    │▲│                                    │   │ │
│  │  │  │ ♦ DTP___.__ │ │                                    │   │ │
│  │  │  │ ♦ PICTURES.__│ │                                   │   │ │
│  │  │  │ ♦ STORIES_.__│ │                                   │   │ │
│  │  │  │  ___.__      │ │                                    │   │ │
│  │  │  │  ___.__      │ │           ┌────────┐              │   │ │
│  │  │  │  ___.__      │ │           │   OK   │              │   │ │
│  │  │  │  ___.__      │ │           └────────┘              │   │ │
│  │  │  │  ___.__      │ │           ┌────────┐              │   │ │
│  │  │  │  ___.__      │▼│           │ Cancel │              │   │ │
│  │  └──┴─────────────┴─┘           └────────┘              │   │ │
│  └──────────────────────────────────────────────────────────┘   │ │
└─────────────────────────────────────────────────────────────────┴─┘
```

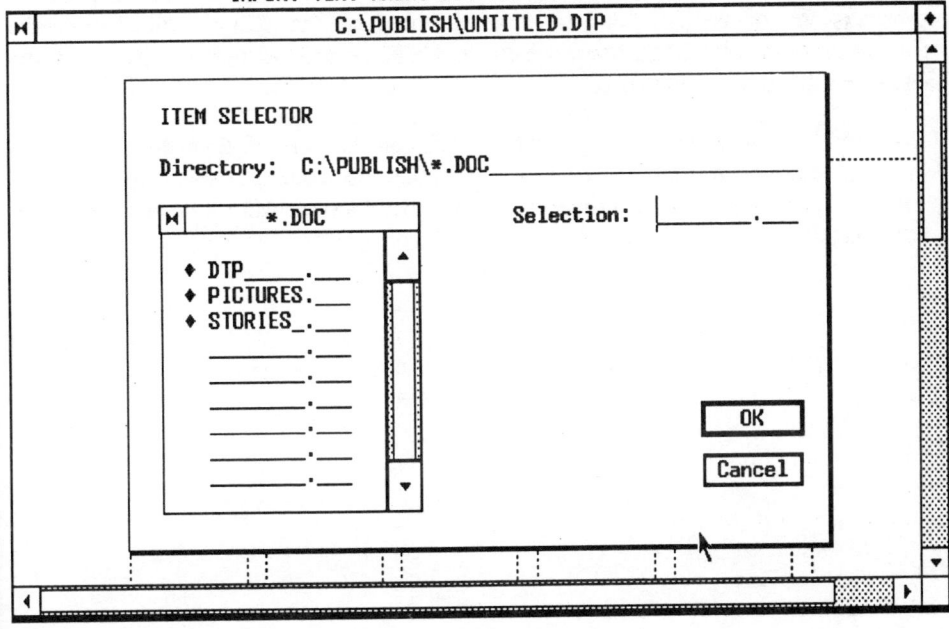

Figure 9.20 Item Selector Screen

Selection Line: Once a directory has been selected then the file SELECTION line can be completed. This can be done by moving the text cursor onto that line, and entering the appropriate filename and extension. Alternatively, if the file is listed in the panel, clicking on this will transfer the data onto the selection line. When entering the filename directly, pressing on the (.) will immediately move the text cursor to the appropriate part of the line, to enter the extension text.

Once the directory and the filename have been fully specified then clicking on the [OK] box will cause the particular load or save operation to be carried out. The sequence can be terminated at any time by clicking on [CANCEL]

Most of the GEM functions, and most of the functions within Timeworks Publisher, can be achieved through the selection of various menus OR by using appropriate key combinations. As you become more familiar with the applications it becomes of benefit, in terms of speed, to learn these alternatives. With GEM, these are illustrated in the menus, along side the particular function. This is the same with Timeworks Publisher, but in addition there is an appendix to the manual which lists all of the 'QUICK KEY' functions, and it is well worth referring to these frequently.

With all of the above information tucked safely under your hat you should now be in a position to make full use of the GEM system as an operating enviroment for much of your computer work.

Timeworks Publisher is a GEM-based program which makes full use of the graphics representations of GEM. You can operate most of the features of Timeworks Publisher without any direct reference to the GEM system, as it stays quietly in the background for most of the time.

If you are a long time user of DOS, and you are familiar with it, then there is little to be gained from the use of GEM directly. For the new computer user, however, the learning process for GEM is probably less painful than for MS-DOS, and generally worth the effort.

Index

A
A4 format, 11, 24
accept (mouse click), 13, 204
ALT key, 64
Apple LaserWriter, 151
ascenders, 10
ASCII, 69, 99
aspect ratio, 122
AUTOEXEC.BAT, 17, 20, 202, 204

B
baseline, 10
Bitstream fonts, 181, 182
box (graphics function), 113
box (GEM), close, 22
box (GEM), full, 22
BRING TO FRONT, 50, 114
browser, 22, 24, 33, 34
bullet, 15, 82, 85, 92, 104, 105
bus mouse, 202

C
CANCEL, 13, 204
capitals, 10
changing your printer, 179
character, 9
character set, extended, 70
character set, GEM International, 70
circle, 116
click, 13, 203
click, double, 13
clip art, 119, 171
clipboard, 31, 32, 65
close box, 22, 212, 214
column guides, 22, 30, 44, 154
communication port, 206
CONFIG.SYS, 204
configuring the system, 227
COPY, 31, 31, 32, 64, 220
copy files, 221
crop picture, 123
cursor, 29
CUT, 32, 64

D
daisy wheel, 1, 2
default style sheet, 106
DEFAULT.STY, 41, 45

DELETE, 220, 224
delete style, 97
descenders, 10
design, aspects of, 130
desktop publishing, 1, 4
desktop, GEM, 211, 229
directory, 208, 209, 213
disk,
    floppy, 20
    hard, 16, 17
    RAM, 17, 19, 205
display (monitor) choice of, 205
display fonts, 181
dither, 196
dot image, 119, 122
dot matrix printers, 2, 14, 177
double click, 13, 203
drag (GEM), 13, 203
dropped capitals, 172, 185
DTP, 1, 4, 5, 14
Dutch font, 7

E
EGA, 5
ellipse, 116
ems, 9, 86
extended character set, 70
extension, 210
extensions, 71

F
filename, 210
files, 208
files, fonts, 60
files, formats
    *.GEM, 118
    *.IMG, 39, 118
    *.PCX, 118
    *.PIC, 118
fill styles, 114
floppy disks, 20
folders, 213, 219
font generation software, 181
font files, 60
fonts, 7, 8, 11, 60, 136, 180
    display, 181
    printer, 181
FONTWID, 19, 179
footers, 13, 75, 76, 77, 105
formats — see files

233

frame, 27, 29, 33
frame border, 48
frame padding, 54
frame tint, 54
freehand drawing, 113
full box, 22, 213, 216

G

GEM, 7, 13, 19, 20, 201, 207, 211
GEM International character set, 70
GEM item selector, 230
GEM SETUP, 20
graphics, 2, 4, 16, 107
gutter margin, 12, 42

H

handles, 30
hanging indent, 183, 189
hard disk, 16, 17, 20
hard hyphen, 193
hardware, 14
header, 77, 105
headers, 13, 75, 76
headers and footers, 76
Helvetica, 7
highlight, 34, 61
hot zone, 86
HP LaserJet, 15
hyphen, hard, 193
hyphen, soft, 193
hyphenation, 66, 189, 190, 193
hyphenation hot zone, 194

I

icons, 21, 213, 217
IMPORT, 32, 68
importing graphics files, 118
indent, 87, 88
inner margin, 44
INSTALL, 19, 20, 204
italic text, 7
item selector, 24

J

justification, 82

K

KERN, 67
kerning, 10, 66, 68, 160
key code, 21

L

landscape orientation, 11, 131
laser printers, 3, 14, 175
LaserJet II, 14
LaserJet+, 14

leaders, 104
leading, 10
left hand, 22
letter quality printing, 2
line art, 39, 119
line style, 112
line type, 48
linked line, 112
Lotus 123, 119

M

Macintosh, 151
margin,
    definition of, 11
    gutter, 12, 42
    inner, 44
    outer, 44
master pages, 41, 43, 139, 153
memory, 16
menu options, 21
mode, changing, 22
mouse, 17, 19, 201, 206
mouse, bus, 202
MOUSE.COM, 17
MOVE, 32, 203

N

NEW, 29, 41
newsletters, 171
normal text, 64

O

offsets, 178
OPEN, 203
outer margin, 44

P

page format, 29, 41
page offset, 44
page, master, 139
paragraph, 13, 31, 37, 57, 79, 79, 81, 80
paragraph style, 83
PASTE, 32
PATH, 204, 210, 213, 217
PC Paintbrush, 38
PCX file format, 38
perimeter, 114
Pica, 9
pixel, 124, 126
point (typography), 9, 10, 13, 47, 203
portrait orientation, 11, 131
PostScript printers, 14, 136, 151, 176, 180
preferences, 229
printer, 14, 19, 29, 206
    fonts, 181
    changing, 179
    dot matrix, 2, 175, 177
    laser, 3, 14, 175